D1243729

FOREIGN POLICY

AND THE

DEVELOPING NATION

FOREIGN POLICY

AND THE

DEVELOPING

NATION

RICHARD BUTWELL, Editor

HENRY BIENEN   RUPERT EMERSON

IVO & ROSALIND FEIERABEND

BENJAMIN HIGGINS   LLOYD JENSEN

WILSON CAREY McWILLIAMS

GAYL D. NESS

University of Kentucky Press   Lexington   1969

CONTENTS

1 | INTRODUCTION
CONTEMPORARY INTERNATIONAL RELATIONS
AND DEVELOPMENT
RICHARD BUTWELL

11 | CHAPTER ONE
POLITICAL DEVELOPMENT AND FOREIGN POLICY
WILSON CAREY McWILLIAMS

41 | CHAPTER TWO
FOREIGN POLICY AND SOCIAL CHANGE
GAYL D. NESS

67 | CHAPTER THREE
FOREIGN POLICY, THE MILITARY, AND DEVELOPMENT:
MILITARY ASSISTANCE AND POLITICAL
CHANGE IN AFRICA
HENRY BIENEN

113 | CHAPTER FOUR
FOREIGN ECONOMIC POLICY AND ECONOMIC
DEVELOPMENT
BENJAMIN HIGGINS

135 | CHAPTER FIVE
LEVEL OF DEVELOPMENT AND INTERNATION BEHAVIOR
IVO K. AND ROSALIND L. FEIERABEND
with Frank W. Scanland III and John Stuart Chambers

189 | CHAPTER SIX
LEVELS OF POLITICAL DEVELOPMENT AND
INTERSTATE CONFLICT IN SOUTH ASIA
LLOYD JENSEN

209 | CHAPTER SEVEN
AMERICAN INFLUENCE IN DEVELOPED AND
UNDERDEVELOPED COUNTRIES
RUPERT EMERSON

INTRODUCTION

CONTEMPORARY INTERNATIONAL RELATIONS & DEVELOPMENT

RICHARD BUTWELL

THE SYSTEM of international relations that existed on the eve of World War II was altered considerably in the years which followed that costly conflict. Before the war what was called "international" relations was essentially the relations among the countries of Europe, where the nation-state had developed. The United States and Japan, both located outside Europe, had been drawn into the system and were, as a matter of fact, the major belligerents in the Pacific phase of the war between 1941 and 1945. The other major powers, however, were European states (Britain, France, Germany, and the Soviet Union), and large areas of the world were colonies of the first two countries as well as of such smaller nations as the Netherlands, Portugal, and Spain. The Americans and the Japanese, moreover, had earlier become colonial powers in their own right. The system, which was becoming truly international before World War II, was still nonetheless mainly Europe-centered when the decade of the forties began.

The war accelerated the process of internationalization of the system of relations among countries. The major European colonial powers were so weakened by this most devastating war among themselves that they were unable in the war's wake to maintain their dominance over their subject territories of Asia and Africa, although, with the exception of the United States and Britain, they tried to do so. Japan's conquests in Southeast Asia in particular were to have a catalytic effect in ending European colonial rule in this part of the world, as Burmese, Indonesians, and Vietnamese, among others, vowed never again to allow themselves to be governed by aliens. This surge to independence subsequently spread to other parts of the world, particularly Africa. The nationalist movements of these emergent states thus combined with the weakened circumstances of the European colonial powers to transform the system of international relations in revolutionary ways.

By the start of the 1960's the international system was altogether different from what it had been before the war, although it resembled the old system in enough ways to blind some observers—and even a few participants—to the dimensions of the changes involved. In the old system the participants, whatever their size, were at more or less the same level of development. The concept of the sovereign equality of states was in this sense an accurate reflection of the relations among the nations that made up the system. The admission of the United States and Japan to the system marked the beginning of its revolutionary transformation. Their entrance into the international system was the result primarily of their acquisition of those characteristics that seemed to separate the European states from most of the other peoples of the world, that is, their level of development economically, technologically, and politically.

There are at least three main differences between the nature of the system of international relations as it existed in 1939 and as it functions today: its scope, its decreasing domination by the states of western Europe, and, perhaps most important, the unparalleled variation in the levels of development of the participants in the system. France and Holland may have differed in size (and military power) historically, but never in the history of the European system of international relations did they differ in their levels of general development as, say, Germany and Indonesia or Japan and Algeria do today.

There is today growing recognition of the relationship between development and international relations, however vague and inadequately formulated the perception of this relationship may sometimes be. The contemporary use of aid or assistance as a foreign policy tool is the most conspicuous evidence of this recognition. Immediate postwar American aid to Europe, Japan, and the Philippines was rehabilitative. Later, aid was designed, as some of its critics claimed, to win, if not buy, friends (and American foreign assistance, unfortunately, is even today too frequently defended in such terms to win necessary congressional financing). But those who formulate and direct United States aid programs in the executive branch of the government are, for the most part, concerned with assisting less developed countries through the often painful process of modernization. They see this as a way of making the world more the kind of one in which the United States and other "have" nations can themselves continue to develop and prosper.

Foreign aid, accordingly, may be viewed as testimony to two beliefs existent among American (and other) foreign policymakers: (a) that differing levels of development may influence, possibly adversely, the very system of interstate relations that has become universal in the years since World War II, and (b) that external agents can play a part in raising the level of living—and of the state of the economy and of the governmental and other organizations that direct it—of the less developed states of the world.

The drive to development, on the other hand, is by no means mainly externally stimulated. The nationalist surge to independence was not simply motivated; it sought independence politically from alien rule, but it was also motivated by a belief that low living standards and other dimensions of underdevelopment were primarily the result of foreign control and exploitation. The termination of colonial rule, it was believed, would be followed by a veritable millennium of progress and prosperity. Independence came much earlier than most Asians and Africans believed it would, but, for the most part, it did not prove to be the dramatic beginning of a new and exciting era of rapid material development or improved living standards. But neither did it prove—again, for the most part—to be frustrating to the point of resignation and abandonment. Trying and often bitter setbacks notwithstanding, the new states have remained true to their previously proclaimed goals of modernizing in various ways their still largely underdeveloped societies.

Both the new system of interstate relations and the multifaceted phenomenon of development, achieved and desired, have been studied by growing numbers of scholars. But the relationship between foreign policy and development has been only modestly explored. This is surprising in view of the increasingly emphasized influence of "internal" factors upon foreign policy formulation and execution in the literature of international relations since the early 1950's. The impact upon foreign policy of ideology, public opinion, elite composition, and the press —among other variables—has been studied. But no studies have sought to investigate the influence upon foreign policy of the level of development of a state or states seeking to influence one or more other states, or the states toward which such efforts are directed. Often some of the factors that have come to be considered within the general concept of development, such as the level of technical education in a country, have been treated but almost always as separate factors in their own right.

Development, as is being realized, is by no means wholly an economic phenomenon. Indeed, many of the most exciting studies in the social sciences in recent years have been those that have broken genuinely new ground in the pursuit of greater understanding of political development. And some have even explored the relationship between political and economic development. Development, as employed here, refers to the array of characteristics by which some states are judged to be more advanced than others: the organization and technology by which production is pursued, to be sure—that is, economic development—but also role specialization in general in the society, swift and mass communication and transportation systems, political processes in which whole populations are involved (though the nature of this involvement may vary), and educational facilities that are widespread as well as increasingly technically oriented.

This complex phenomenon, so much the concern of governments and scholars today, has received little more than passing notice in the literature of international relations. This is especially surprising since most of the studies of international relations—and of the foreign policies of particular states—have dealt with Britain or France or the United States or others of the western countries even in the years since the emergence of the new states in Asia and Africa. Given the fact that the European countries dominated most of the rest of the world during the heyday of colonialism largely because of their greater development (including their administrative and political organization as well as their technological and productive superiority), it is surprising that level of development has not been treated as a major variable in any of the leading studies in the international relations field. In part this is a consequence of the unnatural historic division in political science between the fields of "international" relations and "internal" politics (whether the latter be "American" or "comparative" politics). This parochiality is breaking down, but this has been a development of only the last few years. Its legacy, unfortunately, is still very much with us.

Students of the underdeveloped states have played a major role in pioneering the developmental approach to comparative political analysis. The link between level of development, however—political, economic, or technological—and foreign policy has not yet been vigorously pursued. The fact is that we know far too little about the influence of the level of development upon either initiating or responding states in the international political arena. We also need to know much more about the ways in which international politics itself has changed as a consequence of the fact that a majority of its present-day participants would undoubtedly be classified as "underdeveloped" by most scholars. Capability analysts, primarily but not exclusively in government, have long sought to evaluate the influence of diverse domestic factors—ranging from energy resources to imprecisely calculated considerations of national "character" or "will" —upon various countries' warmaking, or defense, capacities. The fact alone of stalemated American military activity in Vietnam ought to raise serious doubts respecting just how much we really know about the complex interaction between "developed" and "underdeveloped" countries.

Behavior—of which foreign policy is a part—is a reaction to stimulus. This has long been recognized in the literature of international relations. However, *what* reacts and *how* it reacts are probably a function of what have conventionally been considered "internal" factors. Of course, they are no longer wholly "internal" factors—being themselves much influenced by external example and even assistance. Indeed, the whole notion of separate spheres of "international" and "internal" politics—or economics, for that matter—appears anachronistic. Recognition of this condition, however, does not make the task of analysis any easier, but it does improve the likelihood of more accurate and realistic answers to any questions that may be posed.

Given ever-increasing relations among peoples across traditional national lines and the widening (rather than narrowing) gap between the more advanced countries and the less developed ones, the questions posed by the relationship between foreign policy and development may be among the most important of our times. For example, how is international politics influenced by the modest levels of economic development and sometimes pronounced political instability of many of its participants who, as former colonies that have been recently emancipated, have yet to achieve effective integration as states in fact as well as in form? Do these states behave differently from those that are more economically advanced and possess increasingly complex and specialized economic, political, and other social institutions? Is level of development—economic, political, or otherwise—a more or less important variable than, say, size, location, or historical animosities and friendships?

States are invariably targets of other countries' foreign policies, which raises other questions of vulnerability or receptivity as a function of the level of development. Is it easier for the United States, for example, to influence the behavior of an underdeveloped country than to influence a more developed country? Or, to put the question in slightly different form, are there special limitations faced by the American government (or those of the U.S.S.R., Britain, or Japan) in seeking to provoke particular responses from nations less advanced than itself? And, if it is easier to influence such states, is success, so to speak, worth the effort in view of the more limited capabilities and contributions of such states to the resolution of the major problems that are the main concerns of international politics today?

If the behavior of a country is influenced by such factors as its landholding arrangements or the nature of its economy, how effectively can another nation induce change in these areas? The United States, for example, is constantly criticized by its own citizens and others for cooperating with governments of countries ruled by narrowly based political elites who allegedly run their lands in veritable feudal fashion. Some say that the United States should not cooperate with such governments, which might mean limited relations with more than half the nations in the world today; others assert that the United States should use the power allegedly implicit in its level of development and wealth as well as its size to force such countries to change themselves in various ways. But, even given the much more developed economy and advanced technology of the United States, can it (or the Soviet Union or any other country) shape in a formative fashion the development of other nations? In what circumstances is it likely to succeed, in what circumstances likely to fail?

There has been disagreement even in the area of economic change, the most extensively studied dimension of development, as to how to go about the task. Should capital-deficient underdeveloped countries encourage, or discourage, foreign private investment? To what extent should an answer to this question be governed by the levels of development of the investing and recipient countries? Can trade, historically an important type of foreign relations, play a major role in economic development, and has it done so in the past? Can too much (as well as too little) economic and technical assistance be given an underdeveloped country? And how is the appropriate level to be determined?

A major controversy has existed for several years in the United States respecting the relative merits of economic and military aid. It has been claimed, among other things, that military aid strengthens recipient states in such ways, and to such an extent, as to prejudice the possibility of the democratic political development of these lands. This in turn raises the question of why military aid is given and also why it is solicited or accepted by new states lacking in so many other dimensions of development. Does foreign military assistance, for example, free internally generated resources for other purposes, or does it increase the likelihood that a country will spend an even higher percentage of its limited resources on its military organization? Does military aid increase the likelihood of soldiers' coming to political power in a developing country?

Foreign policy behaviors almost always are possessed of both political and economic consequences. Because it can be measured more easily and because so much more (at least comparatively) is known about it, economic development has received far more attention to date than has its less easily defined and understood political counterpart. But political development may well influence the economic development of a country at least as much as this same political development is itself affected by the character and state of a country's economy. Military and paramilitary operations may be employed to topple or salvage a friendly government among the developing states, although the case of Vietnam suggests that this may be a very costly and possibly unsuccessful enterprise, while foreign agents have long sought to influence both the policies and the politics of other states. But can outside powers advance to any significant degree the political development of even weaker, less developed states in directions not deemed desirable by the leaders and peoples of these countries? And to what extent do the character and stability of their national politics effect their foreign policy?

Obviously, comprehensive answers to all these questions cannot be given in seven short studies. But the questions are raised in these studies, and suggestions of answers—in some cases quite specific, if tentative, suggestions—are made.

The papers that pose and seek to answer these questions were prepared for a monthlong conference on "Foreign Policy and Development" held in August 1967 at the University of Kentucky by the William Andrew Patterson School of Diplomacy and International Commerce. The participants in this conference were eight distinguished scholars seriously devoted to questions of both foreign policy and development.

Wilson Carey McWilliams of the Department of Political Science, Brooklyn College, deals with the theoretical framework basic to a study of the relationship of foreign policy and political development. Gayl D. Ness of the Department of Sociology, University of Michigan, examines three cases of successful American influence brought to bear in a special area of social change in other countries—and two cases of failure. Henry Bienen of the Department of Politics, Princeton University, concerns himself with the question of United States military assistance and political change on the continent of Africa. Benjamin Higgins of the Department of Economics, University of Montreal, surveys the subject of foreign economic policy and development, particularly the role of the still-young foreign policy tool of aid. Ivo K. and Rosalind L. Feierabend of the Department of Political Science and the Department of Psychology, San Diego State College, present an analysis dealing with all the world's countries which is suggestive of several relationships between the level of development and foreign policy behavior. Lloyd Jensen of the Department of Political Science, University of Kentucky, inquires into the relationship between political stability as an aspect of political development and the conflict behavior of India and Pakistan. Rupert Emerson of the Department of Government, Harvard University, addresses himself to the problem of American relations with the less developed countries and the contrasts between such relations and those with the more developed European states.

These papers are proof not only of the importance of the problems inherent in their subject but also of the value of various methodological approaches used by scholars from the different social sciences. Because the Kentucky conference's main emphasis was upon foreign policy, most of the participants were political scientists. Their approaches to the question differed, however, as did those of the economist and the sociologist. The Feierabends' paper uses gross data analysis, Jensen's is a case study of the Indian-Pakistani relationship, Ness compares American behavior in five situations separated by time and geography, Bienen looks at military aid in a particular regional setting, McWilliams approaches his subject primarily from a theoretical viewpoint, Emerson's contribution is historical and analytical, and that of Higgins is both analytical and prescriptive.

CHAPTER ONE

POLITICAL DEVELOPMENT AND FOREIGN POLICY

—————

WILSON CAREY McWILLIAMS

DE TOCQUEVILLE wrote, "A new science of politics is needed for a new world."[1] In our time, change has created what seems more a bewildering series of unfamiliar worlds than a single new one, and it is no surprise that political scientists have felt the same need. Yet they have not always understood, as de Tocqueville did, that a new science must return to old questions, that the perennial is never more important than in the transition from the obsolete to the untried.

No science of politics is possible without a definition of "the political," yet no satisfactory definition exists among students of political development. It is easy to understand why men eager to confront the fascinating variety and troubling problems of contemporary life are tempted to avoid the question; millennia of debate have not produced agreement among political philosophers. Yet in a new world, confusion is a protection against dogma, a surety against a narrow vision blind to much of reality. In fact, the effort to avoid timeless confusions only results in the pursuit of lines that are time-bound without being less confused.

"Political development" has meant for most social scientists the politics *of* development. Politics, whatever it may mean, has been secondary; development, the direction of historical change, primary. The concept of development has itself been peculiar: as Michael Walzer writes, it is not an idea of progress but of "progress realized" that informs research.[2] Developing states are separated from developed ones in ways which suggest that change, or at least qualitative change, has come to an end in the latter.

Such categories may be useful in the making of policy: a developing state is one that humbles itself sufficiently to ask for assistance from another which may then regard itself as developed.[3] Even in this sense, dichotomy dissolves into continuity: Ghana, Israel, China, and a host of others would have to be classified as developing in comparison to some states and developed in relation to others.

In a more genuine sense, all states are developing, for all are subject to the universal history resulting from the expansion of the European state system into a single, global political process. Associated with that expansion has been the whole complex of tendencies, uncertain at the edges, which has been termed "modern": science, secularism, empathy, social mobilization, mass communication, and the like.[4]

To forget the universality of history is to forget that all states are modern:

the environment of Ghana is not that of England in 1689 but of the superpowers in the 1960's.[5] The demands of that environment are greater on all states than in any past time. Moreover, many problems of the developing states are not specific but general: they result from a total international environment and cannot be solved by those states themselves.

Comparative politics inevitably involves categories of similarity and unlikeness, and the dichotomy between developed and developing states conceals more than it reveals. Moreover, it is a Western doctrine, vaguely contemptuous in tone; it suggests that to learn the universal and general, men should study those states that are developed, whereas to learn the exotic and particular, men should study those states that are developing.

De Tocqueville suggested, by contrast, that in a world of a truly international politics and universal history, the study of the new states may teach the old much about themselves. The forces of change and the direction of movement, he argued, are harder to discern in states insulated by wealth and established institutions, easier in states where the tasks are harder and stark confrontation exists between men and the forces of their times. The new states may, then, be developing not in the direction of the old, but in the direction that will be followed by the old.

Each state is unique in some ways, yet if due allowance is made for such peculiarities, we may be able to perceive in the new states the outlines of our future political condition. Insofar as that condition is unappealing, it may allow us to consider in time measures that may serve to avert it.

For one school of political theorists, politics and foreign policy are essentially identical. Man is isolated, individualistic, self-seeking, and always a foreigner to his fellows. Such states as he contrives are little more than alliances in which men are bound together by fear of foes—of nature, of one another, and of other men —and by hope for gain at the expense of nature and men who remain outside.

The word "foreign" belies the theory. It derives from *foras*, "out-of-doors" or "outside," what is distinct from the hearth and away from home. "Foreign" is a term without content, meaning only "that which is not domestic." At least in the origin of the word, there would have been no foreigners unless there were some with whom a man was "at home."

Man is a social animal in this, if nothing else: that he is born to dependence, and his security depends on inherited things. The "domestic" is that social space which is the given of man's early life. He need only accept the terms of the gift, the habits and commandments of his blood kin, to find it a world that is peaceful, predictable, and even friendly. Ignorant and weak, man approaches the world hesitantly and with suspicion: the domestic order proves to be trustworthy, until man comes to expect it to be hospitable. The "foreign," by contrast, is an environment that has not offered such proof, or that has givens which conflict with and endanger those of domesticity: in either case, the burden of proof lies with the foreigner and peace is not to be expected without some overt act of friendship.

Providing for man's physical survival and emotional security earns for the domestic order man's deepest gratitude. Indeed, so essential are its benefits that man identifies himself with the domestic, a sentiment that is best called patriotism, the devotion to the land and people of one's fathers. De Tocqueville wrote: "There is one sort of patriotic attachment which principally arises from that instinctive, disinterested, and undefined feeling which connects the affections of man with his birthplace. This natural fondness is united to a taste for ancient customs and to a reverence for ancestral traditions; those who cherish it love their country as they love the mansion of their fathers. They enjoy the tranquility which it affords them; they are attached to the reminiscences which it awakens; they cling to the peaceful habits which they have contracted in its bosom; and they are pleased by the state of obedience in which they are placed." [6]

The horror of treason is, in part, that it introduces (or reintroduces) foreignness into domestic space. In early definitions, in fact, crimes against kindred or the peace were as much parts of treason as was betrayal of the state.[7]

Yet as men grow in security, they begin to question the distinction between domestic and foreign things. Patriotism is the first refuge of man but it is also "the last refuge of a scoundrel" because it is at best a low-ranking sentiment in the hierarchy of human excellence.

Socrates found the origins of patriotism by examining the behavior of dogs, not that of men. Dogs, he pointed out, are "by instinct perfectly gentle to those they know and are accustomed to, and fierce to enemies." This, Socrates suggested, is very "philosophic" of the canine: "the only mark by which the dog distinguishes a friendly and an unfriendly face is that he knows one and does not know the other, and if a creature makes that the test of what it finds congenial or otherwise, how can you deny that it has a passion for knowledge and understanding?" [8]

The irony, of course, only calls attention to the radical defect of "knowledge" which is based on no more than appearance and habit. But the patriotic behavior of men is based on a knowledge no more precise. Earlier in *The Republic* the patriotic thesis that justice is helping friends and hurting enemies is defended by Polemarchus who has inherited the argument from his father as most men inherit home, kinsmen, and political loyalties. Men, Polemarchus is forced to admit, often mistake for friends those who are really enemies (and vice versa), and men's obligations lie to their true friends, the good and the just.[9]

Trust of blood kin and of friends-by-inheritance is at best an approximate tool: blood kin may still betray, and strangers may befriend. Moreover, inherited loyalties are impersonal: they are based on a love of my ancestors and not of me and are automatic only at the cost of personal meaning. The painful experience of unexpected betrayal, the joyous encounter with unexpected friendship, the search for affection that is personal, all combine with men's reason to challenge patriotism. Moreover, since patriotism is based on the feeling that loyalties are given, once challenged it can never be recovered.

"Government," Paine once wrote, "is a badge of lost innocence." In this much he was right: that political society emerges only when men become conscious of uncertainty in the meaning of justice and of choice in their relations with their fellows. Blood kinship must be subordinated to the demands of unity with those we believe to be our true friends, who share with us an idea of justice. De Tocqueville observed that in addition to patriotism, "there is another species of attachment to a country which is more rational. . . . It is perhaps less generous and less ardent, but it is more fruitful and more lasting; it is coeval with the spread of knowledge, it is nurtured by the laws, it grows by the exercise of civil rights and, in the end, it is confounded with the personal interest of the citizen."[10]

Relations based on choice and justice make the boundaries of the state permeable: one not born among us may aspire to become a citizen. Moreover, the claims of justice—that we must do what is due another—change relations with outsiders. A citizen must help his friends, who have a claim on him, but he ought not to harm outsiders unless they have proved hostile. In foreign policy, the principle of political society is innocent until proved guilty; the principle of patriotism is the reverse. Hence, aliens may live among citizens without necessarily introducing foreignness among them or threatening the state. (Polemarchus, who was a resident alien in Athens, should have seen as much.)

Yet political society is not simply the empire of reason. Men will demand the good life only when they are certain that mere life is secure: they will not surrender the physical and emotional security of domesticity until those goods are guaranteed by another society. As Ignazio Silone wrote of intellectuals who broke their ties with family in order to devote themselves to the proletarian cause, political loyalty begins with a "choice of comrades" and not of doctrines.[11]

Civic loyalty, being based on choice, is never so secure as patriotism. Those who choose to be with us may choose to desert us; we ourselves may find that an idea of justice that once seemed good now seems inadequate; we may find friends who seem truer than our fellow citizens. Even under the best circumstances, the emotions of man hesitate at the brink of commitment and hold something back: the sentiment, as de Tocqueville remarked, is "less ardent" than patriotism.

The best circumstances require that the security of civic relations be strengthened as much as possible. Oaths and pledges may help to provide it, and the earliest political societies strove to make a man's word so identical with his self that he would regard the breaking of it as moral suicide. (Our modern idea of treason partly derives from *Treubruch*, the breaking of a pledge.) [12]

We can accept the word of another, or can bind ourselves to him, only to the extent that we know him. We can find the security of shared emotions only with those we know within the limited boundaries that are the outer limits of sensation. In this sense, political society can emerge and can be at its most secure only among a comparatively small number of friends and citizens: the population of a *polis*, Aristotle observed, must always be surveyable.[13]

Great states and empires have more than one appeal to men, yet they contain the seeds of political decay. As de Tocqueville put it, "The ambition of the citizens increases with the power of the state; the strength of parties, with the importance of the ends they have in view; but that of devotion to the commonweal . . . is not stronger than in a small republic. It might, indeed, be proved without difficulty to be less powerful and less sincere." [14]

Whatever the devotion of the founders of empire to one another, the second generation—like that of any state—will be born to domesticity: the political order will be an inherited given, a fatherland. In all states, political education must combat this tendency for citizenship to disintegrate into patriotism by seeking to reproduce in the child the experience of the father.

If, to achieve this end, the great empire restricts citizenship to a surveyable few, those who are excluded become, in effect, aliens: the state is many, not one, with all the instability and weakness which follows from that fact. Moreover, the cares of governing will naturally scatter citizens about their domains: they are likely to become emotionally distant from one another.

But, if all men are admitted to citizenship, even if they share political ideals, the commandments of justice and the good to the mind of man will be at war with his emotions. Not only will most of his fellow citizens remain unknown, man will feel himself insignificant, unimportant, and threatened among them. He may obey the dictates of political authority, but he will retain his emotions within the domestic sphere, changing their objects only when he moves from his family of birth to a family of which he is head. In a recent study, Robert Wesson confirms the classic thesis: "it may be considered a bit unnatural that the area of the state should be much larger than the limits of human interaction. It is understandable that those who live and work together and know their common needs should manage their common affairs, defend their community, and give their resources for the general good. On the other hand, that men should obey and give . . . the fruit of their labors to a distant authority that they know only by hearsay, that they should fight and risk their skins to defend far-off borders against peoples of whom they know nothing—all this represents great institutional development over the simpler state of mankind." [15] Yet the "development" to which Wesson refers is that of institutions, not of men: "The empire can tell men, in its accepted ideology or style that they should give of themselves, but it strives in vain to make them feel why. . . . In the city-state, love of homeland means love of the state; in the empire, they are virtually opposites. . . . the empire raises conflicts between conformity to the official order and devotion to one's own. . . . Only a handful can see themselves as responsible and important in making the future of the community. . . . Civic spirit means involvement in something, responsibility before equals, a sense that our world needs us to make justice and prosperity. . . . the great political order . . . turns loose hearts while subjecting minds." [16]

Whatever the dreams of his imagination or the dictates of his reason, the emotions of man would keep all his loyalty in the narrowest compass possible: beyond a certain number of men, he gives no loyalty at all and is induced to act only for gain or fear for self, and neither sentiment is political.

Yet the small state has difficulties of its own. It is weakened when reason sweeps beyond its parochial boundaries and sees justice as a universal and mankind as a kindred; emotion resists loyalties but the mind shatters them. More important, perhaps, is the fact that defeat in war may well mean the extinction of a small state and only an inconvenience for a large one. (In our times, however, this distinction may have almost vanished.)

Fear of defeat is dangerous because it contributes to a concern for the requirements of foreign policy. The proper center for a political society is internal, on its ideal of justice between citizens. In foreign policy, though policy may be guided by justice, the means are commanded not by what is just but by what is necessary. The attitudes of citizens are less important than the attitudes of foreigners. Democracy is most endangered, for foreign policy tends to demand a sure and swift hand and a cosmopolitan expertise. The classical political theorists presumed that a truly excellent state could exist only if it were so situated as to need no foreign policy; it is significant that it is soldiers, men with the virtue of dogs, who Plato predicts would be the first to overthrow the republic. There is, in other words, a conflict between the political and foreign policy.

Political development, then, entails, in addition to its other requirements, a low salience of foreign affairs. That alone is a gloomy conclusion when applied to the circumstances of our time. No more cheering is the belief that a true political order must be a small one: "in this matter, as in many others, the argument derived from the necessity of the case predominates over all others. If none but small nations existed, I do not doubt that mankind would be more happy and more free; but the existence of great nations is unavoidable." [17]

That there is thought to be one process of development for mankind is a reflection of the universalization of politics. The expansion of human power over man and nature, originating in the West, has created an international politics to which all states must respond or perish; the effort to acquire that power provides the logic of development.[18]

The motives that have induced men to pursue such power are plural. In part, the quest has resulted from threat; imperialism made clear, if men's fears had not, that the choices of men had narrowed to the alternatives of changing or being changed. In part, it has been the consequence of ridicule; science has made many of the religions and cosmologies which served as the intellectual bases of human cultures seem a tissue of folly, and men fear to play the fool. Perhaps most basic and original to the pursuit of power has been the desire for physical well-being—for greater health and for the prospect of greater and now nearly unlimited affluence. "Low prices," wrote Karl Marx, "are the heavy artillery of the bourgeoisie," more effective than cannon in inducing change because they undermine walls from within. Yet all these motives share a common quality: they appeal to passions that are essentially individual, if not individualizing, in nature. Moreover, and partly as a consequence, they have implied a decline of the political: they have made foreign policy not only salient but the most vital consideration of political life, and they have commanded the great state which could acquire and protect power as small states could not. The small states of the world survive only as dependencies of, or by the sufferance of, the greater.

Many have observed that the desire for dignity, the yearning to "matter," is a central motive of the developing states.[19] As that term is commonly used, in fact, "developing states" refers to the "undignified states": to the passive units of international life that have been forced to change regardless of their desires, to those that must humble themselves to ask others for assistance. Economic backwardness or military weakness cannot account for the fact that Brazil or Mexico are often classed with the developing states whereas Spain, Portugal, and Greece are not. The latter states, however, once had a moment when they flashed on the pages of universal history and their present feelings of indignity are assuaged, in part, by memories of past glory.[20]

The yearning for dignity, however, is part of a general reaction to the modern world—a product of it and a reaction against it—and is not limited in locale. As it shatters the traditional structures that invested men with dignity, modern life inhibits, where it does not prevent, the formation of new ones.

Reason is largely inadequate for the creative task. The rationalism of modern life is functional, not substantive: it fulfills the needs of the system and not of men. To ignore the emotional needs of men is to undermine the foundation on which reason must rest, and in modern societies groups that are large enough to effect results tend to be too large to be meaningful to the individual. Even groups that might express the deepest desires of many are often stillborn. It is not enough for men to share attitudes: they must be able to communicate that fact to others and, once that has been achieved, they must find the resources of wealth and organizational skill to give these attitudes a political reality. In wide areas of life, citizens of the industrial states become subject to great organizations, public or private, which they did not create and to which they can create no alternative—to which the individual matters very little indeed. Such groups will be resented whatever benefits they convey.[21]

The nation itself, modern man's effort to recapture the atmosphere of the *patria* or the *polis*, is an abstraction and not a community. Cemented by habit, by appearance, or by symbol, it is vastly larger than the emotional universe of men, and their devotion to it is always ambiguous and tinged with resentment. Aggression toward outsiders is not only an outlet for such resentment: our still-greater difference from foreigners provides the major positive basis for loyalty toward those we do not know and who are unlike us in vital respects. The loyalty of men to the *polis* entails hostility as a secondary consequence of affection; nationalism demands it from its very nature, and is necessarily and not incidentally an "anti-feeling." [22]

Private emotion and public reason are radically separated. In the great industrial states, the former may be quieted by affluence; public frustration finds a compensation in private gratification. Yet the "primordial sentiments" which Clifford Geertz observes in developing states are present in all and find expression in moments of economic failure or political anxiety.[23]

Morally confused and uncertain men in the least developed nations, finding no dignified place in modern settings, may find release in internal aggression, asserting the claims of embattled traditionalism against the state. The most developed have shattered traditional groups almost beyond repair but may allow men the luxury of an affluent privatism and familism—sentiments truly primordial. The "mid-modern" state, finding either alternative difficult, may be driven to external aggression in consequence. Yet such assertions and retreats only partly mask the conviction that the self is worthless, a necessary consequence when a state of war exists between emotion and reason and man becomes a foreigner to himself.[24]

The search for dignity in a world of expanded scale and accelerated change tends to reinforce, not to weaken, the direction and pace of change. Seemingly unable to control the process, men have hoped to find dignity by leading it; men find solace for their passivity in being able to compel others to follow their lead.[25]

The new nations, long forced to follow, seek to escape that necessity and, in an ultimate sense, to lead others in their turn. Indeed, the ability to control one's own destiny in an interdependent world requires the ability to control others. Yet it is a sad fact that the undignified men of the great states will regard the self-assertion of the new states as a threat to their own dignity. Indeed, the long history of leadership by the great states only leads their citizens to regard that status as a matter of right and threats to it as a violation, and not a measure, of justice.

Samuel Huntington's model of political development suggests that most developing states have moved from "primitive" or "contained" political systems to a "corrupt" variety based on high mobilization and low institutionalization.[26] This is probably accurate, yet Huntington implies that developed states are in a different, "civic" situation in which institutionalization is high.

Organization, however, is not institution: it may be effective, but it has no claim on the loyalties of men. An institutional system presumes that certain patterns of organization and behavior become so deeply identified with goals and values as to acquire a moral value themselves. Institutionalization, then, tends to require a history of successful action. Yet, as Huntington points out, any transformation of the political environment threatens institutions, for in a new environment prescribed procedures may fail to attain the desired result.

In part, it has been the cumulative effect of change that has forced political scientists to discard institutional models in favor of the study of process. Seventy years ago, if not earlier, political observers noted that politics had evaded the constraints of the American constitutional order.[27] Increasingly, in all states, the statute law, tortuous in enactment and rigid in structure, is replaced by vague statements whose substance is supplied by administrative decision; "unconstitutional delegation of power" has almost vanished as a category of law.[28]

This tendency is especially marked in foreign policy. When war and peace are no longer distinct states, the declaration of war becomes a formality or is ignored. Constitutional dictatorship, once a resort in desperate situations, becomes the rule in an international environment that makes ever greater demands for expertise, speed, and secrecy. Constraints on these tendencies are provided by the unofficial pressures of groups and the inertia of complex organization, not from institutions associated with public values.[29]

That these conditions exist in states with longstanding constitutional traditions, as well as the goods of modern social and economic organization, suggests a general movement in the direction of corrupt systems. The person of the executive bulks large in all systems. Lack of organization may allow the leaders of new states greater latitude in changes of policy and alignment; the smaller latitude of the leaders of great states is more than compensated for by the magnitude of power available to them. The choice between war and peace may be narrow, but dimensions become irrelevant when the result of the choice is human survival.

Charisma is a necessity of all states: where institutions fail, men must trust those men on whom they depend. Indeed, modern charisma emphasizes not the difference between leader and led but their essential identity; the mass audience is on a first-name basis with truly modern leaders.

Political parties are, as Huntington suggests, a possible source for new institutions, but they are not a panacea. The more institutional a party system, the greater its tendency to obsolescence: it may ignore the concerns of its constituents and lose its claim to their loyalty.[30] Moreover, in any moment of crisis it is not the party that decides; decisions must be made by a few men or by one. Nor is the party exempt from the effects of size; to be successful, it must be so large as to threaten its meaningfulness to its partisans.

Modern states demanded institutionalization because the community was too large and fissiparous to act for itself, especially in crisis situations, and required the constraint of institutions to guarantee that government acted within the limits of public purpose. As institutions decline, there is a need for new constraints; those who by situation or by personal character are able to act may have a duty to act for the community. Old concepts are beginning to emerge from the dusty files of political thought: civil disobedience, military intervention, and even tyrannicide. It is suggestive that in the new nations such ideas have completely conquered the barrier between conception and action. Indeed, civil disobedience, now fashionable in the great states, owes much of its modern origin to its success in India. In this, as in many things, the new states may be the prophets for the old.

Ideas are vital to the survival—or to the recovery—of such aspects of politics as may be possible in modern life. To be able to control the process of change, men must overleap events; they must use their minds to foresee the tendency of things and how they may be altered. More important, they must be able to conceive that those tendencies ought to be altered, to construct an ideal of the political good independent of history or probability. It is as essential to human freedom to be able to resist history as to resist the state. Yet the empire of development tends to extend its sway over the minds, as well as the actions, of statesmen and citizens.

The advent of the modern world involved, necessarily, a break with the older notion that had seen time as an almost changeless dimension of human existence through which men sometimes were able to glimpse ultimate reality. It involved an effort by men to control their destiny by mastering the forces of nature. Put another way, it involved a deprecation of aspiration—the longing of men for ideal things—and an elevation of expectation—the anticipation of receiving them. Even at best, however, expectation is a lower standard; it is limited, as aspiration is not, by the standard of probability: "many have imagined principalities and republics which have never been seen or known to exist in reality [wrote Machiavelli]; for how we live is so far removed from how we ought to live that he who abandons what is done for what ought to be done will rather learn to bring about his own ruin than his preservation . . . it is necessary for a prince . . . to learn how not to be good and to use this knowledge or not to use it according to the necessity of the case." [31]

Yet the Florentine hoped that men might control half of the circumstances of their lives; men should seek to understand natural and political necessity in order to master it. Human purpose remained logically sovereign over prediction.

By the nineteenth century, however, the expanded scale of political life, the birth of technology, and the growth of organizational power had so far developed that men began to doubt the capacity of ideas to control history. The ideas of men gain strength slowly, even with expanded facilities for education and communication, and are forced to begin again with each new generation. The forces of technical and organizational power could transform the environment in a historical moment. Ideas tended to be obsolescent: "Minerva's owl takes wing only as dusk descends." Yet the "scientific" historians of the nineteenth century ventured to hope that if men could not control history they could at least predict it; unable to win a victory himself, man could at least be on the winning side. Even Marx, who saw the real task as that of changing the world, felt impelled to base his vision on an inevitable process and to mock the utopians who trusted the force of ideas alone.[32]

Even that creed has been denied to contemporary men. Predicting the advance of science and technology has proved almost impossible; Wohlstetter writes that it amounts to guessing what darkness will reveal when made light.[33] Theories of political progress, moreover, have been rendered desperately uncertain when they have not been shattered beyond repair.

In a period of accelerated change, the past becomes psychologically more distant, the unpredictable future ever more immediate. The safe haven of experience becomes the backwater of obsolescence. Ortega commented that the experience of generations has become so radically distinct as drastically to limit the possibilities of communication between them.[34] Yet that too is a doctrine of the past: in the too-often-quoted advice to distrust those over thirty it is not hard to hear a yearning to be able to trust those under thirty, to escape the boundaries of time which separate one man from his fellows. As the unpredictable future has rushed nearer, thoughts have centered on dark anxieties, a tendency which reflects not only prudence but the growth of human power, which has given men more to fear and more to lose.

The end of ideology is, in fact, the final triumph of development over the frail barriers of doctrine with which men had sought to surround it. The effort to predict history, like the effort to control it, is surrendered and men are counseled to adapt themselves to the present as best they may.

Political life has always moderated the enthusiasm for ideas with the sobriety of responsibility. Amid the perils and uncertainties of the time, it is to be expected that political men should shorten their perspective; each day's survival may seem a sufficient success. Moreover, the intellectual climate of modernity imposes the same result. Expectation is anticipation, a "taking before," laying mental hands on what is not yet possessed. To deny men what they expect is to commit theft, to steal what has already been psychologically acquired; theft, in turn, demands that one locate the thief. Failure to meet expectation is a crime to be punished, and the environment of constantly rising expectations—a nearly universal aspect of modern politics—puts great pressures on government to be successful (or, at least, to locate another thief). Whatever the causes, preoccupation with the day-to-day and with immediate success makes politics, in an age of change, little more than organized drift.

Symbols bulk larger in the politics of developing nations than in those of the industrial states. Yet the importance of symbols is a mark of material weakness, an effort to "tie the hands of one's enemy with his own inhibitions" and to strengthen one's own morale with the inspiration of rhetoric.[35] Doctrines are valued only secondarily for intellectual content or logical structure (the vagueness and incoherence of ideologies in new states would suggest as much). The first principle is simple: those beliefs are felt true which are thought to advance the quest for dignity.

Formal creeds, for example, are heavily influenced by international fashionableness. Fascist doctrines, prominent before World War II, have almost vanished. Nonviolence had a vogue, especially because it is suited to the militarily weak, but India, its principal exponent, has demonstrated few qualms in the use of force when it seemed to further national aims.[36]

New states, insistent on narrowing the "domestic jurisdiction" clause of the U.N. Charter, have been sensitive when that clause touched their own cases, resolving the ambiguity only by the doctrine that colonialism is an "objective crime" and a "permanent aggression." National self-determination, the basis of that doctrine, has always been ambiguous; in multiethnic new states, it has been interpreted so tortuously as to lose almost all meaning.[37]

Even more bizarre cases are available; the doctrinaire Chinese were able to support the feudal aristocracy of Burundi, to trade with South Africa (data are no longer public), and even, according to some reports, to sell steel and equipment to the United States for use in Vietnam.[38]

Leaders of the new states have often assumed striking and propagandistic poses that have appealed to Western intellectuals offended by the lack of symbolic luster in the politics of their own states. Yet such leaders have also demonstrated great agility in deserting one set of symbols for another. Fidel Castro's opportune discovery of his lifelong attachment to Leninism is paralleled by Sékou Touré's announcement that he was returning nationalized industries to private hands, having only assumed control in order to delude communist states into providing aid.[39]

Such rapid changes of front are made possible by the weakness of new states. The same logic of complex society which makes economic costs inflexible downward makes foreign policies inflexible backward; past commitments constrain, change must proceed slowly, tempered by reassurance. This ponderous diplomacy is a mark of power; lack of constraint in new states is a mark of weakness. In fact, leaders in new states are often compelled by the lack of a trained diplomatic service to assume a dominant role in foreign policy.[40] The term "charisma" conceals more than it reveals; as the magnetism of a leader must vary with the followers he would attract, so the style of the statesman differs depending on whether his state is a lion or a fox.

Symbols affect the conduct of policy; they may be indicators of what states prefer. Preference may exclude some forms of action. Modibo Keita's assertion that only states of similar ideology should attempt regional union excludes such attempts where symbols are too radically different. Yet Keita did not promise success where symbols are similar; preference will be abandoned when the costs are too great. Julius Kambarage Nyerere, for example, offered to delay Tanganyikan independence to promote East African Federation, yet felt compelled to follow policies that rendered that federation improbable. Nor will states seek to extract a price, if one can be had, for even painless stands on principle; various abortive West African unions were cemented with Ghanaian loans.[41]

Even at their most powerful, symbols are neither ideologies nor political philosophies, and it seems likely that even symbols will decline in importance as new states develop material and organizational resources. The great states, unable entirely to free themselves from the encumbrance of ideology, lag behind. However peripheral, our continued concern for doctrine is a remnant of a more distant past; the new states are closer to the future.

The concept of a sharp distinction between domestic and foreign politics has close associations with the modern nation-state. It was related to the expansion of central administration until it controlled the entire territory of the state; to the rise of an internal market which decreased the relative economic importance of international trade; most importantly, to the rise of internal communication relative to communication across frontiers.[42]

Even in this period, however, participation in domestic politics (even if only as a conscious observer) entailed participation in international politics. The process of mobilizing men and resources was dual; domestic societies could make no claim on the loyalty of men without making them more attentive to the currents of international life.[43]

To be sure, the early nation-state was assisted by natural and technical barriers in trade, communications, and defense which made it a more autonomous unit and enabled it to place a more exclusive claim on the loyalties of men. Yet as a price of that loyalty, internally mobilized men made claims on foreign policy for the advancement of their own goals, and the uniformity of national policy disappeared with the coherence of its old governing elite. Appealing to journalists and historical romantics, the term "national interest" has been more and more deprived of content as claims and the groups making them have multiplied. The consensual basis of the national interest is likely, insofar as it remains at all, to be so abstract as to be useless as a guide to policy. (The fact that most Americans believe in democracy says little, obviously, about our international behavior.) And, in the twentieth century, the old barriers that supported the territorial state hardly exist; what survives is not a result of human limitations but of the conscious policy of governments imposed on quite different processes.

Sovereignty has been progressively eroded in organizational terms. Once the powers of the sovereign were fragmented among ministers; now, the old state ministries that once monopolized the conduct of war and foreign policy are forced to share their functions with specialized agencies and with private groups. If the mind of the state has become more confused, the problem is exacerbated by the fact that it no longer speaks with one voice.

There is scarcely an area of politics that does not demonstrate the inseparable unity of politics in our time. Ernst Haas has referred to the process by which problems, insoluble inside the state, "spillover" into internation relations. Equally, and often more compellingly, problems insoluble in international politics "spill in" and demand domestic solutions.[44]

One result of this interpenetration is that more and more domestic groups find themselves united to foreign counterparts by similarities of attitude, training, value, and concern which they do not share with their compatriots. This responsiveness, always a part of international politics, has tended to grow and become stronger in our times; *ad hoc* alignments become semipermanent, vague sentiments acquire organized form. The positive appeals of international responsiveness are seconded by feelings of estrangement or alienation from one's own state. The result has been a weakened, if not divided, loyalty responsive to a dual diplomacy in which foreign states contact unofficial as well as official agencies abroad (and, in fact, often pursue diplomacy through unofficial channels).

Tendencies toward dual diplomacy are even more apparent in the developing states. Domestic and international politics are more clearly inseparable; rudimentary consensus and assimilation make it more difficult to speak of a national interest than in states which have some remnants of a past reality of that vague symbol. Such consensus as exists is likely to be negative, hostility to an imperial or foreign foe. In former colonial territories, the politics of independence *was* international politics; domestic support was mobilized to win victories abroad. The foreign offices of such states often developed as party bureaus during the struggle for independence, resulting in a closer tie to domestic politics but also having a greater propensity to dual diplomacy.[45]

New nations pursue the classic aim of economic nationalism: the attempt to decrease dependence on the external sector of the economy in order to maximize control over the conditions of economic life. Yet the means employed only emphasize the change from the environment of past efforts to attain autarchy. The tools of new states are by preference political and not economic; the terms of aid may be more easily manipulated than terms of trade. Aside from the obvious devices—such as threats of aid from the "other side" in the Cold War—states have developed attitudes that are comparatively new. African leaders have been fairly receptive to foreign private investment despite its dubious economic benefits and its violation of the canons of nationalism. They have observed a tendency for aid to follow investment (after all, investment increases the interest of the donor country by adding economic to political considerations) and hope for a stronger position in negotiations because of it. Also, to a socialist planner, the rise of foreign investment may be preferable to the rise of a domestic bourgeoisie; the former, as Lenin was aware, remains politically vulnerable. This last aspect only emphasizes the indivisibility of modern politics.

New attitudes are only encouraged by the fact that new states are heavily influenced by Marxist versions of theories of international "functionalism" which see international politics as determined by international stratification. Such theories may emphasize the common interest of various sectors of the third world; they also suggest that national economies are a thing of the past and that the world is—or will be—a single economic order.[46] Accurate or not, such theories represent a mood that correctly reflects the forces of the time. Great powers may feel it less, but reason should point out that the universality of their interests and concerns, military as well as economic, makes the indivisibility of foreign and domestic politics even more a fact in their political life. If the great powers have not yet learned the lesson, they will find the task of ignoring it increasingly difficult.

More than one political theory has come to grief by trusting the strength of functional loyalties.[47] An individual may share much with, or may fear much from, a distant other; the fear and the threat lack the immediacy of the need for minimal trust and stable expectations in his relations with those he encounters daily. The psychological bases of territorial loyalty remain intact, if challenged by new forces and portents.

Confronted with divided interests or loyalties, men seek to avoid choice. Where possible they will seek to combine the two; specialized residential areas unite, in part, functional and territorial loyalties. Yet even where choice cannot be avoided, men can make themselves believe that loyalty to one set of interests is possible with little or no loss to another. Our experience would indicate that men will give preference to territorial loyalty and will abandon it only in the last extremity.

The importance of territorial loyalty is only one aspect of the choice. It unites with men's desire for dignity, which leads them—all other considerations aside—to prefer the smaller group, in which they matter more, to the larger, in which they are only vague statistical considerations. It unites with resentment of the impersonality of functional loyalties. Finally, it combines with a fear of the unfamiliar in a universe of pervasive and threatening change.

Men have always sought to recapture lost domesticity, and those who have seemed to symbolize the inroads of foreign things into domestic space have been subjected to persecution and to exile. In the twentieth century, this persecution has assumed peculiarly virulent forms. Yet the odious inhumanities of the times reflect both the vulnerability of the state and the desperation of men's desire to protect it.[48] The permeability of the state has not been the means to the liberation of man; that the state is vulnerable only emphasizes to the individual his own defenselessness and makes clear that citizenship in some states is the basis of even a "right to have rights." True political orders may have become impossible, but men will strive to retain or to acquire as close an approximation as possible. Man remains a political animal.

Many an impressive functional argument can be made for regional organization and integration. In Africa, regionalist doctrine has had high symbolic appeal. Leaders have shared experience, friendship, and common political struggles to an unusual extent, and the mass of men feel no inherited loyalty to the nation. Moreover, states are felt to be too small or too weak to meet the needs of individuals. All these factors would seem to remove barriers to integration. In Asia, for example, where states are larger and the beneficiaries of comparatively ancient national traditions, there has been less interest in regional organization.[49]

The fact that the mass has not been assimilated to the state and that it still gives its loyalty to smaller groups of tribe and kindred appears, at first glance, less significant than the factors impelling states toward regionalism. Africa shares a common experience of "cultural shame." More frequently lumped into a single category by Europeans, Africans also felt the brunt of theories of racial and cultural inferiority. A common experience of indignity and a common object of resentment create at least one bond across tribal and state frontiers.[50]

Yet the results of widespread verbal acceptance of pan-African doctrines have been meager. In part, this indicates that common indignity is a poor bond between men. It unites men only on the basis of a shame they seek to escape and can be sustained only by the pressure of necessity. As states in Africa have won independence, the salience of necessity, the common struggle, has declined. In fact, the seeds of division were sown long before independence; not only the diversity of nature and custom in Africa, but the impact of European colonialism produced different values, attitudes, and patterns of communication. Before independence movements were of serious proportion, schisms developed which reflected many of the post-independence divisions of Black Africa.[51] The passing of necessity deprived regionalist argument of much of its impact on men.

To be sure, the functional case for regionalism is debatable. The colonial economies of the developing world, competitive and tied to metropolitan markets, hold out little appeal of immediate economic gain from regionalism. Indeed, if unity involved a loss of protected markets, the result might be economic decline. Such arguments can be countered by the hope of greater gains in the long term, however, and the important political fact is not the economic merits of either case (economic soundness never being a guarantee of policy) but why the former has seemed more compelling than the latter.[52]

In part, the African states (and the other new nations) suffer from a paralysis of hope; weakness overrides it, and states fear to lose the little they possess.[53] In one sense, it is the analogue of an identical paralysis in many of the great powers—the fear of the future, the surrender to the present.

Division into many states also entails an immediate cost. As the votaries of pan-Africanism constantly point out, individual African states are more dependent on, and subject to influence by, non-African powers. The leaders of states, however, have found that dependence, though onerous, is the preferable alternative. They have feared that regional organization would entail a domination of their states by others, and dependence on many states combined with autonomy of decision is felt preferable to the risk of deeper dependence on a few. The African nation may have little meaning to the mass of its citizens and may seem inadequate even to leaders, yet it is some sort of polity and its structure is somewhat familiar. Here the "bond" of indignity becomes divisive indeed; having conquered one form of dominion, men become doubly suspicious of submitting to a new one and losing whatever gains they have achieved. Resentment against indignity is only a negative value; its positive side is the desire for dignity and significance, for a political order in which one matters. And men will not surrender a state in which they matter more for one in which they matter less without the compulsion of perceived necessity.[54]

Indeed, the resolution of the early ideological divisions within Africa in the Organization of African Unity (OAU), never highly successful, owed whatever success it achieved to the adoption of a legitimist formula. Legal governments demanded unqualified acceptance as a price of cooperation. (Recently, the influence of such sentiments has been suggested in the Nigerian crisis: more ideological sympathy with Biafra exists among African states than has appeared, but the OAU has steadily supported the Federal regime.) [55]

The experience of Africa reinforces the conclusion that Haas and Schmitter reached in their study of Latin America: accelerated regional dynamics are unlikely unless alternatives outside the region fail.[56] African states have found the international order at least sufficiently responsive to prevent those dynamics from developing beyond the most embryonic stage. Barring a closing off of alternatives by the industrial states, regional organization would be likely only if the United States or the EEC were to provide powerful economic and diplomatic support—as European regionalism received from the United States.

If the declining salience of resentment limits regional unity, it also endangers the basis of the state itself. Anticolonialism is still the core of legitimacy of most non-Western regimes. Neocolonialism is, at best, an abstract threat and men grow accustomed to any given level of peril if it is prolonged. States based on a reaction *against* foreign policy remain based *on* it; there is a tendency to follow a policy more and more assertive as development progresses, as expectations and frustrations expand, and as the original unifying danger seems more remote. Yet such a policy, which seeks to create (or reveal) dangers that once seemed apparent has a danger of its own: that the escalation of words tends to leak over into deeds,' whether by terrifying the enemy or by words' ceasing to move men. Nasser can survive a defeat by Israel, but not an accommodation with her.[57]

No dilemma is more common to new states than that posed by the second generation. Rapid mobilization makes it much larger than the first; its demands are harder to meet, both from sheer size and from increased expectations. Moreover, the nation-state, the monument of the first generation and its means to dignity,[58] is only a given for the second. Also, since first generations come to power as young men, the second feel the added frustration of long exclusion from the high counsels of the state. They may be better educated than their predecessors and hence contemptuous of them; they will almost certainly be more likely to be educated at home and will lack the cosmopolitan knowledge and contacts so notable among early leaders. Not only will they be less likely to accept the international order as a given, they are likely to find the state still too undignified and too dependent, its domestic life too subject to impersonal forces and foreign powers. Younger leaders ("generation," though useful, unfortunately combines vagueness with seeming specificity) are likely to create increasing pressures for an assertive foreign policy. Yet this aggression will be the result of frustrations in part less material than those most often measured: the frustration of the desire for dignity and for political society.[59]

Yet the fact is that such frustration and resentment are inherent in development. Modern states, which prohibit interpersonal violence and in which the organizational scale outruns the affections and the sense of dignity of the individual, remain stable only so long as they can guarantee the gratification of private desires. The need for sacrifice is most often justified by the threat of enemy powers. Developing nations, facing a more difficult task with fewer resources, are under great pressure (whether conscious or systemic) to find outlets abroad for resentment which would otherwise find expression at home. As the perils of conflict grow, this may be a harder task to perform, yet the frustrations of development will grow with those perils. Internal disorder, ethnic secessionism, and guerrilla conflict are not only threats to new states; they have made their appearance in the great powers. That too may be part of the future toward which historical development leads mankind.[60]

The prospects for international peace and stability are hardly enhanced by the logic of development. Institutions in international society also decay; international law, difficult to enact and difficult to change, is losing much of its already eroded standing. The cynicism of new states with regard to international law often shocks Westerners, yet Western states have hardly hesitated when they felt that necessity impelled them to a violation of law. Even if new states had participated in the making of international law, it would be a rash policymaker who appealed to *pacta sunt servanda* with any confidence. Change undermines the promises of the past, and states, aware of the danger, hesitate to commit themselves and hedge their pledges with escape clauses. States feel no ability to pit human faith against the forces of change: the cushion of time no longer surrounds states and the perils of trust have reached almost prohibitive levels.[61]

New states, confronting the discontinuity between legal categories and power, have surely been justified in regarding traditional and contemporary appeals to legality as so many shams. Neocolonialism is a doctrine which reflects the gap between legal sovereignty and political independence; it will not do, with the experience of Latin America in mind, to dismiss the doctrine as a communist-inspired fantasy as Crozier does. The doctrine is only a way of stating that some states are immensely more powerful than others; Canada might be ranked among the neocolonies. Yet the fact of that giant difference is the mark of the obsolescence of international legality.

All states are aware of the interdependence of the world; all know that in practice only a few (or only two) states participate in making the decisions that govern mankind. The facts produce anxiety, resentment, and a desire to participate.[62] Yet formal participation solves nothing; it is treated as a gesture of condescension and an indication that the real decisions are being made elsewhere. Great inequalities of power make it impossible for the weak to trust the strong.

Hence, the prevailing tendency for new states to regard alliances with industrial states as inherently degrading. The weak are sensitive about their dignity, and suspicion may become so extreme as to be folly, preventing any accurate calculation of gains and losses. Worse, the suspicion of alliances tends to extend to other developing states if these are somewhat higher on the ladder of development (the relations of Africa with Asia are a case in point).[63]

Neutralism is one effort to discover an alternative to alliance which does not neglect interdependence. The political attitudes on which the policy is based are starkly "realistic"; nonalignment is the balance-of-power of the comparatively powerless. Its major prescription is that new states have an interest in the most intense form of great power competition short of war.[64]

The theory of national liberation wars is the same theory in more violent form. It presumes that the increasing threat of war and the rise of affluence have lessened the importance of values other than peace for the great powers. It sees the world balance and the structure of opinion as restricting or preventing the use of nuclear weapons in peripheral states. Even at the next stage of the argument it remains realistic; guerrilla insurrection cannot hope to defeat even the conventional weapons of a great power. Yet by throwing the nonutilitarian sentiments of patriotism and revolutionary zeal into the scales, a national liberation war may make an area so costly to conquer as to seem not worth the effort. Human will can prevail over unequal power.

The theory, obviously, requires continued conflict between the great powers, the more intense the better—so long as nuclear war does not occur. Yet it also requires that the great powers, and their citizens, operate by a standard of utilitarian rationalism. Whatever the result, the Vietnam war demonstrates that this is a risky supposition. The cost of war makes all states—the great powers as well—anxious for their security; change and unpredictability only heighten fear. This, in turn, makes the great states sensitive to changes in the relative distribution of power; security and dignity are associated in more than one way. Such sensitivity may become inordinate, especially if some groups become convinced that "time is against us" and that is essential to "draw the line." The old-style realism of theorists of national liberation wars is inaccurate in a new reality.[65]

Both neutralism and national liberation wars tend to become a variety of brinkmanship requiring policymakers of supremely great talent. Leaders of new states are often chided for yielding to the normal tendency to overrate the importance of their states to the world balance. Yet, except rhetorically, such ethnocentrism is unlikely to be extreme in new states, which are most often painfully aware of weakness. China assailed the Soviet Union for failure to take advantage of what the Chinese felt were the Soviet Union's opportunities after Sputnik; they did not believe themselves capable of acting and did not attempt it. In fact, the habit of weakness is more dangerous. Breeding resentment, it also generates irresponsibility. It may lead states to exaggerate the givenness of the international system and to pursue policies of local or regional assertion which may, in particular cases, endanger the stability of the whole.[66]

Such policies of regional self-assertion are only too likely, especially among the more confident, but still frustrated, transitional or semimodernized states. The temptation results from the indignities of development combined with the near impossibility of imitating the means by which states in the past achieved great power status. The task is now more difficult than for such late-arrivers as Germany or Japan. States confront a weapons matrix in which qualitative differences in weapons are crucial. Moreover, even if a state can keep the pace of innovation, she must be able to afford the cost of obsolescence, which entails repeated junking and replacing of entire weapons systems. The costs are beyond the capability of any new nation.[67]

Conflicts remain likely, especially for states with an early record of diplomatic success or foreign policy triumph. Such a history often reinforces the inherent resentments and conflicts of foreign policy with a propensity to seek solutions for recalcitrant domestic problems through action in international politics.[68] Politics often follows the course of least anticipated resistance.

For that reason, however, conflict with the great powers is unlikely no matter how resented their status and pretension. Before the recent disastrous campaign against Israel, Nasser found it useful to assert that Britain and France, not Israel, had defeated Egypt in 1956; afterward, he pleaded American and British intervention as the cause of disaster. Defeat, even by the secondary powers who intervened in 1956, was only to be expected in a conflict between an industrial and a developing state. That assumption, however, suggests that such conflicts will be avoided even by the bellicose.

There are, however, developing states that can be taken to symbolize the Western, imperial states ("creatures of neocolonialism"); there are also peripheral or weak Western powers—Israel, Portugal, South Africa. Local conflicts are not only likely with such states, they tend to be total because the states in question are symbolically equated with the source of indignity and frustration.

Some more genuinely local disputes are of serious proportion (Kashmir and the Somali dispute are obvious examples), but many are comparatively petty, both because the stakes are small and because the opponent is not identified with the indignity of the past. Tribal irredentas may, as Zartman argues, come to seem less significant as national integration advances.[69] Yet, that prospect is darkened by the history of similar disputes in eastern Europe. National integration may create pressures to assimilate minority ethnic groups which only stimulate such groups to resist or to seek assistance from kinsmen in neighboring states; national integration may also create competitive efforts to assimilate disputed ethnic minorities. Most probably, governments may feel compelled to pursue irredentist disputes by the fear that their prestige is too weak to survive concession or compromise.[70]

The short record of contemporary affairs only strengthens this prediction. The oau was able to halt the Algero-Moroccan conflict but only by accepting the Algerian stipulation that a cease-fire be based on the principle of "non-adjustment of existing frontiers," which made any resolution of the dispute impossible. Other international agencies have had no more success in similar disputes. And, as Zartman observes, if settlements are not made in times of comparative prosperity and peace, they are likely to detonate in periods of crisis.

Yet it may be less serious to allow local conflicts, within limits, than to impose an iron peace. The resentments of developing states are real and prohibition of foreign conflict—made ever more likely by the interdependence of the world and the risks of conflict itself—may only lead to increased tendencies toward internal division and civil strife.

However, it is not so easy to adopt a permissive attitude to local conflict. A serious consequence of contemporary politics is that, despite extremely high costs, the development of nuclear weapons is likely to seem worthwhile to many states. Undeniably, nuclear status is the high road to greater consideration by the great powers and greater international status generally, though nuclear forces are likely to be too small and too backward to change a new state's position of military inferiority.[71]

Moreover, nuclear-armed neighbors (China is the obvious case) may arouse fears for one's own security. The great powers, menaced themselves with annihilation, are perceived as less willing to honor their commitments than in the past. The "new realism" of Indian and Pakistani commentators reflects this attitude, as does the corollary proposition that each state must develop a deterrent of its own.[72] Banning nuclear diffusion would achieve little, even if it involved a guarantee to India by the U.S.S.R. and the U.S.; if a post-Mao China came to terms with the Soviet Union, would the Soviets honor their commitments? Would the U.S. protect India at the risk of general war? Even if she did, would this not force India to forfeit her nonaligned position? None of these questions can be answered with a resounding affirmative, and not the least of the costs of development is that the risks of error and the uncertainty of the future combine to make just such an affirmation necessary.[73]

The alternatives involve equally dark portents. Perhaps the great powers may contrive to find a solution that will reassure non-Western states sufficiently to deter nuclear armament and to exclude the threat of local aggression. Yet such a result is likely to increase feelings of dependence and resentment. In any case, it would be likely to direct the expression of existing frustrations and resentments in domestic violence and conflict. It is a comment on the gray landscape of the age that this is probably the optimist's hope, for the alternative is an expanding nuclear race, the possibility of local nuclear conflicts, and the constant risk that the great powers will be drawn in. War has become intolerable and indignity, ubiquitous; men who cannot fight foreigners may become foreign to their fellow citizens, and the streets become the new boundaries over which battles are fought. That possibility, it need hardly be said, is the grimmest of the ways in which the present of the new states may forecast the future of the old.

Modern times have realized in the empirical world the vision of ancient prophets: the unity of human history. Yet the vision realized proves not to be a blissful utopia but a predicament, complex, ambiguous, seemingly insoluble. Many of the solutions offered to men have failed, and others will fail in turn. Any solution must realize that there are no impersonal forces in the political world, whatever they may seem. The forces of change and technology that seem to sweep men onward and the shadowy tides of unreason that resist them are both rooted in human desire and imagination. It is because the drama of history is, in fact, the swirling battle of forces in the soul of man that makes it so resistant to control. Men yearn for the goods produced by the forces they fear; pride speaks the inner language of self-hatred and doubt.

If there exists a solution it lies in the redevelopment—or the development—of politics, though the political is at best a tentative synthesis needing renewal in each generation. Perhaps more than any other, the quest for the political, often inarticulate and fumbling, gives unity to such movements as the search for means of participation and dignity common to the unipartite movements of the non-Western world and to the highly individualistic and antiorganizational "New Left" in the West, to the partisans of guerrilla conflict and those of nonviolent civil disobedience.[74]

Men need to give the visions implicit in such movements more articulate form, and once stated, to seek means for the realization of the political in new techniques and institutions. Success must be judged unlikely. It would require initiative and action by the great powers, which alone have the capacity to control the general international environment; the alternatives in the new states depend on the alternatives made available by the old. Yet the great powers tend to fix their attention on the terms of their present rivalry, partly because of the appalling danger it poses to both, partly because they have sufficient comfort to value the present, partly because old ideas and ideologies provide an illusory security in new times. The new states, which perceive the necessities, tend to an imagination chained by impotence; they too tend to accept the present environment as a given.

Yet, however unlikely, the possibility that men will find a way to control the world of contemporary politics—even that they will find a way to attain the political—cannot be excluded altogether. Crisis is a time of unlikelihood and improbability, and as in all great crises we rely on the unlikely abilities and devotion of citizens and statesmen. Men are never prisoners of events, but only of their folly, and the imperative of de Tocqueville's new science rings true for our time: "Our contemporaries are only too prone to doubt of human freedom because each of them feels confined on every side by his own weakness but they are still willing to acknowledge the strength and independence of men united in society. Do not let this principle be lost sight of, for the great object in our time is to raise the faculties of men, not to complete their prostration."[75]

NOTES

[1] Alexis de Tocqueville, *Democracy in America* (New York, 1961), I, lxiii.

[2] Michael Walzer, "Theories of Modernization," in *The Radical Imagination*, ed. Irving Howe (New York, 1967), 279–80.

[3] The utility of such categories, even for policymakers, is doubtful. See Robert A. Packenham, "Political Development Doctrines in the American Foreign Aid Program," *World Politics*, XVIII (Jan. 1966), 194–235, and R. Clower, *et al.*, *Growth without Development* (Evanston, 1966), 4–5, 75.

[4] David Apter, *The Politics of Modernization* (Chicago, 1965), is one of many efforts to assemble such concepts.

[5] Rupert Emerson, "African States and the Burdens They Bear," *African Studies Bulletin*, X (1967), 3–4.

[6] De Tocqueville, *Democracy in America*, Vol. I, Chap. 14.

[7] F. S. Lear, *Treason in Roman and Germanic Law* (Austin, Tex., 1965), 80, 224–26.

[8] Plato *Republic* II. 376.

[9] *Ibid.*, I. 334.

[10] *Democracy in America*, Vol. I, Chap. 14.

[11] "The Choice of Comrades," in *The Radical Imagination*, ed. Irving Howe (New York, 1967), 14.

[12] Lear, *Treason*, 87.

[13] Aristotle *Politics* VII. 4.

[14] De Tocqueville, *Democracy in America*, Vol. I, Chap. 8.

[15] Robert G. Wesson, *The Imperial Order* (Berkeley and Los Angeles, 1967), 28–29.

[16] *Ibid.*, 333–34, 338, 350.

[17] De Tocqueville, *Democracy in America*, Vol. I, Chap. 8.

[18] Rupert Emerson, *From Empire to Nation* (Cambridge, Mass., 1960).

[19] For one example, see Ali Mazrui, "The U.N. and Some African Political Attitudes," *International Organization*, XVIII (1964), 510, 515.

[20] Wilson C. McWilliams, ed., *Garrisons and Government: Politics and the Military in New States* (San Francisco, 1967), 307.

[21] Grant McConnell, *Private Power and American Democracy* (New York, 1966).

[22] Rupert Emerson, "Nationalism and Political Development," *Journal of Politics*, XXII (1960), 24; see also Mancur Olson, *The Logic of Collective Action* (Cambridge, Mass., 1965).

[23] "The Integrative Revolution: Primordial Sentiments and Civic Patterns in New States," in *Political Modernization*, ed. C. Welch (Belmont, Calif., 1967), 167–87.

[24] Karen Horney, *The Neurotic Personality of Our Time* (New York, 1937); M. J. Field, *The Search for Security* (Evanston, 1961). Compare J. E. Mueller, "The Politics of Fluoridation," *Western Political Quarterly*, XIX (1966), 54–67, and Jack Walker, "A Critique of the Elitist Theory of Democracy," *American Political Science Review*, LX (1966), 285–95.

[25] McWilliams, *Garrisons and Government*, 305, 306.

[26] Samuel P. Huntington, "Political Development and Political Decay," *World Politics*, XVII (1965), 386–430.

[27] John W. Burgess, *Political Science and Comparative Constitutional Law* (New York, 1890), I, 150ff.

[28] Bertrand de Jouvenel, "The Principate," *Political Quarterly*, XXXVI (1965), 20–51.

[29] Stanley Hoffman, "International Systems and International Law," *World Politics*, XIV (1961), 205–37; Clinton Rossiter, *Constitutional Dictatorship* (Ithaca, N.Y., 1958).

[30] Harvey Wheeler, "Constitutional Obsolescence in a Duocratic Party System," *Ethics*, LXVII (1957), 79–88.

[31] *The Prince*, Chap. 15.

[32] W. C. McWilliams, "On Time and History," *Yale Review*, LVI (1966), 91–103.

[33] Albert Wohlstetter, "Technology, Prediction and Disorder" (paper presented to the American Political Science Association, New York, 1963).

[34] J. Ortega y Gassett, *Man in Crisis* (New York, 1965), 20–101.

[35] I. W. Zartman, "National Interest and Ideology," in *African Diplomacy*, ed. V. McKay (New York, 1966), 43, 45.

[36] See S. Rose, ed., *The Politics of Southern Asia* (New York, 1963), 111–12, 127–28, for Fascist doctrines in Asia. See also John Marcum and A. K. Lowenstein, "Force: Its Thrust and Prognosis," in *Southern Africa in Transition*, ed. Davies and Barker (New York, 1966), 247–77.

[37] Mazrui, *International Organization*, XVIII, 510, 515; and "Consent, Colonialism and Sovereignty," *Political Studies*, XI (1963), 36–55.

[38] J. Cooley, *East Wind over Africa* (New York, 1965), 110; the report, originally from the London *Observer*, is discussed in *New Times* (Moscow), XXVIII (July 12, 1967), 22–23.

[39] Brian Crozier, *Neo-Colonialism* (London, 1964), 81.

[40] Vernon McKay, *Africa in World Politics* (New York, 1963), 398–99.

[41] M. Keita, "The Foreign Policy of Mali," *International Affairs*, XXXVII (1961), 432–39; Claude Welch, *The Dream of Unity: Pan Africanism and Political Unification in West Africa* (Ithaca, N.Y., 1966), 20, 306–15, 326, 328, 330; Ali Mazrui, "Tanzania and East Africa," *Journal of Commonwealth Political Studies*, III (1965), 209–15.

[42] Karl W. Deutsch, "Shifts in the Balance of International Communication Flows," *Public Opinion Quarterly*, XX (1956), 143–60.

[43] McWilliams, *Garrisons and Government*, 310–11.

[44] Ernst B. Haas, *Beyond the Nation State* (Stanford, 1964); see also "Dynamic Environment in Static System: Revolutionary Regimes in the U.N.," in *The Revolution in World Politics*, ed. Morton Kaplan (New York, 1964), 267–309.

[45] I. W. Zartman, *International Relations in the New Africa* (Englewood Cliffs, N.J., 1966); M. Quint, "The Idea of Progress in an Iraqi Village," *Middle East Journal*, XII (1958), 369–94; Welch, *Dream of Unity*, 15–18; N. D. Palmer, *The Indian Political System* (Boston, 1961), 238–39; I. Wallerstein, *Africa: The Politics of Unity* (New York, 1967), 179–218; Philip Garigue, "The West African Students Union," *Africa*, XXIII (1953), 55–69.

[46] See Wallerstein, *Africa: The Politics of Unity*, 140.

[47] James P. Sewell, *Functionalism and World Politics* (Princeton, 1965), 3–74, 245–332.

[48] Compare Harold Lasswell, "The Garrison State Hypothesis Today," in *Changing Patterns of Military Politics*, ed. S. Huntington (New York, 1962), 51–70.

[49] William J. Foltz, "Building the Newest Nations," in *Nation Building*, ed. K. Deutsch and W. Foltz (New York, 1963), 117–31.

[50] A. A. Mazrui, "On the Concept, 'We Are All Africans,' " *American Political Science Review*, LXVIII (1963), 88–97.

[51] Kwame Nkrumah, *Ghana: The Autobiography of Kwame Nkrumah* (London, 1957), 43–44; G. Jahoda, "Nationality Preference and National Stereotype in Ghana before Independence," *Journal of Social Psychology*, L (1959), 165–74.

[52] E. B. Haas, "International Organization: The European and the Universal Process," *International Organization*, XV (1961), 366–92; Wallerstein, *Africa: The Politics of Unity*, 144; Joseph Nye, *Pan-Africanism and East African Integration* (Cambridge, Mass., 1965).

[53] Compare E. Berg, "The Economic Basis of Political Choice in French West Africa," *American Political Science Review*, LIV (1960), 391–405.

[54] It is illustrative to compare recent regionalism with similar movements in the Balkans, which also collapsed after definitive victories over Turkey. See W. L. Langer, *European Alliances and Alignments, 1871–1900* (New York, 1931), 61ff.

[55] Wallerstein, *Africa: The Politics of Unity*, 91, 92, 136, 137; Nora McKeon, "The African States and the OAU," *International Affairs*, XLIII (1966), 390–409.

[56] E. B. Haas and Philippe Schmitter, *The Politics of Economics in Latin American Regionalism* (University of Denver Graduate School of International Studies Monographs in World Affairs, 1965). Recent U.S. decisions to restrict aid but to encourage self-help in Latin America might have such an effect.

[57] L. Berkowitz, "Repeated Frustrations and Expectations in Hostility Arousal," *Journal of Abnormal and Social Psychology*, LX (1960), 422–29; Haas, "Dynamic Environment," 267–71, 307–309; and L. Binder, "Egypt's Positive Neutrality," in *The Revolution in World Politics*, 175–91.

[58] Note that for Nkrumah "Ghana" was literally the "autobiography" of Nkrumah himself. See n. 51, above.

[59] McWilliams, *Garrisons and Government*, 312–13.

[60] S. Kuznets, "The State as a Unit of Economic Growth," *Journal of Economic History*, XI (1954), 34; see also Ivo and R. K. Feierabend, "Aggressive Behaviors Within Politics," *Journal of Conflict Resolution*, X (1966), 249–71, and F. von Wieser, *Das Gesetz der Macht* (Vienna, 1926).

[61] R. L. Friedheim, "The Satisfied and Dissatisfied States Negotiate International Law," *World Politics*, XVIII (1965), 20–41.

[62] Eduardo Frei, "Latin America and the World of Today," *International Affairs*, XLII (1966), 373–80.

[63] McKay, *Africa in World Politics*, 105; N. P. Nayan, "Non-Alignment in World Affairs," *India Quarterly*, XVIII (1962), 30, 32.

[64] A. P. Rana, "The Nature of India's Foreign Policy," *India Quarterly*, XXII (1966), 101–39; Raj Krishna, "Proliferation," *ibid.*, 285–92; J. D. Sithi, "India, China and the Vietnam War," *ibid.*, 154–76; Binder, "Egypt's Positive Neutrality," 184–87; Wallerstein, *Africa: The Politics of Unity*, 245–46, 253.

[65] Lasswell, "The Garrison State Hypothesis Today," 57–70.

[66] Binder, "Egypt's Positive Neutrality," 189, 197; A. L. Hsieh, "China's Secret Military Papers," *China Quarterly*, XVIII (1964), 79–99.

[67] W. R. Schilling, "Science, Technology and Foreign Policy," *Journal of International Affairs*, XIII (1959), 7–18.

[68] S. Clough, *The Economic History of Modern Italy* (New York, 1964); I. Wallerstein, "Pan-Africanism as a Protest," in *The Revolution in World Politics*, 149–50; Douglas Ashford, "Politics and Violence in Morocco," *Middle East Journal*, XIII (1959), 11–25.

[69] Zartman, *International Relations in the New Africa*, 166ff. See S. Touval, "Africa's Frontiers," *International Affairs*, XLII (1966), 641–54.

[70] See W. L. Langer, *The Diplomacy of Imperialism* (New York, 1951), 303–15.

[71] *Indian and Foreign Review*, April 1, 4, and 15, 1967, pp. 3, 4, and pp. 3, 4.

[72] N. D. Palmer, *South Asia and U.S. Foreign Policy* (Boston, 1966), 178–79, 259–63.

[73] Wilson C. McWilliams, "Ending the Cold War," *Commonweal*, LXXXV (Jan. 6, 1967), 363–65.

[74] See Mitchell Cohen and Dennis Hale, eds., *The New Student Left* (Boston, 1965).

[75] De Tocqueville, *Democracy in America*, Vol. II, Bk. I, Chap. 20.

CHAPTER TWO

FOREIGN POLICY

AND

SOCIAL CHANGE

––––––

GAYL D. NESS

THE RELATION between large, superordinate states and small, subordinate states provides the most useful setting for the analysis of the relation between foreign policy and social change.[1] The argument for the use of this type of highly simplified dyadic model with considerable power imbalance is largely a strategic one. Social change is a complex process that is shaped by many forces. Normally forces internal to the society will be more important than external forces in determining the speed and direction of social change. Further, the external forces that are important seldom derive from a single society. They are more often a complex amalgam of both identifiable foreign policies and the less formal social and economic affinities of a large number of states standing in various degrees of social proximity to the subject society. The simple dyadic, super-subordinate relationship model allows us to cut through much of this complexity in order to arrive at least at a first approximation of some of the dimensions of variance in the basic relation to be studied.

This is not to argue that relations between states of equal size and power are irrelevant, nor that large and powerful states are insulated against external forces. For example, Denmark provided important shipping and commercial functions for Thailand in the latter part of the nineteenth and the twentieth centuries. Although Denmark has undoubtedly been an important carrier of external forces in Thailand, it would be difficult to argue that Danish foreign policy was really significant in shaping the patterns of social change within Thailand. Similarly, large states may be somewhat insulated against external factors by their sheer size, but they are scarcely islands unto themselves. The foreign policies of western Europe, which promoted imperialism and colonialism since the sixteenth century and facilitated massive emigration especially during the latter eighteenth and the nineteenth centuries, certainly had a profound impact upon the character of social change in the United States. This observation itself draws out more clearly one implication of our model and anticipates some of the findings of this analysis. The impact of foreign policy on social change in a subject country is most dramatic and visible in the case of a special relationship between two states, such as the relationship characterized by super- and subordinate status. Further, this observation calls attention to the characteristics in the subject society that make it more or less vulnerable to external forces. European emigration had an impact on social change in the United States precisely because, and only as long as, immigration was permitted. Thus, it is some congruence of compatible external and internal forces that provide the optimum condition for an external force such as foreign policy to have an impact on internal social change.

Size is not the only determinant of super- or subordinate position. What we are more concerned with is a relationship between societies of highly unequal power. To be sure, sheer size often plays an important role. Disparities in size contributed to the United States' superordinate position over Puerto Rico, the Philippines, and Cuba (up to 1958). It did not require a change in size, however, for Cuba to establish greater independence of the United States after 1958. Further, it was a military defeat rather than simple disparity in size that placed Japan in a subordinate position to the United States. Finally it was the combination of reduced size and Nationalist China's reliance upon United States protection for sheer survival that gave the United States considerable capacity to influence the course of social change in Taiwan. Thus the super- and subordinate relationships that we shall examine are themselves the products of a wide variety of forces, including size disparities and the distinct quality of the relationship.

Social change implies many things.[2] We could mean changes in kinship relations, in stratification patterns, in rural-urban population distribution, in the industrial distribution of the labor force, in patterns of authority, in the size and quality of organizations, or in the character and pervasiveness of norms. Any one of these constitutes an area of social change and could provide the focus for analysis. What we shall be concerned with, however, is a more general and more basic pattern of change in social relations. This is the change from older predominantly agrarian societies to newer predominantly urban and industrial societies.

The observation of this major change is at the base of the emergence of sociology as a distinct discipline and has remained a core interest in the discipline for the past century. From Saint Simon through Emile Durkheim, Max Weber, Herbert Spencer, and to Talcott Parsons, sociologists have been concerned with the changing pattern of social relations when men leave agriculture and the rural areas and take up urban residence and industrial occupations, when relatively small-scale societies are replaced with larger ones, when tasks and the relationships built around them become specialized and divided, and when individuals and groups have larger and more diverse arenas in which to play out their roles.

An important part of this basic social change revolves around the ownership and use of land. In the ideal-typical sense, the old society is one in which land was used for the production of goods that would be more or less immediately consumed. Relationships were generally diffuse and particularistic. Kinship defined a set of horizontal claims and obligations covering a wide range of behavior. Hierarchical relations were based largely on the control over land and also gave men broad mutual obligations. Given this areal dimension of relations and the technological barriers to communication, groups bound under single and direct authority relations were relatively small and of low density.

The change we observe is one in which the products of the land begin to move through a marketplace: agriculture is commercialized. As more and more nonhuman sources of power are used, capital and labor become factors of production more important than land: factory production emerges. Labor becomes specialized and divided, implying that its upward relations are of a more specific and limited nature. Even the diffuse horizontal bonds of kinship give way to the limited and specific bonds of organizational affiliation.[3] The basis of stratification shifts from kinship to organizational relations.[4] As the areal dimension of organization becomes less important, as population densities increase and the technology of communication and transportation improves, the boundaries of authority become less restricted and less particularistic. A more extended and more impersonal public authority emerges.[5] Overall, these changes lie at the heart of what we have recently come to call "modernization," a term at once useful and treacherous.

These changes occur gradually. Even where the most violent revolutions have occurred, they constitute more of a watershed in a slower process than an immediate and radical reordering of society. We can find watersheds in nonrevolutionary as well as in revolutionary societies. They can be sought and found in many aspects of social relations,[6] but from what has been proposed in ideal-typical terms above, it is useful to seek them in the patterns of control over land. This is, further, an area in which foreign policy can have and has had a major impact on patterns of social change, especially in the cases we shall examine.[7]

In Japan, Taiwan, and Puerto Rico, United States foreign policy was directly involved in successful land reform programs that marked the watersheds in longer and more gradual processes of social change. The processes were those in which peasant masses became involved in direct and broadly based political action, in which their interests were articulated and transmitted through new organizations. The new organizations replaced the older limited and particularistic relations with landowners and marked the movement of the peasantry into positions of public authority. How United States foreign policy was so involved and what the determinants of its success were will occupy most of our attention in this paper.

We shall use the contrasting experiences of the Philippines and Cuba to throw into greater relief the role of United States foreign policy in the changes mentioned above. The basic argument will be that the major determinants of foreign policy effecting these basic social changes were the coincidence of powerful reform orientations in U.S. foreign policy *and* both general forces for change and the creation or existence of effective organized agents of change in the host society.

Some of the forces of modern social change in Japan can be found in the Tokugawa period (1603–1867). The political and military stability of the period, together with its restriction of intercourse among the Han (local centers of power and initiative) stimulated the development of a national market with Osaka as its center. This also implied a very considerable commercialization of agriculture.[8] The centralization of the knighthood in stipendary positions in towns and their separation from land ownership precluded the kind of violent resistance to agrarian change witnessed in western Europe. This left considerable leeway for the emergence of powerful economic incentives to change on the land itself, marked especially by the new peasant capitalists that grew up late in the Tokugawa period and were an important force in the changes brought by the Meiji restoration.[9]

The Meiji restoration (1868) removed some obstacles to modern social change and in other ways hastened that process. The end of prohibitions against the sale of land and the change of occupations removed barriers, already considerably weakened in practice, to social mobility. Universal education and conscription similarly worked to weaken further the power of ascribed statuses and to open new avenues of mobility to the population. Economic development also played its role. The level of human productivity increased steadily in all sectors, but especially in agriculture.[10] And agricultural growth helped to pay for growth in the urban industrial sectors, adding geographic dimensions to the new occupational avenues of social mobility.

The period from the restoration onward also saw the development of organizations technically competent to promote the basic social changes that were underway. The Ministry of Agriculture played an important role in the early agricultural growth and at the same time acquired considerable understanding of the determinants of agricultural productivity. Especially in the early Meiji period this role involved primarily attention to the technological and biological aspects of productivity,[11] but by the 1920's the ministry was gaining greater awareness of the class determinants, the problem of tenancy and ownership.[12] Out of this process of bureaucratic development came a large organization competent to plan and to execute, but not to decide upon, a decisive reform that would finally bring to an end the land and tenure conditions that supported the diffuse and particularistic relations of the old order.

Not all the forces worked in the same direction, however. More powerful forces worked to sustain the traditional relations, especially on the land, but with repercussions for the entire society. Agricultural development brought increased political power to the growing class of landlords. But while he was gaining political power, the economic role of the landlord was undergoing change. The Meiji landlord had been an integral part of the progressive structure that brought agricultural development.[13] By 1915 agriculture had lost its position as a dynamic growth sector. Net flows of capital that had previously been from the agricultural to the nonagricultural sector now were reversed.[14] Landlords became absentee owners and the incidence of tenancy rose. After 1920 the landlord class was a solidly entrenched conservative if not reactionary class. It used its political power to buttress its position and thus to sustain, especially in tenancy relations, the diffuse and particularistic relations characteristic of the older order.[15]

In acting as a brake upon social change, however, the landlords also acted as a brake upon economic development in agriculture. Against this braking force was the more economically progressive force in the Ministry of Agriculture. Though the weight was clearly and solidly on the side of the political power of the landlords, the strain in the society did present alternatives for government policy that could be easily exploited by an external and highly superordinate power. The stage was set for the United States occupation forces to force the critical decision for reform upon Japanese society.

The immediate postwar Diet, composed of the more conservative wartime elements, debated and delayed action on a land reform bill presented by the Ministry of Agriculture. Only the fear of Occupation pressures for even greater reform induced the Diet to act favorably on a bill in December of 1945. The Occupation found this bill deficient and procured another, more sweeping in its reform, early the following year.

The reform posture of the Occupation derived from a number of sources. Old Japan hands in the U.S. State Department advised caution in the reform, fearing that the radical disruption of the old system of social relations would open the way to chaos and a communist takeover. Others, such as R. A. Feary and W. I. Ladejinsky, pressed for reform and also obtained positions on MacArthur's staff.[16] Part of the proreform argument in U.S. foreign policy was to provide competitive forces to communist ideology,[17] part was based upon the assumed relation between landlordism and Japanese aggression.[18] There was also MacArthur's own previous experience in the Philippines, which had made him sympathetic to and knowledgeable of the problem of tenancy, and the more technical consideration of the immediate need to increase food production and the known connection between tenancy and low productivity. The convergence of these many political, ideological, and technical considerations made the Occupation's decision for reform a powerful and pervasive one.

However important this reform orientation in U.S. foreign policy, it would have been ineffective without reform forces and the technical and organizational competence previously developed in Japan itself. U.S. foreign policy was only the midwife to an idea that was "as indigenous as the conditions which impelled it."[19]

As important as the idea and the laws was the implementation of the reform. This, too, was almost purely a Japanese accomplishment. Thousands of paid local officials and a million voluntary hamlet auxiliaries were involved in the implementation of the law.[20] Local agricultural committees were given great discretionary powers and proceeded to use them, for the most part in rather full compliance with the law. Peasants had to be instructed in their new rights and induced to pursue them, no easy matter when those new rights violated norms that had been reinforced by strong economic ties. The necessary instruction in and protection of peasants' rights could only be accomplished by functionaries thoroughly involved in and familiar with the pattern of social relations. No occupation force would ever have such a capacity. Like the idea of reform, the implementation "was as indigenous as the conditions which impelled it."

The results were profound. In the removal of landlordism and the widespread redistribution of land, the economic supports for the old pattern of social relationships were destroyed. Diffuse bonds of social and economic obligations of large numbers of farmers to a small class of landlords were replaced by highly specific and impersonal contractual relations. About two million farm families, a third of all farm families, became owner-operators; about a million were removed from the status of pure tenants.[21]

Ladejinsky speaks of this as a great rural renaissance. Land and labor productivity, capital accumulation, and mechanization all increased. The once subordinate masses of the rural scene came to gain significant influence in both local and national politics.

The old order has now been left behind. Although the overall process has been gradual, the land reform of the Occupation marks a significant watershed in the process. And the watershed was one in which reform orientations in U.S. foreign policy coincided with orientations and agents of reform in Japan itself.

For our purposes the modern development of Taiwan commences with Japanese acquisition of the island as a result of the Sino-Japanese war.[22] Japanese colonial policy moved rapidly to make Taiwan a food surplus region for Japan itself.[23] Direct Japanese investments in agriculture and irrigation, experimental work to develop appropriate rice varieties and fertilizer regimes, and organizational work in building farmers' associations through which to inject the new science and technology paid great dividends. In the four decades prior to World War II total rice production rose from about 700,000 metric tons to about 1,800,000 metric tons. The area under cultivation grew from about 400,000 hectares to over 700,000 hectares. And yields per hectare rose from just under 2 metric tons to almost 3 metric tons.[24] This was done partly under direct Japanese land ownership but more through the stimulation of Taiwanese farmers themselves to increase their output. The overall process implied the massive and rapid commercialization of agriculture not unlike the developments in Meiji Japan.

Also similar to the Japanese development was the emergence of the relatively small-scale village landlord, using economic forces to bind in diffuse and particularistic obligations a growing number of tenants and part-tenants. Unlike the case of Japan, however, local political and organizational forces in opposition to this pattern of relationships did not develop or, at any rate, did not show the same power as they did in Japan. Taiwanese landlords and Japanese colonial forces were in control of the society and they acted with little opposition to sustain the old pattern of social relations.

The defeat of Japan and the return of Taiwan to Nationalist China in 1945 constituted the first step in breaking down this old system of relations. More critical, however, was the fall of mainland China to the Communists and the subsequent reform orientations in both the Nationalist government in Taiwan and U.S. foreign policy with respect to Taiwan. Although previous U.S. attempts to induce China's leaders to engage in widespread reforms were largely frustrated, the conditions were now propitious for their success.

At least three aspects of these conditions can be isolated: ideological, political, and organizational. The defeat of the Nationalists on the mainland increased the ideological commitment to reform both in U.S. foreign policy and in the Nationalist government itself. Just as in the case of Japan a major part of the U.S. argument was to provide a reform orientation competitive with the Communists. In this argument even the Nationalist government became highly vulnerable to its own, not insignificant, proponents of change.

The new orientation was easier for the Nationalists to accept because the Taiwanese landlords lacked political power under the new government. Suspect because of their previous association with the Japanese, and never with highly developed institutions to promote their interests such as the Japanese landlords had in the home Diet, the Taiwanese landlords were in no position to resist the central political decision to effect sweeping changes in land organization.

Although local Taiwanese organizational supports for reform had never seriously developed, as they had in the Ministry of Agriculture in Japan, a new organizational force of considerable power and competence was created, largely by the United States. This was the Joint Commission for Rural Reconstruction (JCRR). Established by virtue of an act of the U.S. Congress, which provided independent financial support to an organization for rural reconstruction that would be led jointly by Chinese and Americans, the JCRR began its reform activities on the mainland in 1948. At this time little if any attention was lavished upon reform in Taiwan.

Although the JCRR was brought into being because of an act of the U.S. Congress, the specific creation can also be credited to the special work of Mr. James Y. T. Yen.[25] In addition to this local Chinese inspiration, the JCRR had the added advantage of being able to draw upon a large reservoir of qualified and dedicated agriculturalists, who had been trained partly with American support over the past half-century. This professional competence was to be very critical for reform activities in Taiwan. Another major advantage came with the removal of the Nationalist government to Taiwan. Even the large corps of qualified personnel available to the JCRR could be lost in the sprawling masses of mainland China. In Taiwan, the physical proportions of the problem were reduced to about 2 percent of their former size. Further, the political nature of this province provided a situation in which these professionals could have a major impact.[26]

One of the JCRR's first tasks on Taiwan was to press for the type of land reform with which it had been experimenting on the mainland. The professionals in the JCRR could see that an initial requirement for rural reconstruction and agricultural development was the shift from tenancy to owner operation as the dominant pattern of land control. Thus both the political and professional arguments for land reform were compelling. The decision came rather easily.

Implementation was another matter, however. The organizational apparatus that Japan utilized to implement its land reform program did not exist in as developed a form in Taiwan, but there were important rudiments, especially in the provincial Department of Agriculture. The national Department of Agriculture had been disbanded when the government moved to Taiwan, but its functions in policymaking and advice were largely taken by the JCRR. Together with local agencies, the JCRR helped to organize the local committees for the surveying, record-keeping, and the instructional and inspection procedures necessary to implement the reform.

In the land-reform program Taiwan and the JCRR had a number of advantages in addition to those mentioned above. The experience of Japan was utilized to make the reform more efficient and more equitable.[27] The compensation that had been paid to Japanese landlords was quickly reduced by the rapid inflation of the period.[28] In Taiwan a decision was made to pay 70 percent of the land value in agricultural produce bonds as a hedge against inflation. The additional 30 percent was paid in industrial bonds, financed by the capitalization of confiscated Japanese industries. Essentially, it cost the Chinese government almost nothing not only to compensate the landlords but also to turn them into a class of industrial investors. Finally, a good part of the land redistribution was accomplished by selling off about 170,000 acres of public agricultural land taken from the Japanese.[29]

The overall land reform was carried out in three stages. The first began in 1949 with government regulations for the lease of private lands—a rent-reduction program. This prescribed rents not exceeding 37.5 percent of the total annual yield of the major crop. Existing rents were normally about 50 percent, with some as high as 70 percent. Additional abuses, such as demanding rents in advance and extra payments, were prohibited, and tenants were to be given written contracts that protected their tenure on the land. A hierarchy of committees was established to enforce the law and especially to obtain written contracts for all tenants. Although there were certainly evasions of the law, as would be expected, it did have considerable salutary effect in lowering actual rents. This is seen especially in land prices, which fell about 40 percent in 1949 for most grades of agricultural land.[30]

The second stage involved the sale of public agricultural lands and took place largely from 1951 through 1953. The third stage established a ceiling of about 10 acres on land holdings, purchased individual holdings in excess of this, and sold the land to tenants. The laws for this "Land to the Tiller" stage were enacted in 1952 and were largely implemented during the next two years.

By 1956 the pattern of land ownership had changed radically from that of 1948. More than 200,000 farm families, about 25 percent of all farm families, had joined the ranks of the owner-operators. This group had grown from 33 percent to 57 percent of all farm families. Over 100,000 left the ranks of pure tenants, whose overall proportions diminished from 36 percent to 16 percent of all farm families. As in Japan, the economic supports for the old patterns of social relations were largely destroyed.

The program of social change that the JCRR sponsored was not limited to land reform, although this was the first and most dramatic aspect of the program. Beyond the land reform, the JCRR helped to strengthen farmers' associations and used these as communication channels through which to inject a new technology into agriculture. Although these organizations had been originally created by the Japanese, at the end of the war they were not properly constituted to further social change. They had developed into a set of functionally specific organizations, largely controlled by local and absentee landlords for their own immediate economic benefit. Under the JCRR's leadership the farmers' associations were made into effective channels for communication among the peasants.

The economic results of this series of programs have constituted one of the most impressive fifteen-year growth records Asia has seen, with agriculture providing considerable dynamism in the entire process. The political changes are less apparent but are of no less significance. The availability of the JCRR technical and financial assistance to groups and individuals ready to assume some of the cost themselves stimulated the growth of viable centers of initiative throughout the country. At base was the breakdown of the old dependency relations of tenancy. On the surface was the proliferation of a variety of limited-purpose, specific, action-oriented associations that could and did promote the interests of the peasants.

Montgomery observes that although the political character of the one-party state has not been lessened directly by these changes, the viability of local institutions has been greatly increased. So much so, that they "would seem even better able to survive political change than the national government which has resisted it for so many years."[31] Again, a reform orientation in U.S. foreign policy coincided with the emergence of local forces and organizations competent to effect changes in land ownership, which would lead to a basic change in the patterns of social organization.

In the four centuries of its colonial rule, Spain created a relatively integrated society in Puerto Rico. Although the island was used primarily as a military base, controlling the entrance to the Caribbean and the Spanish colonies in Central America, the land was settled and agriculture developed. The Indian population was destroyed and Spanish colonial policy precluded the inundation by Negro slaves that turned the small-holder colonies of other European powers in the Caribbean into racially bifurcated plantation economies. The slaves that were imported and those that came and remained free as runaways were to a large extent integrated into the colony; Puerto Rico became and remained Spanish.[32]

The mechanism of Spanish settlement was the feudal *encomienda* system, which, unlike the capitalist company mechanism, produced a set of diffuse and particularistic mutually obligatory relations between the owner and the laborer.[33]

Even the reforms of the early nineteenth century, loosening the restrictions on trade and transforming the looser (as it developed in Puerto Rico) *encomienda* system into the somewhat more economically rational *hacienda* system, did not alter the basic pattern of social relations.

Crop changes were of considerable and complementary significance. With Spanish protection of sugar, the large landholding patterns had assumed importance before the mid-nineteenth century. In the later nineteenth century sugar lost its importance in Puerto Rico and coffee became the leading export crop. One result was an increase in the independence of the small farmers that dominated the coffee industry.[34] This shrinking of power of the Puerto Rican gentry occurred just at the time of the American takeover and probably facilitated the transformation of the Puerto Rican countryside into a full-fledged foreign-dominated plantation economy, though it is doubtful if any powers in Puerto Rico would have been sufficient to withstand the tremendous force of the American capital-mobilizing capacity.

The United States acquired Puerto Rico as a result of the Spanish American War. American troops landed on the island in 1898; American sugar investors followed quickly. American companies bought and leased vast tracts of the best sugar land from wealthy Puerto Rican families, cementing a tie of mutual interest that lasted for four decades. The Foraker Act, Puerto Rico's organic act of 1900, carried a prohibition against any company's or person's owning more than 500 acres of land.[35] Whatever the motivations behind this prohibition, the restriction was not enforced for the first four decades.

As the plantation system grew, it brought a fundamental change in social relations for a large number of rural people. The stable, paternalistic *hacienda* system with its diffuse relationships and mutual obligations (however unbalanced these were) was replaced by the dynamic, profit-maximizing, economically rational sugar central, whose pattern of social relations was highly specific and universalistic.[36]

For the first four decades of this century the Puerto Rican sugar industry grew rich and powerful; the Puerto Rican population grew but tasted few if any benefits of this economic transformation.[37] The urban elite and the intellectuals engaged in the freewheeling modern politics that was permitted and encouraged by American tutelage. The issue of status was uppermost in these activities: what was to be Puerto Rico's legal status under the Americans? This was an issue that appealed to the political leaders. It dominated their thoughts and gave them ample opportunity for theoretical and philosophical involution, but it also seemed far removed from the question of the welfare of the large number of people whose basic pattern of relations was determined by the sugar industry.

Thus, unlike Japan and Taiwan, the pattern of social relations in the pre-1940 period was not that associated with small-holder family tenancy arrangements.[38] It was associated with the plantation economy in sugar and with extensive family small-holdings in other crops. Poor, landless, seasonally unemployed workers on vast efficient plantations characterized the sugar industries. On the other hand, there were almost 50,000 small, family-sized farms (under 20 acres; about 30,000 under 10 acres) in tobacco, coffee, and other crops.[39] The most profound social dislocation had taken place in sugar, giving rise to the pattern of organization (including trade union movements) characteristic of a more modern economy.

The influence of the sugar companies was exercised not directly through elected organs, as was the influence of the Japanese landlords, but indirectly through the financing of political parties in Puerto Rico and through lobbying activities in Washington. It was apparently largely sugar money that permitted the parties to engage in the vote-buying practices that were characteristic of the elective system before 1940.

Perhaps the most important pressure for social change in Puerto Rico after the initial plantation development came with the New Deal.[40] President Roosevelt established the Chardon Commission in 1934 to investigate Puerto Rican conditions and to make recommendations for relief and reform. Carlos Chardon recommended, among other things, the enforcement of the 500-acre limit to landholdings. The following year the Roosevelt administration encouraged Governor Blanton Winship to obtain Puerto Rican legislation for this enforcement. The legislation came in the form of two acts in 1935. Test cases were developed, and the sugar companies contested them. It was not until 1940 that the U.S. Supreme Court upheld Puerto Rico's right to enforce the limitation, but even this did not end the effective delaying tactics of the sugar companies.[41]

More important than the actual reform this produced was its effect on local political dynamics. In the late 1930's a new political force emerged. Luis Muñoz-Marin broke from established parties and created the new Popular Democratic party, more commonly known as the Populares. Muñoz also broke with previous party traditions. He eschewed the status issue and took up the issue of welfare;[42] he refused to buy votes and urged the electorate to use their vote for their long-term welfare; and he took his campaign to the rural masses and gave prominence to the land situation and the exploitation of the sugar companies. Muñoz won a narrow victory in 1940 and proceeded to press reforms vigorously. In 1944 he won a landslide victory with two-thirds of the vote and has remained undisputed political leader since that time.

Although Muñoz brought the indigenous political power necessary for reform, his efforts probably would have been frustrated but for the concomitant administrative reforms engineered by Rexford G. Tugwell, governor of Puerto Rico from late 1941 until 1946.[43] The problem Muñoz and Tugwell faced lay in the dominance of the legislature over the executive branch of government and the consequent technical and organizational incapacity of the administration to provide real powers of initiative to any elected executive. Tugwell's reforms laid the groundwork for a competent administration that would be the effective servant of an elected government.

Thus, side by side a new indigenous political organization and a new administration were developed, both actively dedicated to reform. Muñoz drew his power from a new set of articulated mass interests. Tugwell drew his support from progressive elements in the American polity.[44]

The reform that ensued differed considerably from the land redistribution of Japan and Taiwan. There was some early and highly dramatized settlement of landless agricultural workers on small house lots, and there was also the creation of a unique arrangement in proportional benefit farms. In these, the government bought lands held illegally in excess of the 500-acre limit and leased them in the form of large farms to competent managers, who then shared the profits among the workers in proportion to the amount they actually worked on the farm.

There were also a series of other reforms designed to increase the welfare of the rural masses, but all of this was considerably different from the reforms wrought in Japan and Taiwan. In effect, the reforms signaled the movement of rural masses, already torn asunder from traditional patterns of relations, into the modern political arena, where their interests would be promoted through their activities as a new voting force.

Less than a decade after coming to power, Muñoz' government turned away from agriculture as an area of reform and directed its efforts to the stimulation of a modern industrial economy. Agriculture has remained a fairly dynamic sector,[45] but the real successes have been registered in manufacturing, commerce, and construction. The new economic powers, both local Puerto Rican and from the United States, are concentrated in the modern urban industrial and commercial sectors.[46]

The significance of the Muñoz-Tugwell reforms lay in their reinforcement and extension in the political arena of changes in social relations begun four decades earlier in the economic arena. The plantation system established the economic base for more specific and particularistic patterns of relations, but it did not fully eradicate the *patron-peon* pattern of relations. The political power of the foreign and indigenous investors precluded the development of the modern organizations that were needed to make the new pattern of relations dominant in the society. Without effective protection and articulation of their interests in specialized political organizations, the rural lower classes might be wage laborers working for a huge impersonal organization, but their relations with the functionaries of those organizations and with the owners of land would continue to be highly diffuse and particularistic. Without independent bases of power, they would still be subject to the more wide-ranging demands of the local holders of power, to whom they would continue to look for an equally wide range of assistance.

In this respect the reforms served much the same type of function served by otherwise highly dissimilar reforms in Taiwan and Japan. They were political reforms that made secure changes in social relations that were, however hesitatingly, being induced by other economic changes. That they followed upon earlier economic changes made them no less necessary to complete the process of social change, for it cannot be argued that a grand evolutionary force would have completed the changes simply because they had been introduced by economic forces. We have too many cases of arrested social change to allow us to have much faith in the inevitability of the emergence of new patterns of relations as dominant in a society simply because it is set in a world context of industrializing societies.

The development of Cuban and Philippine societies under Spanish, then American, influence was not unlike the development in Puerto Rico. Spanish mercantilist policy, the tradition of *conquistador* and missionary, and the use of the *encomienda* system for land administration produced societies of considerable similarity.[47] The mutually obligatory, if highly uneven, patrimonial relations of the preponderantly rural populations experienced the same development to more specific and universalistic relations under the impact of commercialization in the late nineteenth century. The process was merely intensified by the American impact. The massive capital-mobilizing capacities of the United States, together with its great demand for sugar, quickly produced more economically rational plantation economies in the early twentieth century.

In many respects this process was more rapid and more complete in Cuba than in the Philippines. By 1925 the Cuban economy had been fully transformed and the period of rapid growth was over. The next four decades saw stagnation in the internal economy, with increasing United States dominance spreading out of agriculture to utilities, transportation, and urban commerce.[48] The full development of the modern sugar industry in the Philippines did not take place until the second decade of the century, and even then sugar did not occupy the position of overall dominance that it held in Cuba. The plantation economy developed largely in the central islands, while Luzon remained dominated by rice production, with landlord-tenancy relations not unlike those in Japan and Taiwan.

The result in Cuba was the development of powerful revolutionary forces, which finally broke through in 1959. The Philippines has experienced considerable growth in urban commerce and industry, but the agricultural sector, together with its social relations, has remained more economically retarded.[49]

It would be impossible to examine all the points at which American policy either could have promoted reform and did not, or tried and was unsuccessful. A brief look at some of the more dramatic points can, however, reveal some of the important determinants of the ability of foreign policy to promote social change.

The economic development of Cuba in the first quarter century was not accompanied by a parallel political development. Political and administrative structures were corrupt and incapable of actively stimulating social change. There were, however, important internal stirrings of reform in the early 1930's under Grau San Martin. The dictatorial repressions of the Machado government from 1924 to 1933 plus the economic collapse of the depression brought wide-scale pressures for reform and a government with considerable responsiveness to that pressure. Without external assistance, this internal reform orientation was destined to be frustrated by the lack of the administrative capacity to implement new programs.[50] External assistance bringing the kind of legislative and administrative change experienced by Puerto Rico at about the same time might have allowed for the successful execution of reform.

The United States did not, however, assist the reform. Preference was given to Batista's ability to secure order rather than to Grau's desires for reform. It is one of the ironies of the period that just when the liberal domestic policies of the New Deal were furthering basic social change in Puerto Rico, the equally liberal foreign policy precluded comparable assistance to Cuba.

An important point to observe is that Cuba and Puerto Rico were in different positions relative to the United States. Cuba was properly foreign, however dependent economically. Puerto Rico was an extension, however special and unique, of the domestic American system. Secretary of State Cordell Hull and Ambassadors Sumner Welles and Jefferson Caffery were in different organizational positions in the United States in directing relations with Cuba than were Harold Ickes and Rexford Tugwell in directing relations with Puerto Rico.

There is an important implication of this difference in the social bases of the American impact in the two cases. By its independence Cuba was politically insulated from the heterogeneous interests that provided the base for the New Deal reforms in the United States. Cuba was thus left to the homogeneous and highly specialized interests of large-scale foreign investment companies. These interests proved powerful enough, together with U.S. diplomatic and military assistance, continually to support instruments of power with a relatively narrow base in Cuba, and thus to preclude the articulation of the heterogeneous interests that emerged with modern economic development.

One of the early American opportunities to readjust land arrangements in the Philippines came in 1902–1903 with the purchase of the Friar lands. This included 410,000 acres which had previously been held by the Church and had provided part of the basis for popular Filipino hatred of the friars.[51] Although this was a comparatively small amount in the more than 7 million acres of cultivated land, it was important in that it was strategically located, especially in areas of rice and tenancy. Effective redistribution of these lands might have provided a model for further land reforms and an opportunity for rural masses to gain an early foothold in the political structure.

The lands were not so distributed. This was partly due to lack of an organization capable of effecting such distribution. There was nothing in the Philippines comparable to the Japanese Ministry of Agriculture or the Taiwanese JCRR. It was also partly due to the stage of development and the character of the ideas that entered into the debate. Tenancy had not yet become a serious and widespread problem. In other ways, too, the time demanded attention to growth and development, not to welfare and distribution. The Secretary of Interior in the Philippines from 1902 to 1913, Dean C. Worcester, constantly pressed for the sale of friar lands to large companies capable of developing new industries such as sugar.[52]

Although the lands were not effectively distributed to the cultivators, they were also not, except from 1908–1914, legally available to companies and persons wishing to acquire large holdings. The original organic act for the Philippines contained limitations on landholdings (16 hectares to an individual and 1,024 hectares to a corporation),[53] just as it did in Puerto Rico. The same U.S. forces were active in both cases: liberal antiimperialists fearing the evils of monopolistic capitalism and sugar beet interests fearing the evils of competition. In the Philippines these American interests were assisted by articulate nationalist, anticlerical leaders, whose counterparts were largely absent in Puerto Rico. The result in the Philippines was something approaching institutionalized hypocrisy; the increasingly independent Philippine legislature continued to maintain its posture against large landholdings, while wealthy Filipino and American interests continued to amass large holdings. This precluded the utilization by Filipino leaders of the visible target that Muñoz had in the government's outright decision not to implement land limitations in Puerto Rico.

By the time reform forces produced the New Deal in the United States, the Philippines had become considerably insulated against the overflow of those domestic forces to the islands. The United States had stimulated the development of political parties and a not inconsiderable administrative system. This produced a push for independence that was largely absent in Puerto Rico. In this early development, however, the parties proved most effective at promoting the interests of the more articulate upper classes, and the administrative system was largely captured and used more as an instrument of patronage than of change. It was sufficient for the U.S. reform orientation of the 1930's that the Filipinos were writing their own liberal democratic constitution and moving rapidly toward full formal political independence. The issues of welfare important domestically in America found little support in the increasingly "foreign" Philippines.

World War II in the Pacific, with both occupation and liberation, brought great material and organizational damage to the Philippines. In the postwar reconstruction period, the United States had another opportunity to promote social change through land reform. Though this was more limited, it was not unlike the opportunity available in Japan and Taiwan. Two forces appear to have prevented success. One was the continuity of power of the Philippine landed elite, who showed remarkable tenacity through the early American government, during the Japanese occupation, and even through the postwar period that saw collaboration arise as a political issue.[54] Although this elite has not been overly reluctant to pass rather liberal land reform legislation, it has also never been at a loss to prevent the implementation of such legislation.

The second force is represented in a set of organizational characteristics, both Filipino and U.S. The Philippines has not yet developed a technical and administrative structure in agricultural agencies capable of providing the guidance needed for an effective policy and the capacity to carry out such a policy. These agencies remain highly centralized in Manila and functionally fragmented into specialized units with little effective coordination among them. Above the administrative structure, executive powers are sufficiently fragmented to preclude the initiation of reform.[55]

On the U.S. side, organizational involvement in reform has been concentrated in the hands of the aid-giving arms of the State Department. It was in part this involvement that obstructed the creation of a Taiwan-like Joint Commission for Rural Reform in the Philippines. Aid officials in the Philippines argued that a joint organization would be inappropriate given Philippine independence, and they succeeded in establishing an alternative all-Filipino organization, the Office of the Presidential Assistant for Community Development (PACD). The financial and status autonomy of the JCRR had been important in developing a high technical capacity to promote agricultural reform in Taiwan.[56]

Without this autonomy the Philippines PACD was actually more dependent upon the local U.S. aid organization and local political pressures. Consequently, it has not developed the necessary technical capacity to promote reform.[57]

In both cases, then, the failures resulted from the lack of appropriate, or available, reform orientations in U.S. policy, and the lack of forces for reform as well as the technical and organizational capacity to effect reform in the host country.

From these five cases, we can make some tentative general observations of the conditions under which foreign policy can have a decisive effect on social change in a subordinate nation. These must be tentative generalizations because the number of cases is small and the analysis has been necessarily cursory. The utility of the general observations will be determined largely by the extent to which the analysis has abstracted the more important aspects of the social process from the mass of details of the actual historical situations. The utility will be tested by the extent to which the propositions that can be drawn from the cases are found to have a more general validity.

During the critical reform periods in Puerto Rico, Taiwan, and Japan, the relationship with the United States was closer than foreign relations normally allow. These were not relations between truly sovereign states, but between a superordinate state and a subordinate territory. The closeness of the relation allowed for the direct intervention into major policy decisions of the society. The insulation of independence in Cuba and the Philippines prevented the United States from intervening sufficiently to promote change, even if it had so desired.

Another aspect of this relationship is the depth and breadth of the intervention allowed. In the three successes, the United States was concerned with effecting basic changes in the character of the societies. This made its intervention diffuse and profound, with relatively few limits on the sectors of the society it could pry into. The intervention in Cuba and the Philippines was highly specific and limited: to maintain order in Cuba, and to contract for specific forms of aid in the postwar Philippines.

We have also seen that an orientation to reform was needed in U.S. policy. This implies both a general and undifferentiated support for reform, and a very specific reform orientation in certain agents capable of having an impact on the host society. The specific agents of change—e.g., Feary, Ladejinsky, Yen, Ickes, and Tugwell—could draw upon the considerable power of the general value of reform in America. But it was also important that they had a more specific expertise and more specific programs that were highly applicable to the situation of the host societies. The liberal, but very general, reforms in foreign policy *per se* during the New Deal were not very effective promoters of change in Cuba. The equally liberal but more specific reforms in domestic policy were, however, highly useful for Puerto Rico.

In the postwar period the general orientation to an antifascist reconstruction provided general support for the promoters of land reform in Japan and Taiwan. But the resistance of the old Japan hands would also indicate that a more technically specialized orientation to particular reforms was more useful than the general knowledge a foreign observer can acquire of a society. The foreign observer probably tends to be more impressed with the equilibrium aspects of a society. A more professionally specific, but geographically generalized, understanding of social processes can lead more easily to an understanding of the strains inherent in any society and the consequent possibilities of change.

There is also what may be a general limitation upon foreign policy *per se* in promoting change in other societies. In its more specific and limited sense, foreign policy is highly concentrated in the office of the U.S. executive. This concentration, plus the lack of direct relevance of most aspects of foreign policy for the home electorate, makes it possible for quite limited and homogeneous interests to dominate relevant aspects of policy. The events in Cuba and the Philippines have been of little direct relevance to most Americans, but they have been of great importance to the homogeneous and economically powerful sugar and investment interests. It has thus been relatively easy for these interests to gain considerable influence in the limited arena of the executive and, to a lesser extent, the legislative offices. This highly concentrated decision-making loci can be used to mobilize a wide range of very powerful forces in support of specific interests.

This picture is certainly overdrawn, to be sure. Interest groups concerned with foreign policy are seldom that homogeneous, and even the forces within the executive offices concerned with foreign policy are rather wide-ranging in their orientations. It remains true, however, that with respect to Cuba, and to a lesser extent Puerto Rico, in the first half of this century the diplomatic history reads much like a Marxist scenario for a bad movie.[58] Diplomatic and military forces promoted the interests of sugar, and later more extensive investments, which especially after 1930 were anything but progressive.

We began by noting that foreign policy is never more than just one in a large set of forces affecting the change of a society. We subsequently argued that the reforms in Japan, Taiwan, and Puerto Rico could never have been effected without strong local support. This has to be available in two arenas. The general characteristics of the society must have already given rise to general forces for reform, and these must be capable of articulation in the polity. There are severe limitations upon the ability of a foreign policy alone to make the decision for local reform.

It is just as important there be effective organizational mechanisms for implementing the reform. This is required both by the extent of the problem and by its subtlety. No occupation force could have provided the million committee members that were involved in implementing the Japanese land reform. The size of the program required a widescale mobilization that was made possible only by using the Japanese themselves. In addition, effecting true reform requires an extensive knowledge of the subtle cohesive and divisive forces in a society. Such knowledge allows for an efficient judo-like operation in which the weight of the society itself can be used to effect changes. Further, such knowledge of a society is generally gained only by a long and intensive involvement in that society. We can see, especially in local politicians who may be very inarticulate, that this knowledge can approach the intuitive in character and can be very difficult to communicate. Thus, the more a foreign reform orientation can rely on local agents to implement the reform, the more efficient and successful it is likely to be.

This raises the double difficulty of either not having local allies available, or of using the wrong groups as allies. Both conditions seem to plague the massive efforts at reform in U.S. foreign aid programs outside of western Europe.

A final brief observation concerns the utility of having available some relatively clear-cut targets or symbols for reforms around which mass support can be mobilized. Such was the case, for example, with Muñoz' use of the U.S. failure to implement the 500-acre limitation in Puerto Rico. The actual social and economic value of the land reform that ensued when this issue was raised was probably far less than the symbolic value of the reform in mobilizing new interests and bringing new groups to power.

In Taiwan and Japan the tenancy issue provided a clear target for reform, which was useful at two levels. At the policymaking level it mobilized support both as a competitor to communist ideology and as a mechanism to preclude the resurgence of Japanese aggression. At the level of implementation it was also useful in mobilizing peasants to come forth with their demands in a pattern of behavior that was deeply antagonistic to traditional interpersonal styles of behavior. Throughout the underdeveloped world, community-development programs have often foundered on the inability to induce peasants to new forms of behavior in electing village councils or cooperating for limited purposes. It is certainly easier to induce a peasant to go against traditional norms of behavior when the stake is land, which has a very clear and immediate interest to him.

There is another type of target that is also considerably useful. Foreign pressures for reform can provide targets to draw the fire of indigenous conservative groups away from indigenous reform leaders. This was very much the case in Puerto Rico and Japan and operated to a lesser extent in Taiwan. There seem to be two useful effects. One is that they draw away what could be fatal attacks upon the precarious new reform leaders. After reform has been accomplished, it can be relied upon to draw new mass support to its leaders. In the early stages of reform the new leaders are often quite precarious, many are fearful of being hurt by change, and no one has yet tasted its benefits. At this time, it is useful for the society if conservative forces have an external target to attack. It not only makes less precarious the immediate position of the reform leaders, but it can also preclude the development of deep conflicts that persist beyond the specific issue of reform. Conflicts that are limited to specific issues, with different issues cross-cutting one another in group allegiances, form the basis for moderate and pragmatic politics. They are, in fact, critical characteristics of systems with a built-in ability to change. Thus, where foreign policy can provide external targets of attack, this can help to produce or support self-corrective mechanisms in a society, providing for a fairly steady pattern of subsequent social change.

NOTES

[1] Because this paper represents an early stage in one research project and more mature stages of others, I am indebted to a number of sources of support. These include grants from the Agricultural Development Council in New York, the University of Michigan's Center for South and Southeast Asian Studies, and the Patterson School of Diplomacy and International Commerce at the University of Kentucky. Members of the latter's seminar on foreign policy and development provided many useful and critical comments on an earlier draft of the paper. The research assistance of Peter and Josefina McDonough is gratefully acknowledged.

[2] Note the lack of a cumulative, directional connotation in the term "social change." It thus lacks the implication of the most common development term, "economic development," which is given to the most precisely measurable aspect of change. Only recently have the other social sciences begun to use the term "development" in their analyses of change.

[3] See, for example, Neil J. Smelser, *Social Change and the Industrial Revolution* (Chicago, 1959), for a detailed case study of such change.

[4] See Arthur Stinchcomb, "Social Structure and Organizations," in *Handbook of Organizations*, ed. G. March Jones (Chicago, 1965), 142–93.

[5] See Reinhard Bendix, *Nation Building and Citizenship* (New York, 1964), *passim*.

[6] Bendix, for example, finds them in the emerging bureaucratic organizations, the agencies or carriers of modern public authority; see *ibid*.

[7] Our focus here has considerable similarity with that of Barrington Moore, Jr. See especially his *Social Origins of Dictatorship and Democracy; Lord and Peasant in the Making of the Modern World* (Boston, 1966). The subtitle of this work is quite revealing.

[8] See, for example, Thomas Smith, *The Agricultural Origins of Modern Japan* (Stanford, 1959).

[9] See Ronald P. Dore, "The Meiji Landlord, Good or Bad?" *Journal of Asian Studies* (May 1959), 343–55. See also Henry Rosovsky, *Capital Formation in Japan* (Glencoe, Ill., 1961).

[10] K. Okawa and H. Rosovsky, "The Role of Agriculture in Modern Japanese Economic Development," *Economic Development and Cultural Change* (Oct. 1960), 43–68.

[11] R. P. Dore, "Agricultural Improvement in Japan: 1870–1900," *Economic Development and Cultural Change* (Oct. 1960), 69–92.

[12] R. P. Dore, *Land Reform in Japan* (London, 1959), esp. Pts. I and II.

[13] Dore, "The Meiji Landlord, Good or Bad?"

[14] Okawa and Rosovsky, "The Role of Agriculture in Modern Japanese Economic Development."

[15] Dore, *Land Reform*, Chap. 2.

[16] *Ibid.*, 131.

[17] W. Ladejinsky, "Agrarian Revolution in Japan," *Foreign Affairs*, XXXVIII (Oct. 1959), 95–109. See also W. M. Gilmartin and W. Ladejinsky, "The Promise of Agrarian Reform in Japan," *Foreign Affairs*, XXVI (Jan. 1948), 312–24.

[18] Dore, *Land Reform*, Chap. 5, and Gilmartin and Ladejinsky, "Promise of Agrarian Reform in Japan."

[19] Ladejinsky, "Agrarian Revolution in Japan," 106, gives credit to Hiroo Wada, socialist and past minister of agriculture, as the architect of the reform.

[20] Dore, *Land Reform*, Chap. 7.

[21] *Ibid.*, 176.

[22] This section draws especially upon T. H. Shen, *Agricultural Development in Taiwan* (Ithaca, N.Y., 1965); John Montgomery, Rufus B. Hughes, and Raymond H. Davis, *Rural Improvement and Political Development: The JCRR Model*, Papers in Comparative Administration, Special Series No. 7 (Washington, D.C., 1966); S. C. Hsieh and V. W. Ruttan, "Technological, Institutional and Environmental Factors in the Growth of Rice Production: Philippines, Thailand, and Taiwan," mimeographed, 1966; Chen Cheng, *Land Reform in Taiwan* (Taipei, 1961); and my own interviews in Taiwan in 1962.

[23] H. Y. Chang and R. H. Meyers, "Japanese Colonial Development Policy: A Case of Bureaucratic Enterpreneurship," *Journal of Asian Studies*, XXII (Aug. 1963), 433–49.

[24] These data are available in many sources; the figures presented here are given in Hsieh and Ruttan, "Factors in the Growth of Rice Production," 13.

[25] The law was P.L. 472, 80th Congress, "The China Aid Act," April 3, 1948. It is significant that Yen made his plea before the U.S. Congress, which may have appeared more sympathetic to the demand for reform in China than was the Nationalist Chinese government itself.

[26] Gerald Wen has reminded me that there will be some argument on the relative importance of the JCRR and the existing Taiwanese Provincial Department of Agriculture. I recognize that my proclivity to see greater importance in the JCRR is just a proclivity. More detailed research will be required to decide upon the case, but the outcome may not really be worth the effort.

[27] Ladejinsky, for example, advised on the program in Taiwan after his Japanese experience.

[28] This gave rise to later reactionary pressures of organized Japanese landlords for a more just compensation. The reform had by this time, however, provided sufficient peasant support to allow the Ministry of Agriculture to withstand this attack; see Dore, *Land Reform*, 431–44.

[29] Chen Cheng, *Land Reform in Taiwan*, 311. This was from a total of 430,000 acres of public land, representing about one-fifth of all farm lands in Taiwan.

[30] *Ibid.*, 46.

[31] Montgomery, *et al.*, *Rural Improvement and Political Development*, 15.

[32] For a sensitive account of the overall settlement patterns in the Caribbean and the effects of different colonial policies, see Ramiro Guerra y Sanchez, *Sugar and Society in the Caribbean* (New Haven, 1964), which also contains an excellent foreword by Sydney Mintz. Also see Julian Steward, ed., *The People of Puerto Rico* (Urbana, 1956).

[33] Thomas D. Curtis has drawn my attention to this in his excellent monograph, *Land Reform, Democracy and Economic Interest in Puerto Rico* (Tucson, 1966).

[34] The decline in sugar resulted partly from European protection of beet sugar and partly from the technological improvements in refining cane. The latter were too expensive for the limited capital-mobilizing capacities of the Puerto Rican economy. On the overall world supply situation of sugar at the time, see V. P. Timoshemko and B. C. Swerling, *The World's Sugar* (Stanford, 1957), Chap. 2.

[35] It is generally believed that this was the result of pressure from U.S. beet sugar interests, who sought to curb the growth of the competitive Caribbean cane industry.

[36] The industrial distribution of the labor force over these four decades will give some indication of the extent to which social relations would be dominated by sugar.

	1910	1920	1930	1940
employment in sugar (000)	240	245	263	229
total employment (000)	393	407	503	512
percentage in sugar	61	60	52	45

From H. S. Perloff, *Puerto Rico's Economic Future: A Study in Planned Development* (Chicago, 1950), 401.

[37] Benefits did accrue, of course, especially in public health, education, and public construction, but this was due more to the political transformation to dependence upon the U.S. than to the economic transformation.

[38] The term is from Arthur Stinchcomb's suggestive classification, presented, among other places, in R. Bendix and S. M. Lipset, *Class Status and Power*, 2nd ed. (New York, 1966), 182–89.

[39] Steward, *People of Puerto Rico*, especially 66–68.

[40] This is, of course, debatable, for there were important changes in the political structure arising out of purely local conditions. Further, it is probably impossible to separate Puerto Rican from mainland politics in any decisive manner. My argument here is simply that the New Deal hastened the emergence of and helped direct indigenous reform agents in Puerto Rico itself.

[41] Curtis, *Land Reform, Democracy and Economic Interest in Puerto Rico*, passim, and Mathew Edel's two excellent articles "Land Reform in Puerto Rico, 1940–59," Part I, *Caribbean Studies*, II (No. 3), 26–60, and Part II in *ibid.* (No. 4), 28–50.

[42] Later he fused these issues in creating the special status of the Commonwealth, more or less designed pragmatically to provide the status that appeared most appropriate to further popular welfare.

[43] On the reforms of the Tugwell administration, see Charles T. Goodsel, *Administration of a Revolution* (Cambridge, Mass., 1965).

[44] These were of considerable importance because the sugar companies did not give up influence easily and they found powerful allies among U.S. conservative legislators who attacked Tugwell for his "fascist" and "communist" activities.

[45] Sugar is declining in importance, but it is being replaced by rather dynamic new milk and egg industries and to a lesser extent by fruits and beef production. Estado Libre Asociado de Puerto Rico, Departmento de Agricultura, *Ingreso Agricultura de Puerto Rico, 1950/51–1965/66* (San Juan, 1967).

[46] See R. L. Scheele, "The Prominent Families of Puerto Rico," in Steward, *People of Puerto Rico*, 418–62; T. C. Cochran, *The Puerto Rican Businessman* (Philadelphia, 1959); and E. E. Maccoby and F. Fiedler, *Savings Among Upper Income Families in Puerto Rico* (San Juan, 1953).

[47] See Guerra, *Sugar and Society*. Puerto Rico and Cuba were more completely and directly Spanish, since the Indian populations had been largely destroyed, but these societies also faced the necessity of integrating large numbers of Negroes. The Philippines was more Hispanized than Spanish. The process was accomplished largely by Spanish friars, with significant implications for later anticlerical sentiment, but here I consider the similarities more important than the differences. On the Philippines, see the excellent bit of ethnohistory, J. L. Phelan, *The Hispanization of the Philippines* (Madison, 1959).

[48] See Dudley Seers, *Cuba: The Economic and Social Revolution* (Chapel Hill, 1964). Also see Maurice Zeitlin and Robert Scheer, *Cuba: Tragedy in Our Hemisphere* (New York, 1963), for an indictment of the U.S. policy in Cuba.

[49] It seems likely, however, that the openness of the urban sector has drawn off considerable revolutionary potential, especially by giving an indigenous modern economic elite sufficient scope for its activities outside of government and politics.

[50] This is brought out more dramatically in the electoral victory of Grau San Martin in 1944. The massive use of patronage the system seemed to require for the consolidation of power also made rational reforms next to impossible. The contrast with Puerto Rico is striking. The great economic windfall of the war boom was dissipated in Cuba; in Puerto Rico it paid for land reform, welfare activities, and other significant development programs. On Cuba see W. MacGaffey and C. R. Barnett, *Twentieth Century Cuba* (New York, 1965), 30ff.

[51] See G. A. Grunder and W. E. Livezey, *The Philippines and the United States* (Norman, Okla., 1951), Chap. 7.

[52] *Ibid.*, 130–35.

[53] *Ibid.*, 130. David Wurfel, "The Philippines," in G. McT. Kahin, *Governments and Politics of Southeast Asia* (Ithaca, N.Y., 1964), 692, gives the figures: 2,530 acres for corporations and 355 acres for individuals.

[54] See David Steinberg, *Philippine Collaboration in World War II* (Ann Arbor, 1967).

[55] In the formal structure the Philippine president has a wide range of very considerable power. See Wurfel, "The Philippines," 724–26, for a general outline and John Romani, *The Philippine Presidency* (Manila, 1956) for a more detailed account. At the same time, the fluid character of the party structure and the economic independence of the legislators considerably fragments the initiative powers of the president, leaving him primarily with obstructive powers.

[56] This produced a constantly strained relation between the JCRR and the U.S. aid organization in Taiwan. This reflects one of the more common sociological insights that organizations always attempt to preserve exclusive rights of access to their constituencies.

[57] If Ramon Magsaysay had lived, he might have been able to buttress his own charismatic powers with this external support from the aid-giving organizations. This might have allowed him to circumvent the internal obstacles to reform in the legislature and to make a considerable impact on the society. Magsaysay's untimely death makes it impossible to test this proposition, but I remain doubtful that he would have had much effect.

[58] The pungent phrase is Peter McDonough's.

CHAPTER THREE

FOREIGN POLICY, THE MILITARY, AND DEVELOPMENT: MILITARY ASSISTANCE AND POLITICAL CHANGE IN AFRICA

———

HENRY BIENEN

POLITICS AND ECONOMICS in the developing countries can be studied as part of international affairs.[1] There has, in fact, been a large literature on colonialism and its inheritances. And those who focus on imperialism or neo-colonialism have analyzed the impact of external forces on the societies of Asia, Africa, and Latin America. More recently, studies of modernization have argued that there are important connections between national political systems and the international system, and the idea of a transnational politics has emerged. Some studies argue that nonindustrialized or traditional societies are changing under the impact of modern, industrial systems; their concern is to show a world transformation which manifests itself as a generalized Westernizing process.[2] But there has been more interest in analyzing a worldwide process than in examining the specific impact the foreign policies of great powers are having on new or developing states. The imbalance should be rectified because twentieth-century foreign aid may be as significant for domestic political change in recipient countries as nineteenth-century colonialism was. Insofar as this is currently admitted, it is maintained by analysts who see the CIA or the KGB subverting domestic polities, or by those who see the capture of elites via technical assistance and have a cosmic view that the expansion of American, Soviet, or Chinese "influence" somehow changes the patterns of politics in the receiving country so that they emulate the patterns in the donor state.

We can account for the paucity of studies on the impact foreign policies have on political and economic development in the third world. We have had a hard enough time describing the aims and scope of foreign policies; it has been even more difficult to analyze political development in given countries, not to say regions.[3] We have not been able to say with confidence what political development is in the most simple sense of political happenings. We have been hard put to determine priorities of various factors in the development of a polity.

But perhaps we are now able to define more clearly what political development means, as we get better monographs on national politics and as concepts are tested for a generality of application sufficient to permit comparative analysis of their precision and relevance. Thus, we begin to understand better the conditions for development. But, as Robert Packenham points out, it is important to distinguish between knowledge of the conditions for development and knowledge of the ways to bring development about, especially by the instruments of foreign policy.[4] The reluctance to assess the impact of foreign policies on development may be traced, in part, to a belief that very many variables are at work and that policies can cut very many ways, producing intended and unintended effects and long-run and short-run consequences.[5] Furthermore, there may well be operating among American academics, as well as foreign policymakers and implementors, the belief that foreign aid, and even direct intervention via occupation, has been and will be marginal to an indigenous development process.[6] Our own claims to nonintervention in domestic affairs of other states along with the futility that has been felt over our inability to intervene effectively to change domestic patterns of certain states strengthens this belief in the marginality of impact.

My own view is that the United States is the most heavily engaged, or implicated, of all the great powers in the process of development, or nondevelopment, in the *tiers monde*. This is because the United States has the largest economic and military assistance programs, exports the most personnel, governmental and nongovernmental, and is the great power with the most significant trading relations for the Latin American states and for some of the African and Asian states. Furthermore, it is intervening directly and massively in Vietnam.

Here I focus primarily on United States policy in one sphere: military assistance. And I examine some connections between military assistance and political development in tropical Africa. Of all the conventionally delimited areas of the world, Africa has been the least studied in terms of the link between national and international [7] systems and more specifically in terms of the connection between foreign aid and political development. Some attention has been given to foreign aid and economic development in Africa because it has been inescapable for anyone who wanted to write about five-year plans or growth rates to neglect the large foreign component in government or private domestic investment.[8] Similarly, it should be required for anyone who wants to explore the military coups that took place in Africa in the 1960's and to assess the prospects for political change that the military poses in Africa to examine patterns and influences of military assistance. For not only have the nature and scope of postwar military aid programs had significant consequences for the level of armament and tension in Africa and for the balance of power regionally and on the continent as a whole, but within African states military assistance programs have affected the domestic political configuration.[9]

It is particularly hard to assess the impact of various military assistance programs. Along with problems of evaluation in multifactor situations and the lack of rigorous schemes available for assessing the role of military assistance, we are in a realm where the basic data is especially hard to come by. Much of it is classified. The United States and Britain publish more of their military assistance facts than France, the Soviet Union, or China, and in the absence of hard data on the scope of French military assistance, one could not hope to carry out the kinds of correlations between military assistance and coups that Charles Wolfe, Robert Putnam, and Charles Wheatley have done—the last two using Latin American data.[10] Furthermore, with a sample restricted to African countries who have had coups, we would be on thinner statistical ice than the universe of countries with military coups puts us. (The African militaries are providing us with more samples every few months, however.) Even if we had good enough statistical analysis to give us correlations between military assistance and certain political phenomena, like coups, and even if we could make some statistically backed statements about the direction of relationships, e.g., a coup occurs after military assistance rises, we would surely not be satisfied with extensive statistical analysis. We need intensive studies of the impact of specific military assistance programs on political development in single countries.[11] Since I have here neither utilized the data I have to make the kinds of correlations Wheatley and Wolfe have made, and since I do not examine any one country's political development in terms of military assistance, I do not claim this as a study of the impact of military assistance on political development in Africa. Rather, I point to certain aspects of political development in Africa and describe the evolving military assistance programs, with emphasis on American military aid, in the hope of noting implications of aid programs and drawing some connections.

We shall see that the United States military assistance programs are small in absolute terms and relative to American military assistance in other regions. We shall also see that the number of armed forces, but not police forces, the United States is aiding is declining. But the fact that the programs are small in United States terms does not mean they are unimportant for African political development. And the fact that at present there are dominant voices in Congress and in the Departments of State and Defense for limiting American military assistance in Africa does not mean this will always be the case. We can be certain the pressure for assistance from Africa will become more intense. For example, in July 1967, both Congo (Kinshasa) and Nigeria asked for American assistance in domestic crises. Thus, what is said now may be useful for policy formulation later.

Furthermore, military assistance in Africa is very interesting in its own right. The arguments for and against military assistance in Africa revolve around the role of the military as modernizer in Africa rather than as bulwark against foreign aggression or subversion from internal Communist parties. Issues of international politics arise where there are African arms races—northern Africa, the Horn, or where great powers are involved in domestic strife, e.g. Nigeria and the Congo. The confrontation of white minority regimes in southern Africa with independent black states raises a host of important questions in the military assistance realm. Still, it is the role of the military as a ruling group which already confronts policymakers who must frame assistance programs. Military regimes rule in six of fourteen western African states, and three of eight central African states (see Table 1); the Sudan has had military rule; the military is a powerful coalition partner in Uganda and the Somali Republic. The prospects for military rule are good in these and other countries, notably Ethiopia. The scope and nature of assistance becomes both a matter between donor states and recipient ruling military regimes and a question of the further evolution of military regimes.

The discussion of the impact of military assistance on developing countries has been concerned largely with the incidence of coups and the scope of assistance; [12] the literature on military intervention has been concerned with exploring the correlations between intervention and political development and the role of the military as modernizer.[13] We suggest here exploring the relationship directly between military assistance and political development.[14] In this context, assistance to ruling military elites is not our entire concern. The way civilian rulers use the military is certainly another. This use can be for development purposes or civic action. It can be for counterinsurgency purposes. And it can be for maintaining or changing the domestic political balance through employing the military directly against one's opponents. For, as one author has suggested, "Although *coups* which result in change of government attract the most attention, the most frequent *coups* in Africa are probably those initiated by an incumbent government against threatening individuals or groups (real or alleged), and those launched by a ruler or dominant faction against their associates." [15] Obviously, in this regard, the police and paramilitary forces and thus assistance programs run by the Agency for International Development will interest us also.

African armies are for the most part small and lightly equipped.[16] The largest tropical African armed force was well under 40,000 (Ethiopia) until the expansion of the Nigerian army; and on a scale for inhabitants per serviceman and serviceman per square mile of territory, African armies rank low in world area comparisons.[17] The ratio of total men in the armed forces to the combined populations of the thirty-five countries listed in Table 2 is 1:900; France is 1:780; China 1:260; and the United States is 1:65. Somali Republic has the highest ratio of 1:242 and Liberia the lowest of 1:4,956. These thirty-five countries south of the Sahara have armed forces totaling around 300,000 and low reserves forces of about 126,000. There are around another 250,000 men in *gendarmeries* and national police. Thus, the security forces for Africa amount to approximately the same number as those of South Korea.[18]

The African armies are almost exclusively infantry battalions; some have light artillery. With the exception of the north African countries and Ethiopia, air forces are small. Few African countries have anything in the way of a navy. Military manpower usually comprises less than 1 percent of the population. The police forces and *gendarmeries*, which have been neglected in the study of armed forces in Africa, are often larger than the armies proper and often do not have significantly less fire-power.

In many French-speaking African states, the *gendarmerie* functions as a national constabulary, although it is sometimes integrated into the armed forces. There are both fixed and mobile units with responsibilities for public order and internal security. Internal security is usually the *de facto* mission of the armed forces as well since few African armies can as yet carry out foreign operations. African armies have, however, served with United Nations forces in the Congo and do man the borders of their countries. Thus, their function is not purely internal. And in the future they will probably be involved in local or regional conflicts. Since many police forces are on a par with or outnumber the armed forces, and since their missions are overlapping, it is to be expected that the police as well as the army would be involved in politics. And, in fact, ruling military regimes have been coalitions of police, army, and civil servants in Ghana and Nigeria. Until 1962, the *gendarmerie* of Senegal was under the Ministry of the Interior but after M. Dia's coup against President Leopold Sédar Senghor failed, the *gendarmerie* was put directly under the Minister of the Armed Forces. The Sûreté and the Republican Guard of Senegal remained under the Minister of the Interior; this was an example of balancing the police forces themselves rather than concentrating them within one ministry.[19]

When the costs of defense forces as a share of GNP or of total governmental budgets are calculated, the cost of police expenses are not included. But given the comparability of internal security function for both police and armed forces and given the nature of the *gendarmerie* and mobile police forces as paramilitary units, this may not be the most useful way of calculating defense costs. Because the population in Africa is so predominantly rural and because it is typically scattered, internal security would be a problem whatever the political problems. Since Africa is marked by a host of forms of violence (revolutions, coups, rejection movements; organized group violence for both political ends and robbery; and individual murder and assault as well as guerrilla fighting and border wars), the costs of internal security come very high.[20] (We leave aside for a moment the question of whether the first political leaders of the newly independent states have themselves raised the cost of internal security and whether the military has raised these costs.) In Uganda, for example, about 14 percent of recurrent revenue is devoted to police and prisons.[21] Much of the expenditure of African armies can be counted as internal security expenses.

We see from Table 3 that Africa ranks low for defense expenditures as a percentage of GNP as compared to other world areas. In fact, sub-Saharan Africa would rank even lower because the north African countries pull up the figure for defense spending as a share of GNP.[22] However, the defense costs defrayed through military assistance are not included. These are a very significant share of defense expenditures—and for those countries having defense treaties with France, not only equipment and training but perhaps also deferment of recurrent costs have been taking place. African countries, moreover, are not carrying out research and development programs.

We also see from the figures in Table 1 that a number of African countries have defense expenditures that are comparatively high as a share of GNP for developing countries. Kenya, Congo (Brazzaville), Senegal, and Upper Volta are all above 6 percent. In the figures of the Arms Control and Disarmament Agency (ACDA) for 1964, Congo (then Leopoldville, now Kinshasa) was the only country in all of Africa, excluding the U.A.R., that had more than 6 percent of its GNP accounted for by defense expenditures.[23] That defense expenditures are rising in Africa is certainly true. In countries with major armed forces by sub-Saharan African standards we can see the substantial increases. Calculating the impact of defense costs on the economic growth of developing countries has been a major concern both for ACDA and AID. But, generally, arguments have cut both ways, as they have in discussions of political effects. When military assistance becomes massive, there is a fear that inflation will occur in the recipient country and that domestic budgets will not be able to bear the strain of absorbing the attendant costs of expanding the military. And there has been a recognition within all branches of the aid-giving establishment that the political and social contexts are sometimes such that military assistance will either not be possible by itself or will perhaps be counterproductive unless it is accompanied by economic assistance. Thus, a large component of American aid since World War II has been in the realm of defense support or supporting assistance; 17 percent of the total fiscal year 1966 request to Congress for AID programs were in this category. Supporting assistance is used: ". . . to enable countries to make a contribution to the common defense, or to internal security, greater than their economies can support unaided; . . . to maintain economic stability in countries where the absence or drastic reduction of current support would probably involve disastrous economic and political disintegration; . . . to provide, along with other aid sources, an alternative to Sino-Soviet bloc aid where such aid threatens a country's independence or otherwise conflicts with vital U.S. interests." [24]

Supporting assistance is supposed to go to those countries where "essential growth prerequisites of stability and security must be established." It has largely, but not exclusively, been used in "forward defense" countries that are located on the Chinese or Soviet periphery. As a share of AID programs to Africa, supporting assistance has been declining since 1961, with the exception of 1964 when the Congo received a large dose of it. For individual sub-Saharan countries, supporting assistance was large only in Guinea and the Congo. The latter had major security problems, but for Guinea supporting assistance was a way of getting economic aid into the country under a quasi-defense guise as it has been for many non-African countries. We shall see that military assistance too has been used as a way of getting extra economic aid to Africa.

Indeed, an argument has been made that military assistance can be a spur to economic development. The provision of military equipment on a grant basis avoids the use of foreign exchange. The assumption here is that military expenditures would occur whether aid was given or not and that they would thus come out of development budgets. Many recipients of military assistance are countries where troops are recruited from those who live at subsistence level. If forces were cut back, the economies could not easily absorb the manpower. Furthermore, local demand is said to rise as an effect of assistance programs. Above all, the military can directly increase economic growth via its own programs of social and economic development and through its own internal activities which provide nation-builders, such as literacy programs. Thus, the argument here is for the military as modernizer and for militarily sponsored civic-action programs. On the negative side, along with inflationary pressures mentioned previously, assistance programs are seen as merely whetting the appetites of the military for hardware which is not economically productive and the military is seen as a consumer of scarce resources and services and a utilizer of scarce trained manpower.[25]

It is clear that military assistance has in certain places led to inflation, and domestic unrest has been accentuated by economic dislocations. Military assistance has had positive economic benefits, too. Nothing can be gained from such generalizations and "on the one hand this" kinds of analyses. Similarly, highly generalized discussion of the military as nation-builder or modernizer in developing countries is difficult to sustain because military forces differ in terms of skills, social composition, fire-power, relations with civilian society and political groups, and they differ with regard to their own organizational formats. Above all, the societies in which they operate constrain or allow their activities to develop in various ways. Thus, if we want to be able to deal with these arguments for the economic and the even more obscure political effects of assistance, we must focus on the scope and nature of military assistance to Africa and the role of the African military in political development.[26]

Tropical African countries receive military assistance from the great powers: the United States, the Soviet Union, France, Britain, China, and from many western European countries including West Germany, Belgium, Sweden, Norway, from eastern European countries who both sell arms and supply equipment, from Canada and Israel, and from other developing countries, particularly the United Arab Republic and India.[27] Some African states have received their assistance from one source, for example Liberia; others have begun to lessen their dependency on a single source. Thus, some of the French-speaking countries who have preserved good relations with France have nonetheless requested American assistance, Senegal for one. Other French-speaking countries have received both American and Soviet assistance—Guinea and Mali being cases in point. Ethiopia, too, has non-American sources now. Even where a country has been linked to France by a bilateral defense agreement and regional defense agreements, the United States has given some token assistance, e.g., Dahomey.[28]

The main advantage of widening sources is obvious: the lessening of dependence on a single donor. However, there are real disadvantages, also. Too much diversification leads to lack of standardization of equipment and training. The militaries themselves object to this; moreover, they fear splits within their ranks on the basis of cliques formed during overseas experience in various training programs. They do not want an officer corps that is perhaps already split along regional, ethnic, generational, and career experience lines further fragmented in terms of military assistance sources. And this is not necessarily a matter of receptivity to different ideologies or political influences. Rather, it is a fear that solidarity groups may form simply on the basis of shared experiences in different settings.[29] The civilian rulers may feel ambivalent about diversification, too. Although it may be tempting to try and split the military by tying one segment to one donor and playing it off against another, this is a dangerous game. Disunity is a double-edged sword. Lack of cohesion among military elites may promote coups. Syria and Korea are notable examples. In Ethiopia, splits in the military allowed the emperor to survive the Imperial Bodyguard revolt of 1960 and Nkrumah was building his own professional counterforce to the army when he was overthrown.[30] Moreover, diversification of assistance sources brings its own pressures on the civilian rulers. Consider the following case: after the Tanganyikan army mutinied in January 1964, first British and then Nigerian troops came to provide for public order. By the time the army was in the process of reconstruction, Tanganyika was Tanzania; military assistance was being received from West Germany, East Germany, the Soviet Union, China, Britain, Israel, and Canada. Zanzibar's army was trained and equipped from communist sources. And the United States gave police assistance. The Congo is another example. After the uprisings there, the Armée Nationale Congolaise was receiving assistance from Belgium, the United States, Italy, and Israel. Dissidents, meanwhile, were receiving arms and assistance from the U.A.R., the Soviet Union, and China.

I do not intend to sketch the various assistance programs.[31] We can mention that in certain places the Soviet Union has been the major donor. Its current North African programs are very large. It is attempting to transform the U.A.R. and Algerian armies and is becoming increasingly involved with the Nigerian military. In tropical Africa, it became involved with government-to-government aid to the Congo for a brief time and then its aid was given in clandestine fashion to dissident groups. Currently, its major program is in the Somali Republic where its aid through 1966 was reported to be above $30 million.[32] Close to one hundred Somali officers are supposed to have been trained in the U.S.S.R. The Soviet Union was also involved in aiding the Ghanaian army at one point and in building a special Ghanaian military force outside regular army channels. Guinea, too, received Soviet credits following its break with France. All told, by 1964 total military assistance from communist states was put at over $60 million.[33] Whether all this money was expended is another matter, since Soviet aid is in the form of credits which are not always drawn upon.

Soviet military aid to Africa has not been confined to those states that are either carrying out "radical" domestic policies or even those that have lined up with the U.S.S.R. on many foreign policy issues. Somalia could not be put in either category. Rather, Soviet military assistance to Africa, as its foreign aid in general, seems to be a flexible instrument for trying to further rather short-term Soviet political aims.[34] Although Soviet commentators have maintained that a number of countries south of the Sahara—Dahomey, Nigeria, Upper Volta, and others—in which military governments have come to power have received big amounts of American weapons along with related ideological and political concepts, they have not stated any explicit cause and effect between American assistance and military rule.[35] Nor have Soviet analysts of the African military been categorically negative about their subjects. They have maintained that the view that military coups are merely reactionary and militaristic is unsound; similarly, the view that the army is the only all-national force capable of heading a national liberation movement is also unsound. Rather, armies should be seen as playing the role of weapon of the state where insufficient class differentiation and immaturity of social relations brings about a situation wherein one class cannot direct the revolutionary process singlehandedly. Furthermore, the army did not stand apart from the struggle for national liberation. Algeria's army is cited here and its composition—poor peasants, workers, and petty bourgeoisie—is stressed. The role of parties in former colonies is important in this respect in Soviet eyes. National-front type parties united diverse forces and were not prepared to solve post-independence problems. But the army cannot take the place of a party as the guiding force for society as the army has no clear political or ideological platform and no experience in leading the class struggle. Moreover, the army is not unified socially and ideologically, and it splits over the issue of which paths to development should be followed. The army can turn into a tool of reactionary forces, the more so because "the army is a societal institution in which democratic ideas can live rather placidly alongside reactionary views."[36] This analysis is worth citing at some length because it shows greater awareness of the role of the army and the pitfalls of army rule—albeit pitfalls from Soviet points of view—than many American writers concerned with the role of the military in developing countries have shown.

We move on to United States assistance and will not treat British and French aid in any detail—but not because the latter are unimportant programs. In fact, both have been more important than U.S. military aid in Africa in terms of men trained and impact on internal politics. British officers seconded to African countries commanded armies even after independence and still do for certain states (Malawi, Zambia). And where there are African commanders in chief, Britons may command air forces or navies (Kenya). Some 300 uniformed British still work with Kenya's 5,000-man army.[37] And British troops intervened in Uganda, Kenya, and Tanganyika in 1964 to restore order and to shore up heads of state in the three countries.[38]

French troops, too, have intervened to restore a head of state in Gabon, and they continue to be stationed on African soil, although in declining numbers. France has defense and military assistance treaties with some states, and assistance agreements only with others. Although French cadres do not take command posts, they do fill staff and technical posts in African armies.[39] Between 1960 and 1964, over two thousand African officers and noncommissioned officers were trained by France. And there have been annual quotas for Africans in French officer schools running into the hundreds.[40]

One reason for not dealing with French and British programs is that their published figures for the nature and scope of their assistance are highly inadequate.[41] More important is the fact that their programs seem relatively stable and decided on, whereas American military assistance to Africa seems more an open question (despite the congressional limits imposed on the program). The reason for this is that Britain and France are retrenching in Africa, whereas demands will be made for America to play a steadily growing role. However, present American policy to "supplement" the ex-colonial powers' military and economic aid to Africa and to keep the lead in military assistance may not be maintained.

The distinctions between military assistance and economic aid can be drawn by definition, but since the collateral effects of each impinge on military and economic factors, the interrelatedness of the two is ever-present. We could differentiate between military and economic aid on the basis of the form of the aid: if the item is a howitzer there is little problem; if it is an earth-mover, the use could be economic or military and we would have to consider actual use as well. The basis of distinction could be the objectives of the donor: are we primarily concerned with immediate military effects of assistance? We can also distinguish military and economic assistance in terms of the administering agency of the aid program.[42] Supporting assistance has been considered economic aid in part because it is administered by AID, but, when the aid program is defended before Congress, the military aspects are stressed in order to get congressional support. (Some congressmen have argued for a clear distinction between the military and economic aspects of the foreign assistance program for a long time, with all military assistance separated from the foreign aid bill and put on the budget of the Department of Defense. This has already been done for military assistance to Laos and Thailand, and aid to Vietnam is in a special category, too.)

Arms sales can be considered assistance, too, if the credit provisions are for soft loans. Certainly the political implications of sales have been seen by critics and supporters of our arms sales programs.[43] The share of American arms sales to developing countries has been under 10 percent of total sales. Since 1963, the credit transactions to Africa have been classified. Perhaps the hardest thing to measure is the flow of small arms via private manufacturers and clandestine channels. Biafra has received its small arms in this way, as have a number of African governments and rebel movements. United States sales programs have received less oversight from Congress and less publicity than our military assistance programs.[44] For Africa, United States arms sales have been insignificant, at least south of the Sahara, so we are not concerned with American arms sales at this point.[45]

Military assistance itself can be divided into three categories: (a) military assistance which provides military equipment, training, and related services; (b) supporting assistance, which is at various times described in military terms rather than economic; (c) contingency funds used for the same purpose generally as supporting assistance in those emergency situations which cannot be anticipated.[46]

Until 1963, United States military assistance in tropical Africa was administered by the Department of the Army with the Deputy Chief of Staff for Operations (DCSOPS) having primary responsibilities for these military assistance programs (MAP) normally assigned now to unified commands. (Prior to 1963, the Ethiopian MAP was supervised by the Commander in Chief European Command.) At the end of 1963, the United States Strike Command was assigned additional responsibilities as Commander in Chief (CINC) Middle East, Southern Asia, and Africa South of the Sahara. In this capacity, CINCMEAFSA has unified command responsibilities for planning and administering military assistance programs as well as commanding all military assistance advisory groups (MAAGS) and military missions.[47] The unified command, in this case CINCMEAFSA, reports to the office of the Director of Military Assistance in the Joint Chiefs of Staff and the unified command gets policy objectives and order-of-magnitude dollar guidelines from the director. The director of military assistance receives directives and overall guidelines from both the Joint Chiefs and from the Office of the Assistant Secretary of Defense for International Security Affairs (ISA). The Assistant Secretary of Defense, ISA, is charged with the responsibility of directing and administering the military assistance programs, subject to the direction and authority of the Secretary of Defense. At the same time, the MAP personnel in the field are subject to the authority of the Department of Defense hierarchy; they also work under the authority of the ambassadors and work with members of the country team. The Director of Military Assistance also sends program recommendations to the State Department, AID, and the Bureau of the Budget.

One would expect difficulties in coordination with the various overlapping organizational hierarchies within the civilian and military wings of the Defense Department and between Defense and other agencies. One might also expect that whatever the provisions of the Foreign Assistance Act of 1961, which gives the Secretary of State authority over foreign assistance, which he in turn has delegated to the Administrator of AID, the Department of Defense which exercises primary responsibility in the field of military assistance would dominate the formulation of assistance policy. In the small African programs, both the civilian wing of Defense (ISA) concerned with assistance and State and AID have more impact on the contours of assistance policy than they have where there are big programs. In CINCMEAFSA at the end of 1964 there were thirty-six military personnel and fourteen civilian personnel in military assistance work.

Most of them were not concerned with Africa south of the Sahara.[48] Military personnel in the assistance program for Africa feel that AID and State have considerable say in the administration of military assistance for Africa.[49] The AID personnel, in turn, feel that military assistance is particularly inappropriate for Africa in the light of its stark development needs and its distance from the Sino-Soviet periphery. The AID personnel concerned with Africa have more antipathy for the military as a ruling group than have the military personnel. Yet, many officers involved in assistance programs, both in the field and in Washington, and military personnel seconded to ISA or to political-military affairs desks within the State Department do not have exaggerated ideas about the capacity of African militaries for either maintaining political order or achieving political development.

It is probably true that AID's voice has been heard in interdepartmental meetings on military assistance to Africa more than elsewhere. For one thing, there are no large ongoing programs in tropical Africa. For another, Congress has established a $25-million limit on provision of direct grant equipment to all of Africa,[50] although this can be avoided via interest-free loans. And sub-Saharan Africa has been the area of least American involvement politically and economically as well as militarily. Thus, in the context of a relative lack of interest, AID has comparatively more influence on military assistance policy in Africa than in other areas. (The emphasis on military civic action in Africa, however, has been at least as much, and probably more of, an interest of ISA than AID.) Finally, the police assistance programs are operated by the Office of Public Safety, which is located within AID.

The official statement of AID on police assistance notes that the Public Safety Program seeks: 1. To strengthen the capabilities of civil police and paramilitary forces to enforce the law and maintain public order with a minimum of physical force, and to counter Communist inspired or exploited subversion and insurgency. 2. To encourage the development of responsible and humane police administration and judicial procedure and to improve the effectiveness of civil police and paramilitary forces, and to enable them to become more closely integrated into the community." [51]

In Africa where civil police and *gendarmerie* perform security and para-military functions, and where policemen have been partners in military regimes, AID's public safety programs are important and enhance the role of AID (although the Office of Public Safety has its own separate identity within AID). The public safety funds come out of country budgets. Also, AID provides training for civil police and for field forces. The requests of police for aid tend to be "lighter" (that is, weaponry does not include artillery); it is less expensive.

An American presence can be obtained, a concentration on internal subversion is possible, and arms races are not furthered. This is not to say that there is no danger for political development in aiding police forces. Janowitz raises the possibility that mobile police forces are instruments of potential political intervention. While police forces are less costly, they can be even more disruptive to the internal political balance because they are more likely to rely on local coercive pressure and have less of a sense of national goals.[52] "In fact, it might be argued that, in the absence of the army as a counterforce, the police would tend to expand their political power in new nations with weak political institutions, and their intervention might be highly unstable and fragmentary."[53] Since there are armies in Africa, with the few exceptions of Gambia, Botswana, and Lesotho, there is also the possibility of army-police struggle. Posing hypothetical questions will not be nearly as useful as examining specific police recruitment patterns and analyzing actual police-civilian and police-military relations. The kind of weaponry and training the police receive will affect these relations.

The public safety programs of AID came to $2,541,000 for fiscal year 1966 and $3,550,000 for fiscal year 1967. This was one of the smallest categories of the functional fields into which AID breaks its assistance and it came out of a total project commitment for Africa in 1966 of $141,488,000.[54] During this same fiscal year, 1966, AID provided development loans of close to $100 million and supporting assistance of $26 million. Military assistance for fiscal year 1966 was $24 million. The country breakdown on 1967 can be seen on Table 7.

The United States gives military assistance to Africa for a number of reasons, all of which have been noted in congressional hearings. The official line, as expressed by the men from the military and civilian wings of the Department of Defense, from the State Department, and from AID, who appear before the hearings of the Senate and House Appropriations and Foreign Relations committees, is a true telling. With specific reference to Africa, Secretary of Defense Robert McNamara gave three reasons for military assistance, one of which was deleted from the record of the hearings: (*a*) American interest in the independence of Africa. Military assistance helps counteract communist influence and control; (*b*) Military assistance helps maintain friendly regimes that are capable of maintaining stability, which is a precondition for orderly social and economic development.[55] Secretary McNamara's third and deleted reason, we may speculate, had to do with maintaining American base and overflight rights on African soil.

When General Paul D. Adams, then CINCMEAFSA, appeared before a congressional committee, he neglected to mention base rights and communications facilities but he did cite the following as objectives of United States military assistance to Africa south of the Sahara: first, to foster an anti-Communist, free-world oriented community; second, to assist in the development of an internal security capability and political stability essential to economic growth; third, to contribute to the existence of viable and friendly governments; fourth, to provide recognition of new countries and to assist them in assuming the responsibilities of their independence and sovereignty; and, fifth, to prevent an African arms race.[56] General Adams also noted the importance of creating a United States presence—to give "an alternative to the Chinese and Russians who are competing to take over the countries in time."

A specific program, Ethiopian MAP, was described as "maintaining satisfactory relations with the Ethiopian Government which continues to make important communications facilities available to us. Concurrently our program prevents Soviet encroachment into the military field in this strategically located country. Our assistance provides an internal security capability for the Ethiopian armed forces and provides the capability for these forces to contribute to U.N. operations such as those in Korea and the Congo." [57]

There have been other public allusions to bases in North Africa and to tracking stations, need for worldwide communications net maintenance, and overflight rights.[58] Here, military assistance essentially is used to purchase needed facilities. A communications base in Asmara, Ethiopia, an all-weather air base in Libya (Wheelus), port facilities in Liberia (Roberts), overflight rights and landing privileges in the Sudan, all are related to military assistance programs. This is perhaps the most straightforward exchange. Political influence deriving from military assistance and aid programs as development tools are much less clearly achieved. And whether a country's internal security is furthered by military aid is also a question to be explored empirically. Spokesmen for the aid program do not even suggest that African militaries can directly add to American national security by providing forces that can substitute for American forces. In fact, Congress insisted in 1963 that any aid not strictly needed for purposes of internal security in Africa was prohibited unless the President determined otherwise.

In the 1960's American military assistance has largely been geared to short-term political objectives. Military aid has been provided in small quantities to a number of countries in order to maintain political ties both with African ruling civilian groups and with the potential or actual military ruling elites. The United States has been the primary source of assistance for Liberia and Ethiopia and has been a major donor to the Congo. There have also been military assistance programs in twelve other sub-Saharan states (including the Sudan).

Although these programs are small by comparison with American military assistance programs elsewhere (see Table 8), they grew in size after commencement of assistance to Ethiopia in 1953.[59] By 1967 the proposed military assistance to Africa was $31.8 million (See Table 9). This was 3.1 percent of total United States military aid.

The present level of military assistance at $31 million represents a concentration of programs in fewer countries. The Clay Committee had argued, "We believe that the problems created by military assistance programs in the African countries would be greater than those they would resolve." [60] It argued for an end to small, scattered programs. At the same time, AID was moving toward a concentration of economic aid in fewer African countries.[61] The congressional limit of $25 million on equipment (twelve modern jets amount to about $25 million) militated for phasing out the small programs. Moreover, there was another congressional limitation on the number of countries that could receive American assistance of any kind—forty. Thus, small programs in Senegal, Guinea, and Mali were speeded up and phased out.[62] In tropical Africa, only Ethiopia, Liberia, and the Congo now have MAP, along with Libya, Morocco, and Tunisia in northern Africa. Only Libya could afford to purchase weapons. America has already refused a number of requests for assistance and sales. Assistance to Ghana was terminated in 1964, when relations with Ghana deteriorated. When the late Prime Minister Balewa of Nigeria asked for a jet squadron in 1961, Secretary of State Dean Rusk stressed its unsuitability, and the cost of annual maintenance was pointed out as equaling the cost of educating five million Nigerians.[63] There has been a resistance to meeting such requests for heavy weapons, and those responsible for military assistance in ISA and the Joint Chiefs have maintained that aid to Africa in their realm has been for training and for logistical support, communications equipment, small arms, and the establishing of civic action battalions. A functional breakdown of assistance is given for 1962 in Table 10.

Here training does not emerge as a primary component of military aid. Through 1965, 2,721 Africans (including North Africans) were trained in the United States and another 199 were trained at overseas areas. This does not include, of course, training on the ground via mobile teams and MAP people in formal and informal ways. The costs of training through 1965 were $13.9 million of a total cost of over $1 billion for all American military training programs.[64] This was less than 10 percent of American military assistance in dollar terms. For the relatively large Congo program, which has been justified on the grounds that training is the major need of the Congo's army, through 1966, $830,000 of the $18.8 million the Congo received was for training.[65] Of the $31.2 million proposed for assistance to tropical Africa in 1968, $.5 million will go for training. Furthermore, the average MAP personnel strengths have been very small. In 1967, 17 military and no civilians were in Liberian MAP administrative and mission training. The Congo had 29 military personnel, Guinea 16, Mali 4 (there had been as many as 24 in 1965), Nigeria and Senegal 2 each. Only Ethiopia had a large number of personnel with 187 military and 3 civilians.[66] Ethiopia had the largest number of men training in police programs at the International Police Academy.

It is important to note the limited scope of training in the American military assistance programs, even when we have taken account of the overall limited scope of the military assistance program in Africa, because it was implicitly through training programs that the objectives stated by Secretary McNamara and General Adams for military assistance to Africa were to be achieved. Short-term political influence via ties with the military can be had, perhaps, by provision of equipment. But inculcation of values is presumably achieved through the training process.

Colonel Quintus C. Atkinson has stated: "The United States perhaps recognizing this danger of military coups as a part of the objective of 'Free World Orientation' has engaged wherever possible in the training of selected African military personnel in U.S. service schools and in the education and training of other potential leaders in U.S. civilian college programs. These programs not only supply much needed training and education but also offer the opportunity to develop leaders in the democratic tradition. To many United States officials these leadership programs offer more chance of long range success than the more transitory popularity gained from furnishing hardware."[67]

There has been a debate within the military and civilian agencies concerned with military assistance over the nature of training programs. Many individuals doubt whether democratic values can be inculcated via training programs and whether it is the place of the instructors at the various service schools to do so. Furthermore, there is a belief on the part of civilian and military people alike that coups are going to take place in Africa whatever the nature of American training programs and, for that matter, whatever the nature of military assistance programs. To counter these objections, the argument is made that programs should be geared to exploiting leadership qualities, both in the selection of personnel to be trained and in the latter training.[68] Nation-building qualities and nonmilitary aspects should be stressed. General training in administration, encouragement of precepts of public and social responsibility, and personal ethics should be given.[69] It has been explicitly stated that if the military are going to play political roles, they should be trained to do so.[70]

But how do you train an individual or a group for political roles? The principles of administration can be set forth rather clearly, at least for administering bureaucratic, rationalized organizations. Yet these principles, applied to institutions of state in new nations, do not guarantee success. In Africa, if a civil servant is going to be effective in putting across a local program, he may have to be part community-development officer and part politician. There are no models of bureaucratic behavior that can be transferred simply. Political roles are even harder to define. To be able to teach someone how to be effective politically requires a great deal of knowledge about the indigenous society. Is such knowledge about African societies readily available? If so, it has not been evident in the academic community.[71] Do those who train the trainees have this knowledge? Can you teach military assistance personnel who are going to MAP programs in Africa about their countries in a month at the Military Assistance Institute?[72] Is this knowledge going to be gained at Fort Bragg's Army Special Warfare Center and School or Fort Gordon's Army Civil Affairs School or the United States National Interdepartmental Seminar on Problems of Internal Affairs?[73] I think we can be very skeptical. When Africans come to the United States would they be receptive to such teaching? Will courses in civics be anything more than banal affairs and, where they are, how happy will be the governments and militaries who send their people? This is not to suggest that nothing can be taught concerning development to military personnel, both American and foreign. It is to suggest that we are on strange ground ourselves in this endeavor.

Furthermore, the view that we can teach principles of modernization to foreign military personnel without getting into specific problems of local politics is fatuous. Indeed, the views that the military is the elite best suited to carry out modernization in new states and that "how to modernize" can be taught by stressing good "nation-building" principles—the civic responsibility of the citizen to the state, the role and importance of national symbols, and the identity of views between the people and their government [74]—are both rooted in an apolitical image of development. The idea that United States military assistance should stress training in nation-building so that military assistance will not just have collateral benefits for economic and social development but direct benefits through military nation-building activity gained its impetus from a view of the military as modernizer in the new states.[75] This conception in turn gave rise to military assistance for civic action.

We are by now familiar with the argument that the military is a relatively modernized institution in developing countries and that it is oriented toward industry and professionalism; it is available to outside contact, operates on rational norms with a receptivity to technological change, and is socialized to a wider national set of values. It is argued that an "informed soldiery drawn from all elements of the population is not only well placed to transmit national values to the populace" but that "properly employed the army can become an internal motor for economic growth and socio-political transformation."[76] The rub here is "properly employed." For by now we are also aware that the analyses which considered that discipline and organization were the key qualities necessary for institutions to act with political effect and that because the military could intervene successfully against other groups they could be a dynamic force for modernization and bring order out of chaos have not everywhere been correct.[77] It is one thing to prevail against other political groups through possession of weapons, organization, and discipline. It is another thing to create political order or even to bring about stability. The proposition is well supported that it is easier for the military in developing countries to accumulate power than to govern as a ruling group.[78] We have learned that the coups that bring the military to power often carry the seeds of factionalism within the military, if it is not split already.[79] Furthermore, if the military is to rule, it must be a political actor and cannot stand above politics. Thus, a major claim made for the military—that it represents the entire nation and is perceived to be above political strife—ceases to be viable, once the military gains power (if it had any merit to begin with).

There is another problem. Militaries in many countries are not disciplined and well-organized; they are not melting pots or well-assimilated groups that have been forged into a cohesive entity. In Africa, small militaries of a few thousand men have been able to bring down civilian regimes. But these new rulers make up neither in legitimacy nor coercive ability what they lack in political talent. There is no evidence that African militaries have the political talents requisite for rule in Africa. They are not reaching down to the grass roots. There have been attempts to make African armies nation-builders by changing patterns of recruitment and having the army carry out civic-action programs—building roads, irrigation works, etc.,—and by changing names. Thus the Tanganyika Rifles became the Tanzanian Peoples' Defense Force: youth-wingers and party people were enlisted and the army began economic projects. (The French-speaking armies have carried out economic projects for a long time.)[80] But not all militaries want to carry out civic-action projects, not all do it efficiently. The reliability of a politicized army, both for ruling militaries and for civilian regimes, is doubtful. In Africa, of course, the reliability of the essentially mercenary armies constructed by colonial rulers proved to be tenuous, too.

When armies come to power in Africa, their leaders, be they ex-noncommissioned officers from the colonial forces or new graduates from Sandhurst, St. Cyr, and Fort Gordon, do not show particular skill in manipulating political groups via persuasion, flexible policies, and bargaining abilities. Both the Nigerian and Congolese military elites seem to be lacking in these skills, to name only two glaring examples. Are "political" sentiments expressed, for example, when Colonel Lamizana of Upper Volta, commenting on rumors that the former chief of state, M. Yameogu, would remain in office after military intervention, declared, "This is to know how poorly the military man I am, because my honor as a soldier and my dignity prohibit me from such compromises"? [81]

As different military factions begin to make alliances with various civilian groups, a pattern that has become typical in Latin America and the Middle East may occur: institutionalized intervention of the military does not promote political development and bring about political stability; furthermore, the military does not give up aspirations to rule and in fact cannot disengage from the politics of rule.

When we begin to make concrete what we mean by political development in Africa we should be talking about creating effective political instruments.[82] Public order means domestic tranquillity. Political order means institution-building. It is not a terminal state once reached, forever achieved. There are, as yet, no nationwide political structures in Africa that can enforce the will of ruling national elites, no matter whether these elites are of traditional lineage groups, civilian bureaucracies, the military, or the ruling single-party—where it still exists. Although many African states exhibit a rhetoric of mobilization-for-development through disciplined parties or militaries, it is often these very states where values are not allocated for society as a whole by central authorities. However, highly localized determination of political life need not be synonymous with disorder, anarchy, and chaos. In fact, in Africa it may be the only way to avoid these conditions. For tropical Africa we can agree with Huntington's general point for developing countries that the only organization which can become a source of authority and which can become effectively institutionalized is the political party.[83] This does not commit one to the view that attempts at centralized one-party systems will work. Political competition and nondirectiveness are not necessarily inimical to development. They are required for it in Africa. Indeed, political machines that are competitive and decentralized may well be a useful model for Africa. If this is so, the military will hardly be the group most appropriate for manning the machine.

If we should be highly skeptical about the military as the bearer of modernity and the creator of political development in Africa, then we must look carefully into the consequences of military assistance for the balance of political power in African countries. This argument has particular weight because the many reasons given for military assistance elsewhere are recognized as being inappropriate in Africa. We do not look to African military forces as being useful against external aggression from outside Africa and we are not interested in strengthening the defense forces of the free world by adding African military units; nor do we think that military assistance should be used to stabilize given areas through balance-of-power politics. The places where this might apply, the Horn of Africa and the Maghreb, worry us as they become involved in arms races. Thus, the arguments for military assistance to Africa hinge on: (a) developing the military as modernizer; (b) creating strong military and paramilitary forces to assure the independence of a country against internal subversion; (c) enhancing American political influence through connections with the military and by getting leverage with governments who request assistance. If, however, the present phase of military rule and initial military interventions turns out to be short-lived or highly unstable in Africa, then American political influence might be lessened if relationships with new civilian elites are affected by past military assistance programs. It is also possible that military assistance does not add to internal security in Africa but rather lessens it. And it is at least conceivable that the only way militaries in Africa will successfully contribute to development is by restricting their own growth and the importation of hardware.

We have no hard conclusions to offer, but in order to take account of these questions we must now try to assess certain effects of military assistance in Africa.

It is perhaps easier to see the absence of effects of assistance programs than to specify negative or positive effects. For example, the evidence is as scanty in Africa as elsewhere that Secretary McNamara is correct when he says, "The experience we have indicates that the exposure of the military officers to our schools acquaints them with democratic philosophies and the democratic ways of thinking which they in turn take back to their countries." [84] We do not have good "before" and "after" guages of the attitudes of foreign personnel who come to train in the United States. The impression of some of those who train foreign police and military personnel is that the trainees are hardware oriented. (The impression of observers, too, is that trainers are hardware oriented.) We know the military elites are political actors on home ground, but we have as yet little knowledge of how they are influenced by either training programs or a general socialization process. [85] It may be that interpersonal relations at United States training programs neither supply a basis for communications about United States policy and strategic intentions nor effectively communicate values about the role of the military. This does not mean that career and educational experiences are not important. Janowitz suggests that they may be more important than the traditional categories of social background in explaining political attitudes. But so far, we do not know the impact of our training program on these attitudes.

What we do know is that American-trained officers have participated in coups and that men trained for civic action in Latin America and having career experiences with civic-action activities turn their attention to what may be called coup politics. There is also evidence that personal relations are struck between American military personnel and foreign officers. But we can be wary, as Henry Bryoade was not when he said that "military leaders play an important and in some cases controlling role in most of the states of the area and these leaders are on the whole progressive, friendly to the West, and distrustful of the Soviets." [86] Bryoade was referring to the Middle East.

Insofar as militaries directly carry out nation-building tasks, they do so, in American terms, through civic-action programs. "Civic action" has sometimes been used synonymously with "counterinsurgency" because both involve militaries with civilian populations. Civic action, however, stresses the nonviolent use of the military. "Civic action is the use of indigenous and foreign military and paramilitary forces on projects useful to local populations in fields such as education, public works, agricultural, transportation and other projects which contribute to economic and social improvement." [87] MAP-supported civic action is designed to encourage and support the use of local forces in activities that contribute to economic and social development, and to assist in the prevention and elimination of insurgencies inimical to free-world interest by improving the relations between army and population. Congress amended the Mutual Security Act in 1959 to provide specific legislative endorsement for civic action, and President Kennedy directed the Departments of State and Defense to undertake expanded support of civic action in developing countries in 1961. The increased number of African countries that were receiving American military assistance in 1963 was in part a reflection of interest in civic-action programs in Africa. Civic action also served as a way of getting more economic aid into Africa.

There was support for civic-action programs in Africa by AID personnel because they considered such programs as the least evil among the military assistance alternatives. Within the State and Defense departments interest quickened in the military as a force for development, and civic-action programs were seen as direct contributions to economic development and as useful components of counterinsurgency programs. The economic aspects of development were stressed. "The purpose of the non-military operations, such as civic action, is to help eliminate the economic cause of discontent that provides the breeding ground for insurgency."[88] Although there was no interest within the Defense Department in turning African armed forces into civic-action forces, civic action was seen as an appropriate mission for army contingents. For one thing, there was no danger that civic-action activities would unduly detract from what would be primary military purposes elsewhere, namely, defense. The United States had no interest in building large defense forces in Africa and feared an African arms race. Furthermore, it was felt that civic action would not be contrary to the long-term development of private enterprise and a sound civilian economy since there was so little private enterprise in any case. Military officers, seeing that civic action was "in" at high levels in the government, began to see a new army mission in its sponsorship. And for Africa, it was clear that civic action represented a way to get military assistance established. In fact, the Foreign Assistance Act of 1966 stipulated that military assistance to Africa must be for civic action or internal defense.

The civic-action programs now started in Africa are considered to be in early stages with a large potential for expansion. The civic-action programs in tropical Africa usually take the form of assistance for engineering projects. Engineering battalions are rehabilitating schools, constructing roads, and providing sanitation. The United States has provided the equipment, materials, and training for these projects. Since individual items are not detailed, it is not known here precisely what equipment is called civic-action equipment. The claim is that only light equipment is provided. This has meant, in Latin America at least, patrol boats, training for airborne units, and transport and communication material.[89] Some essentially new battalions are being supported by American civic-action assistance. Military spokesmen have claimed for Liberia that civic-action projects have enhanced the government's program of rural and tribal integration into national life.[90] We have as yet no studies corroborating this or denying it. Skepticism has been evident over the positive results of civic action in Latin America and limitations on civic-action programs have been stated elsewhere.[91] And the warning has been sounded that as the military gets involved with civilians and perhaps some of the least satisfied elements—the youth or the rural populace in particularly underdeveloped areas—and as it gets more control over resources, it might activate those resources against the regime.[92] "However, much depends on how this [civic action] is done, for deep involvement by an army in such non-military matters can also lead to corruption and inefficiency. Foreign advisors who stress the importance of the military's role in nation-building may inadvertently be encouraging the army to judge its record—and its hopes—against that of a lack-luster regime."[93]

However, there has been little calculation in the past of the impact of civic-action programs on politics in countries receiving military assistance. This is undoubtedly related to Packenham's finding that among aid administrators the sociological and psychological dimensions of political change are not perceived or are not salient factors in their implicit models of political change and that the American experience has produced an attitude of disdain toward the idea of a possible technology of political development.[94] Perhaps this lack of calculation also reflected the small concern within the American government over the prospects for military rule in Africa. The "marginality of impact" view,[95] plus the notion of modernizing militaries operating on army corps of engineer principles, has, in the context of the relative absence of American interests in Africa, led to a posture where small military assistance programs were supported to gain short-term political goals without a hard look at the consequences of these programs. Even where there was uneasiness over the wisdom of miltiary assistance, if African leaders wanted token programs, the United States gave them these prior to 1965. If there were stronger political interests, larger programs were undertaken.[96]

The desire for an American presence and for ties between donor and recipients has led to a concern with the impact of American assistance in one important political area: the propensity for coups. Moreover, congressmen are always raising the possibility of a connection between assistance and coups. In the past, Latin American military coups occupied congressional attention; more recently, African military interventions have been prominent.

We have already said that we do not know precisely what values are transmitted by military training programs. But, whatever the struggle of conscience, whatever the reluctance (or keenness), African officers have intervened in politics. And they have intervened in former British colonies as well as former French ones. There is no reason to suspect that American-trained officers have been any less inclined to intervene than their colleagues trained at Sandhurst or St. Cyr.[97] Although there have been American military assistance programs in Liberia, Guinea, Mali, Senegal, Nigeria, Sudan, Ghana, the Congo, and Ethiopia, only in Ethiopia and the Congo was assistance going on at the time of an attempted coup. Since all African armies receive foreign military assistance from somewhere, we can find a perfect correlation between coups and assistance at the grossest level of analysis. Some of the smallest armies have revolted—e.g., Togo, Gabon—and so have the largest (Ghana, Nigeria, and Ethiopia). The claim is probably true that some African armies would intervene even if they were armed with bows and arrows and that they would be strong enough to overthrow civilian regimes even with that kind of weaponry. This argument has been made in support of the null-effect hypothesis of military assistance. In the absence of data on the French and British assistance policies, we cannot thoroughly investigate the proposition that the conduct of armed forces in domestic struggles may be conditioned by institutional and national ties with the outside. But even for small armies receiving small amounts of assistance, it would be very useful to examine the impact on military responsiveness to government control that institutional dependence on foreign military assistance may represent.

Wheatley has done this for 54 countries over the period 1950–1964. (Liberia, Guinea, and Ethiopia were the only sub-Saharan African states included.) He sets up a simple "exchange of services" model where the military provides a responsive means for the use of force in the pursuit of government goals while the government reciprocates by providing human and material resources for the military.[98] He elaborates four hypotheses worth listing: "1) The smaller the proportion of total material resources consumed by the military which derive from domestic sources, the less responsive the military to the domestic regime; 2) The higher the absolute levels of military resource consumption, the stronger the association between the proportion of total resources derived from domestic sources and the degree of military responsiveness to the domestic regime; 3) The greater the proportion of domestic material resources consumed by the military and the smaller the proportion of total military consumption they provide, the less responsive the military to the domestic regime; 4) The greater the number of external sources and the larger the proportion of total military resources these provide, the less responsive the military to the domestic regime."[99] Unresponsiveness, in Wheatley's use, includes failure to resist—or assistance to —insurgents or the calculated attempt to remove government incumbents or to alter the structure of government. We would also want to know the likelihood that the military will take independent positions on foreign and domestic issues. This is harder to establish because infighting may be less well known. But it is especially important in the context of military assistance because the donor may have it in mind to encourage military dissidence in foreign or domestic policy.

Wheatley was concerned with relating the onset of coups to military assistance compared to domestic resource levels.[100] We cannot find out with public figures for enough countries in Africa whether military assistance was rising as a share of defense expenditure before coups.[101] In east Africa, mutinies took place for higher pay and then defense costs went up as salaries were raised. Subsequently, military assistance increased in Tanzania and the numbers of donors proliferated. But what the ratio of assistance to new costs was is not known to me. Similarly, defense costs have gone up both in western African states which had coups, some of which were also pay strikes, notably Togo, and in states that have not had coups. It may be that military assistance has no casuative correlation and that factors completely internal to African politics are more important.

But we should note here that many of the factors mentioned by students of African coups can perhaps be gotten at by looking at military assistance. Changes in size of the military, composition, technology, image of self, all are related to military assistance because African militaries are dependent on aid for carrying out structural changes and increasing the size of the armed forces. The argument made by some proponents of military assistance that armies would get money earmarked for capital development if assistance is not forthcoming can be true only up to a point. Furthermore, internal politics in a given country as well as regional struggles for influence can be related to military assistance because outside powers have an interest in the complexion of regimes and in African external relations. After the coup, the United States determined to furnish Ghana aid to stabilize the nation's economy, to service debts, and to modernize the Ghanaian security forces.[102] Great powers also may intervene in crises of internal security, the Congo and Nigeria being cases in point. Thus, military assistance and coups may be related, but not merely in terms of the resource-mediation/ model-responsiveness that Wheatley posits.[103]

Our concern with development leads us to ask: what happens when the military does take over? Do defense budgets rise and, if so, are they financed out of greater foreign assistance or domestic resources? We are interested in the reasons defense budgets rise, too. Zambia has the fastest-rising defense budget in tropical Africa. But Zambia borders on the Congo and on Rhodesia. Yet, the civilian government may be responding to internal political pressure as well as felt security needs. A military regime in power may spend money on the army in order to make payoffs to its major constituent. Or it may make such a botch of rule that it begins to rely more and more on the coercive apparatus and thus incur high costs for maintaining itself.[104]

It has been argued that African politics already manifest a major transformation: the shift away from political power as a technique of rule to a reliance on force.[105] Rulers resort to force when power and legitimacy fail. If African ruling militaries fail to legitimize themselves they will have to rely on instruments of force rather than the manipulation of political power.[106] Do we then meet spiraling demands for assistance? The Congo already shows this pattern, revealing how hard it is for the United States to extricate itself from military assistance in a continuing crisis. There is evidence that the United States would like to end its Congo military assistance programs or at least curtail them. Nor does the Congo appear to be a country listed for country development support emphasis under new AID concentration policy. Yet, at a time when Congress is particularly uneasy about American interventions and military assistance, air transport and troop support are sent to the Congo (during July 1967) after strong requests from the Congo government for help against a mercenary insurrection. Such a request can be refused. In this case it was felt that political ties required the sending of assistance. Moreover, it was argued, and proved to be true, that even such limited assistance could be crucial for the short-run military situation. In this context, with a history of past military and political support, it is hard to get out.

In other words, military assistance in Africa is not merely the provision of material and services to another state but often means giving aid that can tip domestic political balances precipitously. The Congo is simply the most dramatic example of this because its politics have been violent and military forces have frequently been in struggles with other military and quasi-military groups. The recipient state is willy-nilly in a client relationship in Africa to the donor, who willy-nilly finds himself up to his ears in domestic politics without really seeing how he can direct those politics.

If it turns out to be true, as argued here, that African militaries do not have the political resources to run African polities nor are they modernizers, then assistance which makes the military an ever "heavier" institution in society but that is not able or designed to change the fundamental nature of the militaries will not be conducive to an orderly process of political development.

So far American military assistance has reconstructed certain military forces through massive aid and direct military intervention. Korea and Vietnam are cases in point, although the latter may be more significant for the questions it raises about the limits of American military assistance and intervention. In Africa, it cannot be said that MAP has been used as "one of the most useful available instruments for American foreign policy for meeting the challenges of the systematic revolution in the underdeveloped areas." [107] Nor has MAP been looked on as not only a military program but also a broadly gauged sociological and organizational undertaking.[108] Aid has been used for direct rather than indirect influence.[109] The biggest programs have been where the United States has had bases, and assistance has been in the nature of *quid pro quo*. I have largely ignored the foreign policy aspects of assistance here to concentrate on the possible consequences of these small programs. It is possible for big powers with many huge programs to overlook the impact of small programs on small states with porous and fragile political structures and to concentrate on short-term political influence rather than long-term political development.

TABLE ONE

ARMED FORCES OF SUB-SAHARAN AFRICA

(excluding gendarmeries and police)

Nation	Armed Forces	Inhabitants per Serviceman	Annual Defense Budget *(million dollars)*	% of Total Budget	% of GNP	Active Reserves *(not police)*
EASTERN AFRICA						
Ethiopia	35,000	634	31.2	17.0	2.3	8,000
Sudan	18,500	789	40.0	17.7	4.4	
Somali Republic	9,500	242	6.7	18.1	4.8	
Tanzania	3,000	3,440	7.2	3.8	0.3	4,000
Kenya	4,775	1,906	10.2	6.9	9.8	
Uganda	5,960	1,235	17.0	10.2	1.5	
SOUTHERN AFRICA						
South Africa	23,000	829	322.0	19.9	3.5	53,000
Rhodesia	4,345	963	16.9	6.6	1.9	38,300
Zambia	3,000	1,200	13.5	5.7	2.5	2,000
Malagasy Republic	2,800	2,143	9.1	8.8	1.0	
Malawi	850	4,350	1.5	3.3	1.1	?
Botswana						
Lesotho						
CENTRAL AFRICA						
Congo *	32,000	478	22.5	14.5	1.7	
Cameroon	3,000	1,366	15.8	19.5	4.2	
Burundi *	950	2,737	.97	· 6.9	.7	
Congo (Brazzaville)	1,300	615	3.8	8.9	10.9	
Rwanda	1,500	2,007	1.3	9.7	.7	
Chad	700	3,857	5.8	13.5	1.8	
Central African Republic *	500	2,400	2.3	7.9	.6	700
Gabon	300	2,000	2.5	7.6	5.1	
WESTERN AFRICA						
Nigeria *	11,500	4,956	54.0	9.9	.9	
Ghana *	9,000	844	42.0	7.4	2.5	
Guinea	3,000	685	5.9	8.1	3.1	
Senegal	4,700	659	21.1	11.6	7.6	
Ivory Coast	3,600	972	8.8	6.9	2.4	
Liberia	3,580	698	3.1	6.7	1.8	
Mali	3,500	1,280	8.8	21.2	3.2	
Sierra Leone *	1,360	1,618	2.6	4.9	1.3	
Upper Volta *	1,700	2,470	2.8	14.1	6.1	1,000
Niger	1,500	2,000	3.7	10.8	1.2	
Dahomey *	1,400	1,429	4.1	12.0	2.0	
Mauritania	1,100	909	4.1	17.9	5.1	
Togo	600	2,500	2.8	13.5	4.1	
Gambia *						

* Ruled by military regimes as of June 1967.

Source: Charles Stevenson, "African Armed Forces," *Military Review,* XLVII (March, 1967), 18–24.

COMPARISON OF ARMED FORCES AND CIVIL POLICE GENDARMERIE

Nation	Armed Forces	Civil Police or Gendarmerie
EASTERN AFRICA		
Ethiopia	35,000	28,000 plus 1,200 in frontier guard
Sudan	18,500	10,000
Somali Republic	9,500	5,000
Tanzania	3,000	1,350 (*including a parachute company*)
Kenya	4,775	11,500 (*including a light plane wing*)
Uganda	5,960	5,500 (*including General Service Units and air wing with light transport and helicopters*)
SOUTHERN AFRICA		
South Africa	23,000	28,000 police, plus 15,000 reservists, 51,500 Kommandos (*part-time rural militia*)
Rhodesia	4,345	6,400 active, 28,500 reservists
Zambia	3,000	6,000 (*including 6 platoons of Mobile Police with light aircraft*)
Malagasy Republic	2,800	1,000 gendarmerie & 600 civil police
Malawi	850	3,000
Botswana		
Lesotho		
CENTRAL AFRICA		
Congo	32,000	21,000 civil police, 5 gendarmerie battalions
Cameroun	3,000	3,000 gendarmerie, 5,900 civil police, 1,800 mobile police
Burundi	950	1,000 gendarmerie, 850 civil police
Congo (Brazzaville)	1,300	
Rwanda	1,500	750
Chad	700	550 gendarmerie, 1,950 civil police
Central African Republic	500	500 gendarmerie, 700 Republican Guard and 330 civil police
Gabon	300	600 gendarmerie, 900 civil police
WESTERN AFRICA		
Nigeria	11,500	24,000
Ghana	9,000	9,000
Guinea	5,000	1,000 civil police, 900 gendarmerie
Senegal	4,700	1,500 gendarmerie, 3,000 civil police
Ivory Coast	3,600	1,500 gendarmerie, 800 civil police
Liberia	3,580	700 police, 5,000 militia
Mali	3,500	1,000 gendarmerie, 600 civil police
Sierra Leone	1,360	2,050
Upper Volta	1,700	1,500 gendarmerie, 300 civil police
Niger	1,500	1,300 gendarmerie, 400 civil police
Dahomey	1,400	1,200 gendarmerie, 1,000 civil police
Mauritania	1,100	800 civil police
Togo	600	1,000 gendarmerie, 300 civil police
Gambia	None	150 paramilitary field force

Source: For armed forces I have used Stevenson, *Military Review*, XLVII, 18–24; for police or *gendarmerie* I have used Wood, *The Armed Forces of African States.* Wood and Stevenson have many comparable figures for armed forces, but they disagree in various places, too. Although the publcation date for Stevenson is later than for Wood, some of Wood's figures seem more up to date; others do not.

TABLE THREE

DEFENSE EXPENDITURES AND SELECTED ECONOMIC DATA
FOR LESS DEVELOPED COUNTRIES,[a] BY REGION, 1964

Region	Mid-Year Population	GNP[b]	Defense Expenditures[c]	Defense % of GNP	Public Education Expenditures[d]	Public Health Expenditures[d]
	(in millions)	*(in billions of U.S. dollar equivalents)*				
Europe	109.0	$ 53.0	$ 2.5	4.7	$ 3.2	$ 1.3
Latin America	229.2	74.0	1.7	2.3	2.2	0.9
Far East	1,036.1	105.4	6.8– 9.8	6.5–9.3	3.9	0.9
Near East	82.1	19.2	1.4	7.2	0.9	0.3
South Asia	611.1	55.7	2.1	3.9	1.3	0.4
Africa	222.1	24.2	0.5	2.1	1.0	0.4
Total	2,289.6	$331.5	15.0–18.0	4.5–5.4	$12.5	$ 4.2
% of world total	(71.2)	(17.3)	(12.1–13.0)		(14.3)	(11.1)

[a] For this table, less developed countries include Albania, Bulgaria, Greece, Portugal, Spain, Turkey, Yugoslavia; all of the Near East and Far East except Japan; all of Latin America; and all of Africa except the Republic of South Africa.

[b] For most free-world, less developed countries, GNP statistics are based on U.N. data for prior years. For less developed countries where official national accounts data are not available or are considered to be inadequate, estimates were prepared from available information.

[c] Data have been generally adjusted to concepts used by NATO.

[d] The quality and comprehensiveness of these data vary significantly from country to country. Data generally relate only to central government expenditures. In many countries, provincial and local governments have a major role in education and health.

Source: United States Arms Control and Disarmament Agency, *World Wide Defense Expenditures and Selected Economic Data, Calendar Year 1964,* Research Report 66-1 (Washington, D.C., Jan. 1966), Table III, p. 17.

TABLE FOUR

DEFENSE EXPENDITURES AND GROSS NATIONAL PRODUCT
FOR SELECTED AFRICAN COUNTRIES, 1960, 1962, AND 1964

(in millions of U.S. dollar equivalents)

Country	1960		1962		1964	
	GNP	Defense Expends.	GNP	Defense Expends.	GNP	Defense Expends.
Ethiopia	$ 812	$15	$ 900	$19	$ 982	$22
Ghana	1,324	14	1,518	33	1,675	39
Nigeria	3,300	16	3,715	24	4,120	48

Note: Gross national product and defense expenditures are in current market prices generally converted at official exchange rates. Defense expenditures have been adjusted generally to the concepts and definitions used by NATO.

Source: World Wide Defense Expenditures, 19.

TABLE FIVE

AID EXPENDITURES—APPROPRIATION CATEGORY BY REGION
AND COUNTRY—FISCAL YEAR 1966

(thousands of dollars)

Country	Total	Development Loans	Techincal Coopera- tion/ Develop- ment Grants	Supporting Assistance	Contin- gency Funds	Contributions to Interna- tional Organi- zations
AFRICA	212,140	90,160	76,730	42,954	1,271	1,024
Algeria	834		678	156		
Burundi	292		292			
Cameroon	3,453	2,005	1,135	313		
Central African Republic	1,468		1,468			
Chad	1,164		1,164			
Congo (Brazzaville)	38		38			
Congo (Kinshasha)	22,285		1,423	20,004		858

Country	Total	Development Loans	Technical Coopera-tion/ Develop-ment Grants	Supporting Assistance	Contin-gency Funds	Contributions to Interna-tional Organi-zations
Dahomey	460		460			
Ethiopia	7,830	741	5,803	1,276	10	
Gabon	557		557			
Gambia	102		102			
Ghana	29,545	28,642	903			
Guinea	7,214	141	2,876	4,215	−18	
Ivory Coast	2,340	1,694	646			
Kenya	3,777	448	3,329			
Liberia	21,241	14,565	6,676			
Libya	454	−4	458			
Malagasy	602		602			
Malawi	1,695		1,695			
Mali	1,782	42	951	654	135	
Mauritania	185		185			
Morocco	20,240	6,280	854	12,972	134	
Niger	1,117	339	778			
Nigeria	20,530	4,579	15,951			
Rhodesia and Nyasaland	1		1			
Rwanda	410		410			
Senegal	165		148	17		
Sierra Leone	1,549		1,539		10	
Somali Republic	5,654	1,294	4,360			
S. Rhodesia	7		7			
Sudan	3,493	67	3,426			
Tanzania	3,920	2,062	1,858			
Togo	1,088		1,088			
Tunisia	27,047	24,496	2,551			
Uganda	3,443	1,654	1,789			
Upper Votla	367		367			
Zambia	808		808			
East Africa Regional	3,268	1,116	2,152			
Africa Regional	11,509		6,998	3,346	1,000	165
Regional USAID/Africa	205		205			

TABLE SIX

FRENCH MILITARY ASSISTANCE: 1964

(in millions of dollars, excluding gifts of equipment)

Cameroon	1.84
Central African Republic	1.40
Chad	1.36
Dahomey	——— [a]
Gabon	.88
Ivory Coast	2.00 [b]
Malagasy Republic	11.66
Mauritania	1.30
Niger	1.00
Senegal	1.40
Upper Volta	——— [c]

[a] A French gift of military vehicles was worth $2 million.
[b] There was a 340-man mission in 1963.
[c] No monetary breakdown available from the source.
Source: M. J. V. Bell, *Military Assistance to Africa* ("Adelphi Papers," No. 15, Dec. 1964, ISS). Addenda and Errata Pt. I, March 24, 1965, pp. 1–4. Bell put French military assistance to Africa at $46.6 million in 1963 and $48.4 in 1964.

TABLE SEVEN

AID'S PUBLIC SAFETY ASSISTANCE TO AFRICA

(in thousands of dollars obligated)

	1966	1967	Total through Fiscal Year 1967
Central African Republic	77	4 *	214 *
Chad	141	39 *	312 *
Congo (Kinshasa)	526	2,437	4,207
Dahomey	34		
Ethiopia	408	199	2,378
Kenya	77	46	553
Liberia	211	323	2,526
Malagasy	42	34 *	408 *
Niger	40	18 *	560 *
Rwanda	208	101	661
Somalia	647	320	3,804
Tanzania	64	*	182 *
Tunisia	30	9	150 *
Upper Volta	36		
Total	2,541	3,550	15,955

* As of March 31, 1967.
Sources: Figures for 1966 from the Statistics and Reports Division, Office of Program Coordination, AID, as published in AID, *Report for July 1, 1965–June 30, 1966* (Washington, D.C., 1967), 31. Figures for 1967 and total figures from Office of Development and Planning, Bureau for Africa, AID.

MILITARY GRANT AID PROGRAMS—CHARGEABLE TO APPROPRIATIONS DELIVERIES BY FISCAL YEARS

(millions of dollars)

Africa	1950–1955	1956	1957	1958	1959	1960	1961	1962	1963	1964	1965	1950–1965
Cameroon								.2				.2
Congo (Leo.)									.1	5.0	2.3	7.4
Dahomey							.1	*				.1
Ethiopia	4.8	4.0	4.7	8.8	5.2	7.0	6.0	10.9	10.9	10.3	8.3	80.9
Ghana								*	*	*		*
Guinea											*	*
Ivory Coast								.1	*			*
Liberia			.1		*		.3	.4	1.2	.7	.5	3.1
Libya			1.1	.3	.9		.3	1.3	.4	1.5	2.2	8.1
Mali							.1	.7	.1	.2	.5	1.6
Morocco						.3	2.1	1.5	6.1	6.0	2.3	18.4
Niger								.1	*			.1
Nigeria								*	*	.3	.2	.5
Senegal								.1	1.6	.5	.1	2.3
Sudan							*	*	*	*	*	.1
Tunisia								2.7	2.3	5.7	3.5	.9	15.1
Upper Volta								.1	*		*	1.
Total	4.8	4.0	4.8	9.9	5.5	8.2	11.5	17.8	26.1	28.0	17.4	138.0

* Less than 50,000.

Source: Department of Defense, *Military Assistance Facts* (Washington, D.C., May, 1966), 14. McArdle gives higher figures for U.S. military equipment and training assistance to African states, 1950–1964, putting Ethiopian assistance, for example, at $11.3 million for 1963 and Liberian at $2.0 for the same year. Her sources are cited as U.S. Department of State, *Report to the Congress on the Mutual Security Program for FY 1961*, p. 22, and International Development Agency, *Proposed Mutual Defense and Assistance Program for FY 1964*, p. 177. McArdle's figure may be higher because all training costs are included. See Catherine McArdle, *The Role of Military Assistance in the Problem of Arms Control* ("Center for International Studies," MIT, Aug. 1964), 69, Table a.

TABLE NINE

FISCAL YEAR 1967 PROPOSED MILITARY AID

	Amount	Percent
Europe	36,129	3.5
Near East and South Asia	240,125	23.4
Africa	31,816	3.1
Far East	387,340	37.7
Latin America	71,999	7.0
Regional costs	68,991	6.7
Worldwide costs	190,600	18.6
Total	1,027,000 *	100.0

* This is total obligational authority and includes both $917 million in new obligational authority requested for fiscal year 1967 and $110 million in estimated recoupments and reappropriations from prior year programs.

Source: Military Assistance Facts, 2.

TABLE TEN

FUNCTIONAL BREAKDOWN OF U.S. MILITARY ASSISTANCE TO AFRICA, FISCAL YEAR 1962

(in millions of dollars)

Supply operations and nutritional surveys	2.3
Training	2.8
Total fixed charges	5.1
Spare parts	2.4
Attrition	1.0
Other consumables	.4
Total force maintenance	3.8
Aircraft	.9
Ships	.6
Tanks, vehicles, and weapons	5.4
Missiles	
Electronic and communications equipment	1.3
Special programs	11.2
Other	2.0
Total force improvement	21.5
Total	30.4

Source: U.S. House of Representatives, Appropriations Committee, Subcommittee on Foreign Operations Appropriations, *Hearings for FY 1963*, p. 543, cited in McArdle, 68.

TABLE ELEVEN

NUMBER OF AFRICAN PARTICIPANTS IN PUBLIC SAFETY PROGRAMS IN THE U.S.A.

	1965	1966
Africa	79	101
Chad	2	
Congo (Kinshasa)		6
Ethiopia	29	25
Kenya		3
Liberia	10	5
Sierra Leone		1
Somalia	17	23
Tanzania	13	17
Tunisia	4	17
Uganda	4	
Upper Volta		2

Note: There were no Africans in public safety programs being trained by the U.S. in third countries.

Source: AID, *Operations Report, FY 1966,* p. 108.

TABLE TWELVE

THE NUMBER OF U.S. GOVERNMENT TECHNICIANS IN PUBLIC SAFETY PROGRAMS IN AFRICA AS OF JUNE 30, 1966

Central African Republic *	1
Chad	1
Congo	6
Ethiopia	7
Kenya	7
Morocco	1
Rwanda	2
Somalia	2

* (Listed as East African Republic in AID document.)

TABLE THIRTEEN

U.S. MILITARY ASSISTANCE FUNDS FOR CIVIC-ACTION PROGRAMS IN AFRICA—FISCAL YEARS 1962 THROUGH 1966 *

(in thousands of dollars)

	1962	1963	1964	1965	1966
Congo (Leo.)				**	
Ethiopia			167	6	5
Guinea				783	152
Liberia		463	66	88	9
Libya			6		
Mali			5	230	162
Senegal		183	66	276	306
Sudan			**		
Tunisia			2		
Upper Volta				8	8
Total		646	312	1,391	642

* Fiscal year 1962 was the first year that civic-action assistance was so identified in MAP.

** Less than $500.

Source: U.S. House of Representatives, Committee on Foreign Affairs, *Hearings, Foreign Asisstance Act of 1966*, 89th Cong., 2d Sess., 1966, p. 1040.

NOTES

[1] This present work grows directly out of a concern with American policy that was fore-shadowed in Henry Bienen, ed., *The Military Intervenes: Case Studies in Political Change* (New York, 1968). The Inter-University Seminar on Armed Forces and Society, under the chairmanship of Professor Morris Janowitz, has generously provided financial assistance for the continuous research. Furthermore, discussions with colleagues at formal and informal gatherings of the Inter-University Seminar have been invaluable. As a member of the seminar, I happily acknowledge the debt owed to the Russell Sage Foundation in support of our work. Equally valuable to me has been the support of the Center of International Studies at Princeton. This work could not have been possible without the help I received from many individuals in the Department of State, Agency for International Development, and Department of Defense, particularly in the Office of the Assistant Secretary of Defense for International Security Affairs, and the Office of the Special Assistant for Military Affairs in the Joint Chiefs of Staff. My acknowledgment of thanks to the various organizations and agencies cited in no way is meant to distribute the responsibility for the results here produced.

[2] For a review of some of these works, and a critical analysis of what he calls eurhythmic change (further change toward the characteristics of the society from which the original change derived), see C. S. Whitaker, Jr., "A Dysrhythmic Process of Political Change," *World Politics*, XIX (Jan. 1967), 190–217.

[3] See my "What Does Political Development Mean in Africa," *World Politics*, XIX (Oct. 1967), 128–41.

[4] Robert A. Packenham, "Political Development Doctrines in the American Foreign Aid Program," *World Politics*, XVIII (Jan. 1966), 230.

[5] Among the few studies that have tried to come to grips with the impact of foreign aid on development in recipient countries are Amos Jordan, *Foreign Aid and the Defense of Southeast Asia* (New York, 1962); Charles Wolf, *Foreign Aid: Theory and Practice in Southeast Asia* (Princeton, 1960). These are more cost-effectiveness studies of various combinations

of United States deployments than analyses of impacts. Wolf's *United States Policy and the Third World* (Boston, 1966) does the latter.

[6] Packenham's study of Agency for International Development middle-level personnel established that one important segment of the government at least views foreign economic aid as having marginal effects on internal development (*World Politics*, XVIII, 228).

[7] There have been studies of Africa as a subsystem in the international system, e.g., I. William Zartmann, "Africa as a Subordinate State System in International Relations," unpublished paper, and I. William Zartmann, *International Relations in the New Africa* (Englewood Cliffs, N.J., 1966).

[8] See Andrew M. Kamarck, *The Economics of African Development* (New York, 1967).

[9] Catherine McArdle, in *The Role of Military Assistance in the Problem of Arms Control* ("Center for International Studies," MIT, Aug. 1964), has addressed herself more to the consequences of military assistance for the balance of power between states because she believed the nature of the difficulties precluded the possibility of assessing impacts of military assistance programs (pp. 8–10). Another study with an arms control focus is Lincoln P. Bloomfield and Amelia C. Leiss, "Arms Control and the Developing Countries," *World Politics*, XVIII (Oct. 1965), 1–19.

[10] Charles Wolf, "The Political Effects of Military Programs: Some Indications From Latin America," *Orbis*, VIII (1965), 871–93; Charles Wheatley, "Some Inter-National Dimensions of the Role of National Military Forces in Internal Political Conflict," paper prepared for the 1965 meetings of the American Sociological Association, Session on the Sociology of War and Peace; Robert Putnam, "Toward Explaining Military Intervention in Latin American Politics," *World Politics*, XX (Oct. 1967), 83–110.

[11] We are only now getting studies of the genesis of particular coups in depth. See, for example, Bienen, ed., *The Military Intervenes.*

[12] Among those who argue that American military assistance does not create coups are Wolf in both of the studies alluded to and Captain David Zook, Jr., "United States Military Assistance to Latin America," *Air University Review*, XIV (Sept.–Oct. 1963), 82–85. Among those who argue that there are positive correlations between coups and American military aid are Herbert Mathews, "When Generals Take Over in Latin America," *New York Times Magazine*, Sept. 9, 1962, and many congressmen as well as academics. See, for example, U.S. Senate, Committee on Foreign Relations, *Hearings, International Development and Security*, 87th Cong., 1st sess., Pt. II, May 1961, pp. 610–12, 681, 669.

[13] On military intervention and political development, see Martin Needler, "Political Development and Military Intervention in Latin America," *American Political Science Review*, IX (Sept. 1966), 616–22; Edwin Lieuwen, *Arms and Politics in Latin America* (New York, 1965); Morris Janowitz, *The Military in the Political Development of New Nations* (Chicago, 1964); Henry Bienen, "Public Order and the Military in Africa; Mutinies in Kenya, Uganda, and Tanganyika," in *The Military Intervenes.* Many books have been concerned with the role of the military as modernizer, including those just cited. Also see the following bibliographies: Peter B. Riddleberger, "Military Roles in Developing Countries: An Inventory of Past Research and Analysis" (Special Operations Research Office, March 1965); and Moshe Lissak, "Selected Literature on Revolutions and Coups d'Etat in the Developing Nations," in *The New Military: Changing Patterns of Organization*, ed. Morris Janowitz (New York, 1965).

[14] To some extent Wolf has dealt with this subject and others have written of fundamental changes in the balance of power which military assistance brings about. There has been less analysis of the effect of military assistance on ruling elites. A recent study which takes this up is Willard F. Barber and C. Neale Ronning, *Internal Security and Military Power: Counterinsurgency and Civic Action in Latin America* (Columbus, 1966). Also see Annex D, *Report of the President's Committee to Study the United States Military Assistance Program* (the Draper Report), Washington, D.C., 1959, Vol. II, by the Foreign Policy Research Institute of the University of Pennsylvania. I have not seen a report by W. P. Davison, "Political Side Effects of Military Assistance Programs" (RAND Corporation, 1960).

[15] Aristide Zolberg, "The Structure of Political Conflict in the New States of Tropical Africa," paper prepared for delivery at the 1966 Annual Meeting of the American Political Science Association, New York, Sept. 6–10, 1966, p. 13.

[16] For material on African armies, the source I have found most useful is the publications of the Institute for Strategic Studies (ISS) in London, particularly, David Wood, *The Armed Forces of African States* ("Adelphi Paper," No. 27, April 1966); M. J. V. Bell, *Army and Nation in Sub-Saharan Africa* ("Adelphi Papers," No. 21, Aug. 1965); M. J. V. Bell, *Military*

Assistance to the African States ("Adelphi Papers," No. 15, Dec. 1964); also M. J. V. Bell, "The Military in the New States of Africa," paper given to the working session, "The Professional Military and Militarism," Sixth World Congress of Sociology, Sept. 1966; James S. Coleman and Belmont Bryce, Jr., "The Role of the Military in Sub-Saharan Africa," in *The Role of the Military in Underdeveloped Countries*, ed. John J. Johnson (Princeton, 1962), 359–405; William Foltz, "Military Influences," in *African Diplomacy*, ed. Vernon McKay (New York, 1966), 69–90; George Weeks, "The Armies of Africa" in *A Handbook of African Affairs*, ed. Helen Kitchen (New York, 1964), 188–236.

[17] For armies of other areas, see ISS, *The Military Balance, 1965–66* (Nov. 1965).

[18] Charles Stevenson, "African Armed Forces," *Military Review*, XLVII (March 1967), 18–24.

[19] For a good description of a police force in Africa see Foreign Areas Studies Division of the Special Operations Research Office, *United States Army Handbook for Senegal* (Washington, D.C.: American University, Aug. 1963), 443–54.

[20] Colin Leys has given us a most useful typology of violence in Africa in his "Violence in Africa," *Transition*, IV (1965), 17–20. War subsystems refer to the feuding of tribes and clans as a way of life.

[21] *Ibid.*, 19.

[22] Algeria, with an armed force of 48,000 men, was spending 3.2 percent of GNP in 1964. For the same year Morocco, with an army of close to 45,000, was spending 4.8 percent; Tunisia, with an army of 16,000, was spending 3.1 percent, and Libya, with an army of 6,000, was spending 3.6 percent. See United States Arms Control and Disarmament Agency, *World Wide Defense Expenditures and Selected Economic Data, Calendar Year 1964*, Research Report 66-1 (Washington, D.C., Jan. 1966), 11–12.

[23] Stevenson's figures for defense budget as a share of GNP were published in 1967. The Arms Control and Disarmament Agency's were published in 1966 using 1964 calendar year. There are many discrepancies between them which perhaps may be accounted for by rapid shifts in government spending. The governments' figures upon which they are based are variable also. For some countries the same data are used.

[24] AID, *Principles of Foreign Economic Assistance* (Washington, D.C., 1965), 20.

[25] These arguments are summarized, among other places in Harold Hovey, *United States Military Assistance* (New York, 1965), 219–24.

[26] See Janowitz, *The Military in Political Development*, for a comparative study on the military in new nations.

[27] Stevenson, "African Armed Forces," Stevenson, 22, notes that 23 nations give military assistance to African countries.

[28] For French defense agreements see *West Africa* (London) Aug. 24, 1963, reprinted in Kitchen, *Handbook of African Affairs*, 233–35. For the texts of certain published agreements see *Collective Defense Treaties* (Washington, D.C., 1967), 165–66. Also see Wood, *Armed Forces of African States*, for a brief résumé of aid for individual African states.

[29] See Philip B. Springer, "Disunity and Disorder, Factional Politics in the Argentine Military," in *The Military Intervenes*, 145–68.

[30] See Colonel A. A. Afrifa, *The Ghana Coup* (New York, 1966).

[31] This can be found in Bell, *Military Assistance to the African States*; Wood, *Armed Forces of African States*; McArdle, *Role of Military Assistance in Arms Control*; and in the ISS publication by John Sutton and Geoffrey Kemp, *Arms to Developing Countries* ("Adelphi Papers," No. 28, Oct. 1966).

[32] Marshal Schulman, *Soviet Foreign Aid* (New York, 1967), 180.

[33] McArdle, *Role of Military Assistance in Arms Control*, 78.

[34] For a discussion of Soviet military aid programs and their motives, see *The Soviet Military Aid Program as a Reflection of Soviet Objectives* ("Georgetown Research Project," Atlantic Research Corporation, June 1965).

[35] V. Sibirsky, "Washington's New Frontiers in Africa," *International Affairs* (Moscow), II (Feb. 1967), 73–77.

[36] A. Iskendrov, "The Army, Politics, and the People," *Izvestia*, Jan. 17, 1967, p. 2.

[37] *The Economist*, May 27, 1967, p. 900.

[38] See Bienen, "Public Order," in *The Military Intervenes*, 35–70.

[39] Lt. Col. Bernard L. Pujo, "South of the Sahara: Defense Problems in French Speaking Africa," *Military Review*, Feb. 1966, p. 33.

[40] *Ibid.*, 34.

[41] Press and periodical reports can be assembled. Sutton and Kemp have done this and they provide material on origin of aircraft, tanks, etc. House of Commons, Papers, *Civil Appropriations Accounts* and *Civil Estimates* reported military aid to Africa where there were small programs: Libya, Sudan, Somalia, Mali. Nigeria was not reported after 1960; Ghana and Kenya were not reported. Data on Tanganyika and Uganda were incomplete; Sierra Leone was not reported.

[42] John H. Ohly, "A Study of Certain Aspects of Foreign Aid," Annex G of the *Draper Report*, 282–83.

[43] Henry Kuss, Deputy Assistant Secretary of State for International Security Affairs and the man in charge of arms sales, has argued that from the military point of view we stand to lose all the major international relationships paid for with grant aid money unless we can establish professional military relationships through the sales media. U.S. Senate, Committee on Foreign Relations, Subcommittee on Disarmament, *Hearings, United States Armament and Disarmament Problems*, 90th Cong., 1st Sess., 197, p. 147.

[44] A staff study prepared for the use of the Committee on Foreign Relations, *Arms Sales and Foreign Policy* (Washington, D.C., 1967), argues that at a time of increasing congressional oversight of military grant assistance, emphasis has shifted from these programs to a concentration on military sales. In fiscal year 1961 sales were 43.4 percent of grant aid; in 1966 sales stood at 235.1 of aid (p. 2).

[45] Reported sales for Africa south of the Sahara were: $1.3 million for Liberia between 1956 and 1965 and $.3 million for Nigeria in 1965. Ethiopia acquired some naval vessels and some jets with interest-free loans. McArdle, *Role of Military Assistance in Arms Control*, 74. Total receipts from military sales for all Africa from 1961 to 1965 were $11.2 million. They were estimated at $1 million for 1966 and 1967. Total sales 1961–1965 were $4.6 billion. From Department of Defense, *Military Assistance Facts* (Washington, D.C., May 1966), 19.

[46] AID and Department of Defense, *Proposed Mutual Defense and Development Programs, FY 1965* (Washington, D.C., April 1964), 30.

[47] Detailed descriptions of the administration of military assistance can be found in Hovey, *U.S. Military Assistance*, 139–40, and *Information and Guidance on Military Assistance* prepared by the Evaluation Division of Military Assistance, Deputy Chief of Staff, S and L Headquarters, United States Air Force, 10th ed. (Washington, D.C., 1966), 15–22. A very valuable commentary on administration of MAP in Africa is provided by Colonel Quintus C. Atkinson, "Military Assistance in sub-Saharan Africa" (unpublished M.B.A. thesis, George Washington University, 1966). I am grateful for Colonel Atkinson's making this work available.

[48] Hovey, *U.S. Military Assistance*, 144. The unified command for the Pacific had 80 military personnel; for Europe it was 60 military and 29 civilians. For Latin America it was 24 military and 7 civilian personnel.

[49] Atkinson, "Military Assistance in sub-Saharan Africa," notes that AID is both a referee in economic and military assistance plans and competes with Department of Defense for funds, p. 23.

[50] AID can fund equipment which normally would be furnished under military aid. It can pay part of the costs of training military personnel. Economic funds can be used to build local production facilities for the military. On the other hand, military aid can pay for paramilitary unit buildup, and military aid can be used for provision of consumable items which are needed for strengthening the military.

[51] AID, *Information on the Office of Public Safety and the International Police Academy* (Washington, D.C., 1966).

[52] Janowitz, The Military in Political Development, 101.

[53] *Ibid.*

[54] Figures for 1966 are from the Statistics and Reports Division, Office of Program Coordinator, AID, as published in AID's *Report for July 1, 1965–June 20, 1966* (Washington, D.C., 1967), 31; 1967 figures are from AID's Office of Development Planning, Bureau for Africa.

[55] Statement of Secretary of Defense Robert McNamara, in U.S. House of Representatives, Subcommittee on Appropriations, *Hearings, Foreign Assistance and Related Agencies Appropriations for 1967*, 89th Cong., 2d Sess., 1967, Pt. I, p. 513.

[56] Hovey, *U.S. Military Assistance*, 107–108, citing General Adam's testimony before the House Foreign Affairs Committee in 1964.

[57] U.S. House of Representatives, Committee on Appropriations, *Hearings, Foreign Operations Appropriations, 1964*, 88th Cong., 1st Sess., 1963, p. 296, cited by Atkinson, 57.

[58] G. Mennen Williams, "U.S. Policy in Africa," *For Commanders*, V (July 1965), 1.

[59] McArdle claimed that the United States was the largest single donor of military assistance in Africa through 1964. McArdle, *Role of Military Assistance in Arms Control*, 67. This may not have been true for Africa south of the Sahara as compared to French assistance, although the Ethiopian program was undoubtedly the largest effort by far until the Soviet program in the Somali Republic. France gave $81 million worth of equipment to African countries as "independence gifts." Bell, *Military Assistance to Africa*.

[60] Department of State, *Report to the President from the Committee to Strengthen the Security of the Free World* (Clay Report) (Washington, D.C., 1963), 10.

[61] As ambassador to Ethiopia, E. Korry, in an unpublished report, argued that this should be done. Also see President Johnson's Special Message to Congress on Aid to Foreign Lands, in New York *Times*, Feb. 10, 1967, p. 16. And Anthony Astrachan, "AID Reslices the Pie," *Africa Report*, XII (June 1967), 8–15.

[62] There actually was a time lag between the Clay Committee's recommendations and the weeding out of countries in MAP because programs negotiated in 1963 had to be completed and because the idea of civic action and counterinsurgency took hold in Africa.

[63] Vernon McKay, ed., *Africa In World Politics* (Chicago, 1963), 40, cited in McArdle, *Role of Military Assistance in Arms Control*, 77.

[64] *Military Assistance Facts*, 31.

[65] *Foreign Assistance and Related Agencies*, 1967, p. 731.

[66] *Military Assistance Facts*, 24. In the small programs with two or four MAP people, individuals will plan programs, be involved in selection of indigenous personnel for training, and be watchdogs in program implementation.

[67] Atkinson, "Military Assistance in sub-Saharan Africa," 72, citing United States Department of Air Force, *Information and Guidance on Military Assistance*, 9th ed. (Washington, D.C., 1965), 15.

[68] One interesting example is the selection of African students to attend college in the U.S. and then go on to military training here. Socialization and training theoretically are combined. What this will mean for the careers of those who do it remains to be seen, both with respect to their values and the vulnerability of their political position.

[69] Annex E of *Draper Report*, "Training and Education Under the Assistance Programs," by the staff of the committee, 137–60.

[70] See also C. Windle and T. Vallance, "Optimizing Military Assistance Training," *World Politics*, XV (Oct. 1962), 91–107.

[71] See Henry Bienen, "What Does Political Development Mean in Africa?"

[72] Hovey, *U.S. Military Assistance*, 146, gives some material on Military Assistance Institute (MAI) courses. American military assistance personnel are now passing through MAI, which has its own staff and also has guests from agencies of the government and the academic community for lectures. Military attachés do not pass through MAI but go to other institutes for training. There is great sensitivity within both AID and the Defense Department to the need for getting military and police assistance personnel who can train men in the intricacies of modern weapons or criminalistics, police or military administration, and the development tasks. As Byron Engle, the director of the Office of Public Safety, has said, "The man we are looking for doesn't really exist. He must have executive police experience or he won't go very far as an advisor. He must also know something of military affairs, intelligence, language, and international politics." *Information on the Office of Public Safety and the International Police Academy*.

[73] For a brief sketch of curriculum at training centers, see Barber and Ronning, *Internal Security and Military Power*, 148–56, and Lt. Doyle C. Ruff, "Win Friends . . . Defeat Communism," *Instructors Journal*, II (July 1964), 25–34. Also see *Military Assistance and Training Programs of the U.S. Government* (New York, 1964).

[74] *Draper Report*, Annex E, p. 154.

[75] Windle and Vallance, "Optimizing Military Assistance Training," 91–107.

[76] *Draper Report*, Annex E, p. 151.

[77] See Lucien Pye, "Armies in the Process of Political Modernization," in *The Role of the Military in Underdeveloped Countries*, ed. John J. Johnson (Princeton, 1962), 69–90, and Guy Pauker, "Southeast Asia as a Problem Area in the Next Decade," *World Politics*, XI (April 1959), esp. 339–44.

[78] Morris Janowitz, "Organizing Multiple Goals: War Making and Arms Control," in *The New Military: Changing Patterns of Organization*, ed. Morris Janowitz (New York, 1965), 29.

[79] Bienen, *The Military Intervenes*.

[80] The Ivory Coast Army's insignia is a badge and a hoe.

[81] Quoted by Walter A. E. Skurnik, "Political Instability and Military Intervention in Dahomey and Upper Volta," paper presented at the annual meeting of the African Studies Association, Bloomington, Ind., Oct. 1966, p. 15.

[82] See Bienen, "What Does Political Development Mean in Africa?" and Aristide Zolberg, *Creating Political Order: The Party States of West Africa* (Chicago, 1966), 93.

[83] Samuel Huntington, "Political Development and Political Decay," *World Politics*, XVII (April 1965), 429. Huntington argues that military juntas may spur modernization, that is, industrialization, urbanization, increased literacy, rise in income, but that they cannot bring about political development, which he defines as the institutionalization of political organizations and procedures (p. 393). African militaries are not likely to bring modernization, in Huntington's terms, either. And in certain cases, rather than bringing about public order, they accentuate tendencies toward chaos (Nigeria) or create disorder (East Africa in 1964).

[84] U.S. Senate, Committee on Foreign Relations, *Hearings, Foreign Assistance Act of 1962*, 87th Cong., 2d Sess., 1962, 76, cited in Barber and Ronning, *Internal Security and Military Power*, 218.

[85] There is the aphorism attributed to F. Houphouet-Boigny: if you want a man to be a good bourgeois, send him to Lumumba university in Moscow, but if you want to radicalize him, send him to the Sorbonne.

[86] U.S. Senate, Committee on Appropriations, *Hearings, Mutual Security Appropriations Act for 1954*, 83rd Cong., 2d Sess., 1954, 921–22, cited by Edgar Furniss, *Some Perspectives on American Military Assistance* (Center of International Studies, Princeton University, June 1957), 17.

[87] *Information and Guidance on Military Assistance*, 10th ed., 12.

[88] Gen. Curtis Lemay, "Strategic Advantage is Key to All Tasks" (Air Force Information Policy Letter: Supplement for Commanders, No. 125, Internal Information Division, SAF) 11, Pentagon, cited by Barber and Ronning, *Internal Security and Military Power*, 162. Barber and Ronning noted that economic aspects of development were stressed by military officers in personal conversations. Packenham concluded the same thing for AID officials. Some officials that I met in the Office of Public Safety and the International Police Academy were very sensitive to what an AID pamphlet calls "the social climate of stability and security." (See AID, *Information on the Office of Public Safety and the International Police Academy*, 2.)

[89] Barber and Ronning, *Internal Security and Military Power*, 240.

[90] U.S. House of Representatives, Committee on Foreign Affairs, *Hearings, Foreign Assistance Act of 1966*, 89th Cong., 2d Sess., 1966, p. 1045.

[91] See Davis B. Bobrow, "Limitations on Civic Action," in *Arms Controls in the Developing Areas*, ed. Edward W. Gude, Davis B. Bobrow, Clark A. Abt ("A Unicorn Study," Phase II Report, for the Directorate for Arms Control, Office of the Assistant Secretary of Defense for International Security Affairs, Contract Number SD-125, prepared by the Strategic Studies Department, Missile and Space Division, Raytheon Company, Bedford, Mass.), 131–41.

[92] William Foltz, "Military Influences," 88.

[93] Fred Greene, "Toward Understanding Military Coups," *Africa Report*, Feb. 1966, p. 11.

[94] Packenham, "Political Development Doctrines in American Foreign Aid," 232–33. Aid administrators now feel that they are beginning systematically to look at the impact of U.S. AID programs. Indeed, recent meetings with AID personnel indicated pronounced concern for the impact of programs. It may well have been the instructions of Congress, more than the urgings of academics or individuals within AID, that has led to this concern. For Title IX of the Foreign Assistance Act of 1961, as amended, now states (from 1966): "In carrying out programs authorized in this chapter, emphasis shall be placed on assuring maximum participation in the task of economic development on the part of the people of the developing countries, through encouragement of democratic private and local government institutions." The House Committee on Foreign Affairs asked AID to develop new criteria by which the agency could evaluate its success in implementing Title IX. AID's *Report to the Congress on the Implementation of Title IX* (Washington, D.C., May 10, 1967) shows a broader approach to the development process than heretofore.

[95] The new policy of concentrating aid in target countries in Africa will lead to an erosion of the "marginality of impact" view.

[96] We must distinguish between token programs—for example, sending eight jeeps and eight trucks to Dahomey in 1962 and 1963—and those like the assistance program to Liberia which, though small by American standards, would have impact on internal developments.

[97] Whatever the legitimacy of intervention in the eyes of British, French, and American

trainers, it is probable that barracks talk about politicians is not too respectful, although Peter Calvocoressi assures us that in Britain "it would be repugnant to the military mind to become involved in the dissemination of political ideas." *World Order and the New States* (London, 1962), 55.

[98] Wheatley, "Role of National Military Forces in Internal Political Conflict," 1–2. The exchange of services schema has been put forward by Moshe Lissak, "Social Change, Mobilization, and Exchange of Services Between the Military Establishment and the Civil Society: The Burmese Case," *Economic Development and Cultural Change*, XIII (Oct. 1964), 1–19.

[99] Wheatley, "Role of National Military Forces in Internal Political Conflict," 3–6.

[100] Wolf had a similar concern in "Political Effects of Military Programs." He concluded that large military aid programs do not seem to be associated with more restrictive and authoritarian institutions. Aside from problems of talking about political development in these terms (derived from Russell H. Fitzgibbon and Kenneth F. Johnson's "Measurement of Latin American Political Change," *American Political Science Review*, LV [Sept. 1961], 515–26), coups are not dealt with *per se*. Needler has related military overthrows of governments to deteriorating economic conditions but not at all to military assistance. He concludes that because of internal military factionalism, U.S. positions can influence "swing men" among the Latin American militaries. But his discussion here is of recognition and nonrecognition, not of assistance policies. Needler, "Political Development and Military Intervention in Latin America," 624–25. Wheatley found that Latin American states diverged from the correlations he found elsewhere with regard to the connection between military responsiveness and indicators of the salience and effectiveness of government mediation of resource flow. Janowitz in *The Military in Political Development* has suggested that fundamental differences in the history of militarism in South America make that area atypical of developing areas. It may be that when American spokesmen have denied the connection between military assistance and military takeovers, the Latin American experience has been uppermost in their minds.

[101] To my knowledge, none of those who have dealt with coups in Africa have even attempted to relate assistance to their onset.

[102] New York *Times*, May 16, 1967.

[103] As Wheatley himself notes, "Role of National Military Forces in Internal Political Conflict," 27.

[104] David Apter has posited a situation where there is an inverse relationship between information and coercion in a system. *The Politics of Modernization* (Chicago, 1966), 40.

[105] Aristide Zolberg, "Military Intervention in the New States of Tropical Africa," in *The Military Intervenes*, 71–102.

[106] The distinction between power and force is made by Zolberg, who utilizes Talcott Parson's analysis, "Some Reflections on the Place of Force in Social Process," in *Internal War*, ed. Harry Eckstein (New York, 1964), 59.

[107] *Draper Report*, Annex C, "A Study of United States Military Assistance Programs in Underdeveloped Areas," 51.

[108] As the *Draper Report* suggested should be done; *ibid.*

[109] Edward C. Banfield, *American Foreign Aid Doctrine* (Washington, D.C., 1964) has noted that aid can bring some desired condition through a transformation of society. That is, via indirect means a political culture might be altered; in direct influence, culture is taken as a given and direct political results are the goal.

CHAPTER FOUR

FOREIGN ECONOMIC POLICY & ECONOMIC DEVELOPMENT

———

BENJAMIN HIGGINS

FOUR ASPECTS of foreign economic policy are of importance for the development of underdeveloped countries: foreign aid, foreign trade, stabilization, and encouragement (or discouragement) of private investment.

Foreign aid has been much more in the public eye in recent years than any of the other three types of policy, and controversy concerning it has been much keener. It might also be said that thinking about it has been much more confused. For this state of affairs social scientists are partly to blame. There is little truly sophisticated literature on the theory of foreign aid, and it could hardly be claimed that in practice foreign aid programs have been shaped by such theories as there are. Foreign aid policy developed first on an *ad hoc* basis, and social scientists have tried to provide a logically consistent rationale afterward.

It is not even clear as to why the donor countries believe foreign aid should be provided. Moral obligation to help the poor, the threat to national security entailed in the widening gap between rich and poor nations, the desire to win allies, and the possibilities of expanding world trade have all been cited as reasons for helping the underdeveloped countries with their development programs.

In his inaugural address, President Kennedy stressed the moral obligation to help less prosperous peoples: "To those peoples in the huts and villages of half the globe struggling to break the bonds of mass misery, we pledge our best efforts to help them to help themselves, for whatever period is required—not because the Communists may be doing it, not because we seek their votes, but because it is right. If a free society cannot help the many who are poor, it cannot save the few who are rich."

Most statements of the objectives of foreign economic policy are general and vague. There is no lack of such statements: speeches by Presidents, secretaries of state, and foreign policy administrators; the documents arising out of work of the Draper Committee;[1] the various submissions to the Special Committee of the United States Senate to Study the Foreign Aid Program;[2] the later submissions to the Senate Foreign Relations Committee;[3] and statements by independent research organizations and scholars.[4] Nearly all these statements have a common stamp. For the purposes of an earlier study,[5] I summarized the essence of these statements as follows:

1. The major aim of American foreign economic policy is to accelerate economic growth in underdeveloped countries, on the grounds that poverty-stricken nations are a threat to the security, peace, and freedom of the American

people. In addition, however, it is desired to demonstrate to the underdeveloped countries and to the world that high rates of growth can be achieved within a noncommunist economic framework and with a democratic political system. The political objective, in other words, is to achieve the economic goals in a fashion that will contribute to the growth of representative, responsible, and independent governments, which are not hostile to the West, and which can be expected either to remain neutral or to support the United States in a major war. It may also be—although this is a question for analysis—that stagnation elsewhere in the world may become a drag on the economic development of the United States itself.

2. A secondary objective is to assist in the economic stabilization of other countries on the grounds that economic instability hampers development and is also a threat to security, peace, and freedom. Instability elsewhere may also aggravate the problem of maintaining steady growth in the American economy, although this too is a question for analysis.

In stating the political objective of U.S. aid, I have avoided any blunt statement that United States foreign economic policy is designed to combat communism. The United States has given aid to both Yugoslavia and Poland. It would presumably be contrary to American principles to combat communism in countries where it is clear that the majority of the people support a communist government and where the government is representative of the people, responsible to its wishes, and independent of foreign domination. It may be questioned whether such a nation is conceivable, but that is another matter.

I have also avoided stating the U.S. economic objective to be one of "closing the gap between the levels of per capita incomes in the United States and other countries." It is extremely unlikely that this aim could be accomplished in less than a century, if ever. Since the United States starts from a level of per capita income so much higher than that of underdeveloped countries, growth rates would have to be several times as high in underdeveloped countries as in the United States, if the absolute difference between American incomes and their incomes were to be reduced. The technical difficulties involved in generating such a process are enormous, and for the advanced countries to promise the impossible would in the end prove contrary to the interests of the advanced countries. Moreover, just as in any one country the presence of a few rich people would not be a very serious matter if no one were poor, the fact that some nations are richer than others would not be very serious if there were no poor nations. The economic goal is to eliminate poverty everywhere rather than to close the gap between American and foreign incomes.

I have also rejected the idea that the aim of foreign economic policy is to buy friends. Friendship cannot be bought; the motto most clearly established by foreign aid experience would seem to be "the feeding hand shall be bitten."

France continues to provide more bilateral assistance, relative to gross national product, than any other country. The bulk of French aid goes to French colonies and territories, the rest goes almost entirely to ex-colonies. In France, therefore, the question is not only "Why aid?" but also "Why aid concentrated in these few countries?" The most thorough review of French foreign aid policy to date is the Jeanneney Report.[6] The report attaches little importance to any economic gains from aid. The basis for the relatively generous French aid program is simply the necessity of cooperation with underdeveloped countries for the purpose of "human solidarity." There is also a responsibility for the spreading of French civilization and keeping alive the French tongue as an international language. Finally, France must join other Western powers in preventing the emergence of a bloc of developing countries hostile to the West. The report recommended broadening the geographic scope of French aid but felt that French-speaking Africa should continue to enjoy priority. France's revolutionary tradition gives her special advantages in dealing with developing countries, the report argues.

The United Kingdom also provides most of its assistance to colonies or ex-colonies. A White Paper of September 1963 pointed out that half the increase in British aid between 1957–1958 and 1961–1962 went to colonial territories. Most of the rest of the increase went to independent Commonwealth countries; both aid to other countries and contributions to multilateral programs remained small. The White Paper had little to say about why aid is given; the British people feel a responsibility for development of the remaining colonies and a continuing responsibility toward independent Commonwealth countries. Having helped these countries to political independence, "it is a natural and fitting continuation of the earlier relationship that we should now assist them in their efforts to achieve balanced and self-sustaining economies" (p. 16).

The German approach to foreign aid policy seems even more simple. As Goran Ohlin puts it, "No strategic or security considerations are given much weight, and no historic ties of any importance have guided the direction of aid. . . . Repeatedly, the present Minister for Economic Co-operation, Herr Scheel, has described it as 'welfare policy on an international scale.' "[7] Japan stresses the diplomatic aspects of aid. The prime minister stated to the Diet in October 1963, "It is quite natural that Japan should extend assistance to other countries as she herself has attained such remarkable economic growth, and Japan must also make a greater effort to establish friendly relations of solidarity with Asian countries, bearing in mind the necessity for stability and peace in all of Asia."[8]

In the smaller countries, like Norway, Sweden, Belgium, Italy, and Canada, the expectations of diplomatic gains from aid are somewhat diluted; the major motives seem to be a feeling that all advanced countries share the responsibility of helping the poor ones and a general desire to be in on the act.

In the complex process of interacting economic, social, and political forces which brings economic development, what contribution can capital assistance make? It is quite clear that capital assistance cannot begin to do the job alone. At the same time, the availability or absence of foreign aid of the right kinds and in the right amounts might make the difference between success or failure of a country's own efforts to launch a process of sustained economic growth.

The most obvious thing that foreign aid can do is to fill the gap between capital requirements for a "take-off" into sustained growth and domestic capacity for savings and investment.[9] There is no use in providing a country with more capital than it can effectively use. On the other hand, an ideal international economic policy would see to it that all countries were able to invest annually an amount equal to their absorptive capacities. They would then be able to maximize income over a long-run planning period, given the supplies of factors of production other than capital, and the institutional, political, and economic framework. Capital assistance would be "on tap" in such quantities that lack of capital would never cause a bottleneck in the economic development of any country.

We can imagine that the planning authorities estimate the net contribution to national income, direct and indirect, from now to infinity, resulting from the addition of successive blocks of investment to the total investment program planned for the next five years.[10] The additional blocks of investment for which estimates of contribution to income are made should be big enough to take care of the relevant economic, political, and social discontinuities in the development process of the country concerned. In calculating the contribution to the national income of a particular extra block of investment, allowance must be made, of course, for maintaining the capital stock at its new, higher level thereafter. We shall call the addition to income of each successive block of investment the "marginal contribution" of investment to distinguish it from the "marginal productivity" of capital in its ordinary meaning and also from "marginal efficiency." The marginal contribution includes all the changes that would accompany a substantial addition to the developmental investment program.

We can then define "absorptive capacity" as the amount of investment that can be undertaken, within a five-year program, without reducing the marginal contribution of the last block of capital below x. In other words, it is the amount that can be undertaken without raising the incremental capital-output ratio (ICOR) of the last block of investment, or marginal ICOR, above $\frac{1}{x}$. In this context we are concerned with investment over a five-to-ten-year planning period and the resulting increase in income over a very long period—twenty years or more.

The question, then, is how high do we put x? One could make a strong case for making x equal to zero. Absorptive capacity would then be the total amount of capital that could be invested during the planning period and still add something to future income. Putting it the other way round, it is the amount that can be invested without raising the marginal ICOR to infinity. In most countries, the real obstacles to acceleration of growth are lack of entrepreneurship, inefficiency of public and private administration, shortage of technicians and skilled workers, lack of commitment of government and people to economic development, resistance to social change, and the like. As the investment budget is increased, a point is reached where the inadequate supplies of these other factors of production will reduce the marginal contribution of additional investment sharply to zero. Given the discontinuities in the supply of new capital (one cannot build half a railroad or half a power plant), it is doubtful whether the amount of investment that would raise the marginal ICOR to infinity would be very different from the amount that would raise it to, say, 30:1.

If foreign capital assistance is provided in the form of hard loans carrying a rate of interest of y percent, it seems clear that x should not be set lower than y. That is, investment financed by foreign aid should not be carried beyond the point where the addition to national income offsets the increase in cost of servicing the debt.

An operational manual of the U.S. Agency for International Development suggests that in determining the cost-benefit ratio of projects proposed for AID support, an interest rate of 3.5 percent should be applied to the foreign component of the cost; for the domestic component local interest rates should be used, or, if no accurate local rate can be isolated, a "shadow price" of 6 percent should be applied.[11] John H. Adler, commenting on this suggestion, maintains that its economic rationale is doubtful. The use of a different rate of return on foreign and on domestic capital, he argues, presupposes that: "(a) a project suitable for partial financing by foreign aid with a rate of return at or above the cut-off rate cannot be developed because (b) the supply of co-operant factors cannot be increased in the short run, but (c) the undertaking of the project itself will somehow stimulate the supply of deficient co-operant factors, and (d) that this cannot be brought forth by any other method, such as import or technical assistance." [12] Dr. Adler agrees, of course, that certain projects can increase the flow of domestic resources and thus raise rates of return above initial levels. In such cases it may be justified to accept the lower rate of return in the first place. But it is justified only if the internal rate of return over the entire life of the project is above the "cut-off rate." "In that event," he insists, "the project itself is 'good' and what is bad, or inadequate, is the cost-benefit analysis which does not permit systematic and rational determination of the rate of return allowing for the lapse of time." [13] Adler accordingly favors a single "acceptable rate of return applied to total capital," but he does not tell us precisely how the "acceptable rate of return" is to be established.

What about the gestation period? Is it a matter of indifference how long it takes before increases in income start to accrue? If the capital is costless to the receiving country, it is a matter of indifference—not in assigning priorities to projects, when a discount factor should be applied to future income, but in deciding on the total amount of investment to be undertaken. If the capital involves a future debt service, of course, the addition to income must be compared with this debt service. The rate of capital accumulation should be pushed to the point where the increase in income *net* of debt service is zero. But no interest rate prevailing within the underdeveloped countries themselves seems pertinent so long as the capital comes from abroad and represents savings performed outside the economy. The marginal contribution of additional investment within the economy is certainly relevant, but there is no internal "cost of capital" with which this rate might be meaningfully compared.

It may be, of course, that different time-paths of income yield different total income, from now to infinity, with the same total investment over the next five years but differing allocations between saving and consumption in subsequent five-year plans. This fact raises the problem of the country's "welfare function" regarding income now and income later. Ultimately, such decisions must be made by the government; no purely economic analysis can provide an answer as to what time-path is optimal. [14] The selection of a discount factor, of course, is essentially a determination of the optimal time-path of income.

If a substantial proportion of capital assistance is to take the form of loans, perhaps the best definition of x would be the rate of interest at which the aid-giving government can borrow. This interest rate provides a rough measure of the value to the people in donor countries of this marginal use of savings. Clearly, this interest rate is a highly institutionalized phenomenon and depends a good deal on the monetary and fiscal policies currently pursued by the governments of donor countries. Nevertheless, this measure is probably as good as any available. Let us therefore define absorptive capacity as the amount of investment that can be undertaken, over a five-year planning period beginning from the present, without reducing the addition to perpetual national income below 3 percent. Or, putting it once more the other way round, absorptive capacity is the amount of investment that can be undertaken in five years without the marginal ICOR rising above 30:1.

It has been suggested to me that the concept of absorptive capacity involves a time limit on the period during which aid must be continued. This idea has some validity but must be applied with care. When should a country stop borrowing? Canada was a net borrowing nation for nearly a century after confederation. It became a net lending nation during World War II and is now expanding rapidly as a net borrowing country once more. Could it possibly be argued that Canada's recourse to international capital markets to finance recurrent phases of development indicates that the capital inflow between 1880 and 1910 was too high?

It could perhaps be said that, if the amount of foreign aid is so great that at the end of a twenty-year planning period further capial inflows are necessary merely to maintain per capita income, absorptive capacity has been exceeded in the interim. It is easy enough to spot countries where this situation has prevailed: Korea, Vietnam, Laos, Libya. Foreign aid is itself part of per capita income, and, if it can be counted upon to increase steadily, there may be no limit to absorptive capacity in this distorted sense.

However, our definition really takes care of this problem. It involves a comparison of the addition to the stock of capital with the addition to national income in perpetuity which it produces. Military aid with no offsetting increase in domestic savings, or support to current consumption, involves no addition to the stock of capital and no permanent addition to national income. The ICOR involved is infinite, and it cannot be justified at all on economic policy grounds. In short, such assistance falls outside the scope of foreign economic policy.

There is some level of domestic investment which represents a "maximum effort." "Effort" is partly a matter of saving and investing more and partly a matter of working harder or better, but both can be expressed in terms of investment inputs.

It is possible for the level of investment to be too low in the important sense that it requires no fundamental policy decisions, no changes in attitudes or behavior patterns, no acquisitions of skills or improvements in technique, and no improvement in business or public administration. All these things, once in motion, tend to have a cumulative effect on future growth. On the other hand, it is possible for a country to try to invest too much. Some degree of austerity may so destroy incentives that growth is retarded rather than accelerated. Obviously, no country should try to invest more from its own resources than it can absorb.

As a rule, the maximum domestic effort will be below absorptive capacity for several reasons:

1. It is usually necessary to feed and clothe a growing population either through production of consumers' goods at home or production of exports to finance imports of food and textiles.

2. The sacrifice entailed may go beyond what is indicated by the domestic welfare function, destroying incentives and reducing output, capital accumulation, and welfare below potential levels.

3. The structure of inherited capital (and future comparative advantage) may be such that certain increases in production of consumers' goods are necessary in the near future, if excess capacity is to be avoided. In other words, some existing capital, of a kind that should be reproduced, or some types of new capital recommended by future comparative advantage may be specific to the production of exports or consumers' goods.

An ideal international policy, then, would be one which guaranteed that foreign capital would always fill any gap between absorptive capacity and the maximum domestic effort, provided domestic investment is actually equal to the latter. Subtracting the amount of foreign private investment that is acceptable and forthcoming from the gap, we obtain the amount of foreign capital assistance to be provided to each country.

The increase in total aid involved in applying this criterion would probably not be very great. It would, however, mean considerable geographic redistribution of foreign aid. As things are now, some countries are clearly getting more than enough to fill the gap between absorptive capacity and maximum domestic effort. If this criterion were universally understood and recognized as being wholly without political strings, its application could greatly improve the atmosphere in which foreign aid programs are administered.

It is unlikely that absorptive capacity will exceed maximum domestic effort by very much in most countries. A big gap will occur only where the supply of skills of all sorts is unusually high relative to the current level of income, as in India.

If a country needs capital assistance, by definition its maximum domestic effort is below the minimum effort required for a take-off into sustained growth. If the country is worthy of capital assistance, on the other hand, it must have an absorptive capacity that is at least equal to this minimum effort. The really difficult cases are those in which both absorptive capacity and the maximum domestic effort are below the minimum effort required. In these cases, foreign economic assistance must be concentrated on technical assistance, designed to raise both the maximum domestic effort and absorptive capacity by training workers, managers, public administrators, and technicians, and providing expertise directly in the short run.

W. Arthur Lewis suggests in effect providing foreign aid as a reward for increasing the domestic effort. He would make aid equal to the growth in the ratio of savings (S) to gross domestic product (GDP) over three years: Aid $= S_1/GDP_1 - S_4/GDP_4$. If total public and private capital formation from domestic sources is 24 percent of GDP last year whereas three years earlier it was 22 percent, aid for next year would be 2 percent of GDP. The necessary computations would be made annually on agreed definitions by an international team of national income statisticians. Lewis regards his proposal as "just about the simplest self-policing aid formula that one could devise." [15]

Simple it may be, but it is hard to fathom the rationale except in terms of the Protestant ethic—to him who hath shall be given, virtue is its own reward, waste not want not, make what you can and save what you can. Rigorous application of the formula would mean that a country that has just struck oil, like Libya, with more capital than can be effectively used already, would stand high on the list for aid in per capita terms because she could hardly help but have a rapid increase in the ratio of developmental investment to GDP. But a country in trouble, like India during the second plan, finding itself unable to sustain its rate of domestic investment because of bad harvests, collapse of world markets, or other disaster, would suffer a cut in its foreign aid as well. A more flexible method of deciding whether, under existing conditions, a country is making a maximum domestic effort or not, with aid provided in amounts equal to the difference between that maximum and absorptive capacity, seems better designed to achieve the objectives of international economic policy.

John Fei and Douglas Paauw raise a somewhat different question: [16] assuming that the objective of international economic policy is to bring all countries to a situation of self-sustained growth, where the per capita marginal savings ratio (PMSR) is high enough in itself to permit target growth rates to be achieved indefinitely, how many years of gap-filling aid will be needed before this type of "bliss" is achieved? The question was answered for thirty-one countries for which data were available for the key variables: initial savings ratio, PMSR, capital-output ratio, rate of population growth, and target rates of growth. The results were rather startling. Among the thirty-one countries, Yugoslavia alone had already reached "bliss." In seven other countries, a policy such as recommended above of filling the gap between domestic effort and requirements for reaching targets (assuming the targets accurately reflect absorptive capacity) would produce self-sustained growth, where no further aid would be needed, in due course. Mexico, for example, is only four years away from "bliss" and the Philippines only six; but with the present parameters Colombia will need sixteen years to achieve self-sustained growth, Greece will need seventeen years, and Taiwan thirty-two years. The other twenty-three countries, with the values ascribed to the key variables, will never reach "bliss" at all; aid requirements will continue to increase forever. This group of countries includes Argentina, Brazil, Chile, India, Indonesia, and Burma, among others. No African country in the sample can attain "bliss."

The eight "successful" countries divide again into two subgroups. Some are already on a "glide path"; foreign aid can fall monotonically to the termination date. Others belong to the "hump scale" group, where aid must increase for some time before starting its slide down the "glide path."

In the "successful" cases, aid should be provided to fill the gap. In the others, international economic policy must be directed toward reducing the gap —in our terms, toward raising both the maximum domestic effort and absorptive capacity. Here technical assistance can play an important role.

The United States and other donor countries, the World Bank, and the International Development Association are all providing small amounts of capital assistance for education projects. It is clear, however, that the role of foreign capital in the field of education is limited, for the simple reason that the scarce resources needed to expand education programs are normally supplied through domestic rather than foreign channels. Ultimately, the question is the same: to what extent can the supply of trained teachers, classroom space, textbooks, and laboratory equipment be built up through the expenditure of foreign exchange provided by external assistance?

First, it is apparent that schoolteachers cannot be provided from abroad to any significant extent. Certainly, technical assistance programs can provide limited numbers of foreign teachers in special fields where the need is particularly pressing, and where the supply in other countries is relatively abundant. It must be recognized, however, that all countries face a shortage of teaching personnel over the next ten years. The relative cost of providing large numbers of teachers from abroad makes such an approach impossible. Similarly, the extent to which teachers can be provided to students from underdeveloped countries by sending students abroad is severely limited. Schools in many advanced countries are crowded to capacity, and the number of foreign students that can be accepted, even at the university level, is severely restricted. The limitations on provisions of textbooks and laboratory equipment from countries with a different language, culture, and technology are obvious. As for the classroom space, most countries have adequate supplies of building materials appropriate for construction of schools, and it is doubtful that it would be appropriate overall development policy to allocate any significant proportion of foreign aid budgets to the purchase abroad of building materials or equipment for the construction of schools.

It is clear enough from some of the statements regarding external financing of education that those interested in expanding educational programs, and particularly ministers of education, really have in mind increased allocations in domestic currency to acquire human and physical resources domestically available, while the foreign exchange is utilized for other projects within the overall economic and social development program. Certainly, insofar as expansion of the education program requires the attraction of human and physical resources from other fields of activity, thus reducing the output of other goods and services and adding to inflationary pressure, increased foreign exchange may be used to import raw materials and equipment for other projects, or even to import final consumers goods, thus offsetting inflationary pressure. In this way any harmful effects of expanding the educational program may be offset. However, it should be noted that in this event there is absolutely no significance in first attaching the foreign assistance to educational programs. The ultimate result is exactly the same if the external assistance is provided against the economic and social development program as a whole, and in that event there is less likelihood of misallocation of the actual foreign exchange provided. Ministries of education seldom have particular expertise in overall economic and social development programming, and accordingly it is preferable that foreign exchange which will not in fact be utilized for educational purposes should not be allocated to Ministries of Education.

In the short space of fifteen years, attitudes toward the contribution of technical cooperation to economic development have gone full circle.[17] When President Truman announced his Point Four program in 1949, much was expected from simple transfer of know-how from technologically advanced to technologically retarded countries. The attitude was well expressed at the time by an American undersecretary of state: "It is important to us and to the rest of the world that people in these areas realize that, through perseverance, hard work, and a little assistance, they can develop the means of taking care of their material needs and at the same time can preserve and strengthen their individual freedoms."[18] Technical assistance in agriculture was expected to be particularly productive, bringing back "one hundred fold" the modest outlays required.[19]

As time went by and the bilateral and multilateral technical assistance programs failed to produce spectacular results in developing countries, while understanding of the development process accumulated and the large-scale capital assistance under the Marshall Plan brought impressive increases in productivity in Europe, emphasis shifted for a while to industrialization and to massive transfers of capital. But with new disappointments and still deeper understanding of the complexities of economic development, it was recognized that the capacity of developing countries to absorb capital effectively was sharply limited by shortages of skills both in technical and scientific activities, and in everyday application of manpower in the productive process. Thus, although the importance of capital assistance—as a supplement to domestic investment, a source of foreign exchange, and a vehicle for transfer of technology—is not being overlooked, emphasis is once again shifting to technical assistance. One symptom of this new interest in technical assistance is the series of evaluation missions carried out under the auspices of the United Nations and the Organization for Economic Cooperation and Development.

Absorptive capacity is limited by the supply of technical, managerial, scientific, entrepreneurial, and labor skills; by the willingness to accept the risks of investment in durable productive capacity; by the supply of natural resources; by the stability of the government, its commitment to development goals, the honesty and efficiency of the civil service, the quality and scope of the educational system, the appropriateness of development plans and stabilization policies, and the like. The maximum domestic effort is affected by these factors and also by the commitment of the population to the goals of development, their savings and consumption habits, attitudes toward work and leisure, and confidence in their government. It is clear, therefore, that well-conceived technical assistance programs can raise both absorptive capacity and maximum domestic effort. Indeed, within the context of an ideal international foreign aid program, it could be said that the function of technical assistance is to do just that.

More effective programming and evaluation of technical assistance can be obtained by concentrating on the quantitative rather than on the qualitative aspects of the international flow of human resources. A clearer picture of technical assistance as an aspect of economic and social development may be obtained by drawing analogies between trade in skills and trade in commodities. In the first place, just as no country, whatever its stage of development, is expected to be exclusively an exporter or an importer of goods, or even of capital, so no country should be expected to be exclusively an exporter or an importer of human resources. All countries can be expected to be both exporters and importers. However, the pattern of international trade, the terms of trade, the balance of trade, and the overall balance of payments are all important aspects of a country's economic situation.

The composition of international trade in skills should reflect comparative economic advantage. Even developing countries with overall shortages of skilled manpower have surpluses of certain types of skill, sometimes at a very high level, as indicated by the presence of the educated unemployed. Until the developing countries with such surpluses reach the level of development that permits them to absorb all their own trained people, it makes good sense to export surplus skills to countries with shortages of the same categories of trained personnel, whether through organized technical assistance programs or in some other fashion. To some degree, the existence of surplus skills reflects past inadequacies in the educational system, in the sense that it has failed to adapt to the occupational needs of the country at each stage of development. However, there may be a case for continuing to produce skills for export. Greece, for example, might continue to turn out archeologists, ancient historians, and scholars of Greek literature and language in excess of its own immediate needs.

Of particular importance to developing countries are the terms of trade—whether in commodities or in skills. It is by no means clear that the terms of trade in skills of developing countries have been universally favorable in the sense that the average cost, in man-years of training, of people coming into the country is higher than that of people going out. Unfortunately, among the emigrants from developing countries are some of their most highly educated people—and these not always in the categories with surpluses at home. Consequently, the terms of trade in skills are not as favorable for developing countries as they might be.

It is sometimes said that the optimal balance-of-payments situation for a developing country is an import surplus offset by a net capital inflow. An analogy can be obtained for human resources if we think of trained adults as capital goods and the educational system as the basic stock of capital. We could then say that the optimal balance-of-payments situation for a developing country is an import surplus of human resources (in terms of value rather than volume) offset by a net capital inflow in the form of educational facilities. The latter can be accomplished either by foreign-financed fellowships to train students abroad or by the development of the domestic educational and training facilities through foreign aid.

When cast in terms such as these, it is clear that technical assistance is one part—an important one—of a much broader spectrum. It is apparent, for example, that technical assistance policy cannot be properly formulated independently from the international exchange of human resources through the private sector. Information regarding import and export of skills by private institutions should be continuously available to the authorities, to assist them in formulating technical assistance policy. It is also clear that the international flow of human resources should be adjusted to the flow from the domestic educational system. Given the stock of human skills and the flow from the educational system, technical assistance in all its forms should aim at filling the gap between available skills and skills needed to execute the development program.

Some developing countries, concerned with maintaining their independence of the "economic imperialists," have raised the cry of "trade, not aid." Sometimes it appears that what these spokesmen have in mind is "aid *through* trade"—that is, guaranteeing quantities for their major exports. If "trade" means merely removing any remaining barriers to the importation of major exports of developing countries, there is little reason to believe that it can contribute significantly to accelerated growth of underdeveloped countries. Indeed, one of the reasons that these countries remain poor is that foreign trade has proved to be an engine of growth of very low horsepower. There are few developing countries that have not enjoyed substantial growth of foreign trade in the past.

Let us look at Southeast Asia, the region that remains the most stagnant and troublesome of all major groupings of countries. Whether we take the whole century since 1900 or only the period since World War II, Southeast Asia is the region that seems to frustrate most obdurately efforts to raise per capita income. Yet all countries in Southeast Asia have had at one time or another one or more strong exports to serve as leading sectors for vigorous growth of the entire economy. In Indonesia, most recalcitrant of all Southeast Asian countries, there has been a whole succession of strong exports, from spices in the sixteenth century to rubber and petroleum in the twentieth. Between 1880 and 1920 Indonesian exports grew 1300 percent. Similarly, Malaya enjoyed a 440 percent growth of exports in the three decades between 1906 and 1925. In the 54-year span between 1906 and 1960 Malayan exports grew by 1400 percent. The exports of tea from Ceylon grew 1100 percent between 1849 and 1875–1879. In Taiwan total exports grew 500 percent in 25 years (1915–1917–1940–1942). These periods are selected so as not to begin with a year when exports were so low that large percentage growth means little; the initial year in each case is some time after the major new exports were well established. Throughout the whole of the latter nineteenth and early twentieth centuries the percentage growth of exports was considerably higher than the percentage growth of total output. There was, in fact, little structural change; the new export sector was superimposed on a stagnant traditional agricultural sector, where little happened except population pressure and a shift from slash-and-burn to irrigated agriculture. Except for Malaya, the proportion of the labor force engaged in traditional agriculture scarcely fell. The story is much the same in other underdeveloped regions.

The postwar picture is much the same, perhaps worse. There is no significant correlation between postwar growth rates in Southeast Asia and either the ratio of exports to national income or the rate of growth of exports. Moreover, exports which once were strong are strong no longer. According to Economic Commission for Asia and the Far East (ECAFE) projections (which are certainly optimistic, since they ignore supply and marketing problems), even if we assumed that total income would grow as fast as exports, only petroleum exports are likely to grow enough between now and 1980 to yield a 3 percent average annual increase in per capita income. If we accept instead a 2 percent growth target, then sugar may be added to the list.

In short, it is clear that instead of expecting expanded trade to solve the development problem, we should realize that development is needed to solve the trade problem. The countries with the largest proportion of their labor force in agriculture are precisely those with the biggest comparative disadvantage in agriculture and with a more marked comparative disadvantage in agriculture than in other sectors. In the United States, on the contrary, comparative advantage is most marked precisely in the agricultural sector.

With the mounting food crisis and industrialization of developing countries, sharp shifts in the structure of international trade can be expected, unless our policy prevents them. What seems most important in the field of foreign trade policy is that as the poor countries prove their ability to undersell us in industrial products—as they certainly will—we do not impose barriers on the importation of their industrial products. The myth that low wages reflect low productivity has long since been exploded. Industrial technology has proved highly mobile among countries. If anything, the level of technology in the new industries of developing countries is higher than in advanced countries, and real wages will remain lower for a long time to come. Our proper role may well prove to be that of becoming the "bread-rice-soybean basket of the world."

Even if expansion of traditional exports cannot be expected to make a fundamental contribution to accelerated growth of developing countries, it remains true that the stability of export earnings complicates the problem of formulating, financing, and implementing development programs. It took the United States a long time to recognize this fact. As late as 1958, while President Eisenhower was urging more liberal foreign aid, his brother Milton was insisting in an

official report that United States participation in international commodity stabilization schemes be limited to technical assistance to study groups. His advice
was apparently heeded, and it was not until the Kennedy administration and the
Act of Bogota that the United States was officially committed to participation in
schemes "to deal with the problem of instability of exchange earnings of countries heavily dependent upon the exportation of primary products." [20] Since that
time the United Nations Conference on Trade and Development has devoted
considerable attention to this problem, but so far nothing in the way of a general
scheme for international stabilization has emerged.

Among the various proposals, my own favorite remains the one suggested
in 1958 by the General Agreement on Trades and Tariffs (GATT) Panel of
Experts.[21] The International Fund, in consultation with experts from the major
exporting and importing countries, would study long-run trends in prices of the
major exports of developing countries. The Fund and the governments involved
would agree on an appropriate trend price for some years to come and revise
this price as needed in the light of new developments. An alternative—theoretically less attractive but possibly more workable—would be simply to take the
average price during several years in the recent past as evidence of the long-run
trend. If the market for any commodity included in the agreements suffers a
temporary setback, the governments of the exporting countries would buy for
stocks and make such payments as they wished, in domestic currency, to their
own producers. To provide the foreign exchange needed to permit development
programs to be carried out despite the decline in foreign exchange earnings, the
International Monetary Fund would permit drawings on its reserves up to some
stipulated percentage of the value of stockpiles at the predetermined "normal"
price. The loans would be repaid and stockpiles reduced when prices in world
markets rose again. If producing countries did not "play the game" properly, or
if it appeared that the break in the market was permanent and consequently
stockpiles overhanging the market continued to grow, the "trend" or "normal"
price would of course be revised downward.

As a minimum contribution to international stabilization, the advanced
countries should presumably endeavor to make sure that their efforts to stabilize
their own economies do not have the effect of destabilizing the economies of the
developing countries. Worst offender on this score has been the administration
of U.S. Public Law 480. Complaints that the disposal of U.S. agricultural surpluses has disrupted the export markets of other countries have come from
Argentina, Spain, India, Pakistan, Japan, and even Canada. The accumulation of
counterpart funds from PL 480 sales, as recipient countries discover that local
currency generated by their own borrowing from their own central banks is no

more inflationary than spending counterpart funds and is subject to no control but their own, is becoming an embarrassment to the U.S. government. At the same time, it is clear that surplus commodity disposal has a useful role to play in the whole nexus of policies designed to accelerate growth of developing countries. As the food crisis mounts, this role is likely to become increasingly vital. It would seem clear that surplus commodity disposal should be continued but within an international framework and as an integral part of an overall international policy for stabilization and development.

Policy regarding private foreign investment has been left to the end for several reasons.

First, the international flow of U.S. capital is a tiny trickle and seems likely to remain so, no matter what is done about it. To get some sense of scale, we might revise upward the figures suggested some years ago by Alex Cairncross and say that, if U.S. foreign investment were to play the role today that U.K. investment played in the nineteenth century, relative to the total scale of the world economy, U.S. foreign investments today would amount to some $1,000 billions, and the U.S. would receive a net income from foreign investments of about $50 billion per year. Instead, total U.S. foreign private investment is not much more than $50 billion, and net foreign investment runs at $1 billion to $2 billion per year, even less than foreign aid.

Second, such foreign investment as there is tends to go to advanced rather than developing countries. Canada and Europe have proved much more attractive to U.S. investors than the underdeveloped countries, and among the latter the relatively advanced countries of Latin America have been more attractive than the poorer countries whose dependence on outside capital for development may be greater.

Third, the policies of the developing countries themselves toward foreign investment are likely to prove much more significant for investment decisions than anything the advanced countries can do. The measures used by advanced countries to date have consisted mainly in guarantees against expropriation, devaluation, and the like, plus tax incentives (or disincentives). These measures have proved somewhat impotent where the general climate for foreign investment has been unfavorable. It is still true today that "nothing is so shy as one million dollars," and the countries most in need of foreign capital (and of the entrepreneurial, managerial, and scientific expertise that comes with it) are precisely those that are most reluctant to make the kind of passes needed to seduce millions.

Finally, there is a continuing controversy among Western economists as to whether or not foreign private investment makes a net contribution to development of underdeveloped countries. Some, like Martin Bronfenbrenner, maintain that not only should developing countries be uninterested in attracting new foreign investment but also that they should confiscate the foreign enterprises already there. The gain in funds that could be locally reinvested, instead of being transferred abroad as profits and repatriation, would likely substantially exceed any new inflow of capital from abroad—especially in countries where property income is high and landowners are prone to consume rather than invest.[22] Others, like Wendell Gordon, go less far, but argue that the point is soon reached in borrowing countries where the cost of servicing the old debt exceeds any possible net inflow of new capital and that foreign enterprise delays the formation of domestic cadres of entrepreneurs, managers, scientists, and technicians.[23] On the other side of the controversy, there are economists who point out that the debt service is met out of the higher gross national product that the foreign investment itself helps to produce and which could not be attained without it. The proponents of foreign investment also insist that foreign capital brings with it foreign skills, especially of the entrepreneurial and managerial variety, not otherwise available. The cadre of foreign expertise that accompanies foreign investment raises absorptive capacity and thus has a chain effect.

Probably one ought not to generalize about the potential contribution of foreign investment to development of developing countries but should consider each case on its merits. Being impressed by the enormous difficulty of generating an adequate supply of entrepreneurial and managerial skills in countries where they are now almost totally absent, I am inclined to favor foreign investment in such countries. The need for effective economic leadership seems to be especially pressing in mixed economies. At the same time, it must be recognized that most developing countries have had substantial foreign investment in the past and that foreign enterprise has fallen far short of solving the development problem in many of these countries.

From the foregoing review of major aspects of foreign economic policy in relation to economic development, one major conclusion stands out: if the policy of advanced countries is to be truly one of assisting poor countries with their economic development, foreign aid must be the major instrument. Liberalization of foreign trade (especially ready acceptance of new industrial products) and international stabilization measures can help. Foreign private investment still has a role, at least in some countries. But the major need of poor countries is rapid structural change, and in many of them the requirements are such that they cannot do the job alone, if population growth is to be outrun by a big enough margin and for long enough to put them on the road to self-sustained growth. In this context, aid must mean grants or very soft loans, not fifteen-year loans at 6 percent. Technical assistance has a major contribution to make in raising both absorptive capacity and the maximum domestic effort, but it must henceforth be programmed as part of a general human resource policy and continuously integrated with overall development planning and programming. The scale of assistance needed is such as to make it unwelcome in many countries if it is on a bilateral basis. Some overhauling of the machinery for international aid is clearly and urgently required.

NOTES

[1] See especially, The President's Committee to Study the United States Military Assistance Program, *Letter to the President of the United States, and the Committee's Third Interim Report* (Washington, D.C., July 13, 1959).

[2] See, for example, U.S. Senate, *The Objectives of United States Economic Assistance Programs*, prepared at the request of the Special Committee to Study the Foreign Aid Program by the Center for International Studies, M.I.T., Senate Doc. 1 (Washington, D.C., 1957).

[3] See, for example, *Basic Aims of United States Foreign Policy*, prepared by the Council on Foreign Relations (Washington, D.C., Nov. 25, 1959).

[4] See, for example, Max F. Millikan and Walt W. Rostow, *A Proposal: Key to an Effective Foreign Policy* (New York, 1957), and Harland Cleveland, *The Theory and Practice of Foreign Aid* (prepared for the special-studies project of the Rockefeller Brothers Fund, Nov. 1, 1956), 31–32.

[5] Benjamin Higgins, *The United Nations and U.S. Foreign Economic Policy* (Glencoe, Ill., 1963).

[6] Ministère d'État Chargé de la Réforme Administrative, *La Politique de Coopération avec les Pays en Voie de Développement*, Rapport de la Commission d'Étude instituée par le Décret du 12 mars 1963, remis au Gouvernement le 18 juillet 1963.

[7] *Foreign Aid Policies Reconsidered* (Paris, 1966), 39.

[8] *Ibid.*, 49.

[9] A somewhat longer and more technical version of the analysis on capital assistance and absorptive capacity can be found in Benjamin Higgins, "Assistance étrangère et capacité d'absorption," *Développement et Civilisations*, Oct.–Dec. 1960, pp. 28–43. See also P. N. Rosenstein-Rodan, *International Aid for Underdeveloped Countries* (CENIS, Jan. 1961).

[10] In practice, projections of income would probably not be carried beyond 20 to 25 years, but, if an appropriate discount factor is applied, additions to income in the next generation will not be a very important consideration.

[11] AID, *Benefit-Cost Evaluations as Applied to Aid Financed Water or Related Land Use Projects*, Supplement No. 1 to Feasibility Studies (Washington, D.C., 1964).

[12] John H. Adler, *Absorptive Capacity: The Concept and Its Determinants*, Brookings Institution Staff Paper (Washington, D.C., June 1965), p. 7.

[13] *Ibid.*

[14] Cf. ECAFE, *Report of the Expert Group on Development Programming Techniques* (Bangkok, 1960).

[15] W. Arthur Lewis, "Allocating Foreign Aid to Promote Self-Sustained Economic Growth," in *Motivations and Methods in Development and Foreign Aid*, ed. Geiger and Solomon, Proceedings of the Sixth World Conference of the Society for International Development (Washington, D.C., March 1964), p. 23.

[16] John C. H. Fei and Douglas S. Paauw, "Foreign Assistance and Self-Help: A Reappraisal of Development Finance," *Review of Economics and Statistics*, Aug. 1965, pp. 251–67.

[17] This section is a byproduct of a mission undertaken by OECD to evaluate technical assistance to Greece and a United Nations mission to evaluate technical assistance to Libya. The report of the Greek mission by A. Maddison, A. Stavrionopoulos, and B. Higgins is published under the title *Technical Assistance and the Economic Development of Greece* (Paris, 1965). The report of the U.N. mission has not been published for general distribution.

[18] Undersecretary of State Webb, quoted in Charles Wolf, Jr., *Foreign Aid: Theory and Practice in Southern Asia* (Princeton, 1960), 59.

[19] Secretary of Agriculture Brannon, quoted in *ibid.*, 63.

[20] "Act of Bogota," Sec. IV, para. 2.

[21] *Trends in International Trade* (Geneva, 1958).

[22] Martin Bronfenbrenner, "The Appeal of Confiscation in Economic Development," *Economic Development and Cultural Change*, April 1955.

[23] Wendell C. Gordon, "Foreign Investment," *Business Review* (University of Houston), Fall 1962.

134

CHAPTER FIVE

LEVEL OF DEVELOPMENT AND INTERNATION BEHAVIOR

———

IVO K. & ROSALIND L., FEIERABEND

with Frank W. Scanland III & John Stuart Chambers

THIS DISCUSSION concerns the relationship between levels of socioeconomic development achieved by nations of the world and their behavior within the international political system.[1] The study includes 84 nations (all independent polities in 1948), which are scrutinized for the period following World War II. The variables employed derive generally from the period 1948–1962. The discussion is based on a consideration of 27 variables in all, giving the study a global scope although a limited historical perspective.

A major portion of the analysis centers on three categories of internation behavior: hostile transactions, amicable transactions, and degree of involvement in the international arena (or transactional level). Events such as wars, economic sanctions, mobilizations, accusations, treaties, alliances, state visits, and others may serve as typical examples of hostile and amicable behaviors occurring between nations in the international system. Their frequency of occurrence, and also the extent to which they are directed toward a wide variety of other nations, gives an indication of the level of international involvement of a nation within the system. These broad transactional categories are then related to a variety of ecological and structural variables of political systems. In particular, level of socioeconomic development is related to type and level of internation transactions.

With this broad and general focus, a great many nuances of international and national behavior are lost, including styles and varieties of foreign policies, actions and reactions in the international arena, specific idiosyncracies of nations, and their unique physical, social, and historical backgrounds. A macroscopic look at the entire universe of nations, as here conceived, sacrifices the richness of social and political reality preserved in case studies. Yet, a macroscopic view also has its merits. The entire universe may be surveyed, making comparisons possible that are not available to case studies, which often argue the uniqueness of events. Also, generalizations are difficult to uphold on the basis of a single case or a few cases. Such a macroscopic approach provides a panoramic view of the world, revealing global patterns and relationships between levels of development and hostile and amicable transactions in the international sphere.

The questions we are seeking to answer empirically vary in complexity. At the simplest level, we ask whether the nations at various levels of attained development also vary in the amount of external hostility expressed toward others, in level of diplomatic and other interactions, and in level of amicability.

We also attempt to distinguish empirically a limited number of types of transactional postures characterizing the nations of the world, an approach which perhaps comes the closest to the notion of a generalized foreign policy pattern. These postures are also related to developmental level. Furthermore, we analyze a set of variables which might serve to predict internation behavior to see whether they have the same predictive power for nations at different levels of development. Finally, we also analyze dimensions of hostile behavior to determine whether they are by and large the same for nations at different developmental levels.

A final introductory word is in order. The larger portion of the discussion and analysis is descriptive and statistics are used in the descriptive rather than in the inferential sense. The prevalent question asked is what patterns persist at mid-twentieth century, rather than why they persist. In the last section of the study, however, we attempt to interpret at least a portion of our global empirical findings in terms of explanatory variables. Some theoretical insights are suggested inductively from the descriptive data, and a few hypotheses are formulated and compared with our empirical findings.

The data used in this analysis fall into two basic categories: The first consists of both internation and intranation behaviors; the second comprises a variety of ecological characteristics including socioeconomic, demographic, political, and military indicators.

The behavioral data deal with different transactions among nations. These include hostile and friendly transactions as well as a measure of the level of internation interaction. Transactional behavioral data must be collected from various sources, and the first step in establishing a data collection of this type is a delimitation of the acts which will be included for study. This in turn depends upon prior definition of the variables selected for inquiry.

Behaviors signifying aggressive or hostile relations between nations are of various types and differ in the level of threat or severity implied. Thus, one may distinguish war, or armed conflict, as the most intense instance of internation hostility, whereas at the other end of an internation hostility continuum, one might place a mild diplomatic maneuver, such as a request for clarification or a verbal protest. In between these two extremes, a number of different actions may be distinguished. Rummel and Tanter, for example, selected twelve types of such behaviors for study: antiforeign demonstrations; the expulsion or recall of diplomatic officials of lesser than ambassador's rank; threats; presence of military action; war; troop movements; mobilizations; accusations; negative sanctions; protests; the severance of diplomatic relations; and the expulsion or recall of ambassadors.[2]

Having defined the actions, the task is to peruse news sources and other chronicles of events and to record the occurrence of internation behaviors falling within the specified categories. In this way, the Rummel and Tanter studies developed a data bank covering 75 nations for the period 1955–1960. Data for the collection were drawn from five sources.[3]

Chambers completed a collection of internation hostility behaviors which expanded the Rummel and Tanter bank in a number of ways, although unfortunately not in terms of data sources.[4] The categories of events were the same as in the Rummel-Tanter collection, with the addition of two new events (quasi-military acts and requests for assistance of third parties against target countries) and a narrowing of the category "threats" into three subtypes of different intensity (nonspecific threat, semispecific threat, and specific threat). Chambers also retrieved and stored the data in terms of dyadic relations, naming the initiator and target country for each event, and qualified some events further in terms of such factors as the amount of violence, number of persons involved, amount of property damage, etc.

In his data collection, Chambers also sought to amass information on internation relations of a nonhostile character. For this purpose, he defined thirteen categories of amicable internation events: offers; talks, negotiations, conferences; expressions of support; social and cultural agreements; economic agreements; political agreements; scientific agreements; military agreements; official visits; diplomatic recognition; state visits; alliance in the presence of military action or war; agreements for adjudication or mediation by a third party; and conferences between member countries of an international organization.

Data on these amicable interactions were collected, categorized, qualified, and stored in the same fashion as the hostile interactions. The Chambers complete data bank of both hostile and amicable internation interactions covers 84 nations for a six-year period, 1955–1961.

The level of political unrest characterizing a society may also be determined in terms of behaviors such as riots, strikes, demonstrations, coups, civil wars, etc. Following the definition of political instability as aggressive behavior directed by politically relevant individuals or groups within the polity against the officeholders, by the officeholders against such individuals and groups or, finally, among the officeholders themselves, the Feierabends distinguished 28 categories of political instability events: dissolution of legislatures; resignation of politically significant persons; dismissal of politically significant persons; fall of cabinets; significant changes of laws; plebiscites; appointment of politically significant persons; organization of new governments; reshuffle of governments; severe trouble within a nongovernmental organization; organization of opposition party; governmental action against specific groups; strikes; demonstrations;

boycotts; arrests; suicides of significant political persons; martial law; executions; assassinations; terrorism, sabotage; guerrilla warfare; civil war; coups; revolts; and exile.[5]

Occurrences of these events were recorded from two data sources,[6] and each event was qualified in terms of a number of subcategories including duration; violence; number of people involved, injured, killed, and arrested; whether significant people were involved, etc. The data collection includes 84 countries for the fifteen-year period, 1948–1962.[7]

A scaling or profiling of nations on the behavioral variables of internation hostility and amity and internal political instability was also needed. For this purpose we used a scaling method based on frequency and intensity-weighting of events.[8] The first step was to scale the behavioral events in terms of their intensity value. This scaling was based on a construct-validity analysis of the meaning of amity and aggression (both external and internal). For internal political unrest, for example, events were placed on a 7-point scale in terms of the amount of violence and severity of disturbance connoted by each. Thus, civil war fell at point 6 and elections at point 0 on the scale. In between these two extremes, events were ranged at the various scale positions. Consensual validation was obtained for this scaling by the technique used for assigning values in the judgmental method of attitude scaling.[9] In similar fashion, intensity scale values were determined for acts of external aggression and amity.

Finally, countries were profiled on the behavioral dimensions by weighting the frequency of events in terms of their intensity values. Countries were first grouped according to the most extreme event (unstable, hostile, or amicable) occurring within the country during the time period under study. Then the frequency of events weighted for intensity was summed to yield the country's position within its scale group. Countries were profiled on a 7-point scale for internal political unrest and on a 5-point scale for internation amity. Two different scales were developed for internation hostility. A 7-point scale was used in which the highest scale value, 7, was reserved for military action, declaration of war, and total blockade.[10] A 4-point scale was also developed and applied to the Rummel-Tanter collection of data.[11] Point 4 on this scale included war, military action, and severance of diplomatic relations. Thus, the main differences between these two measuring instruments and the resultant country profiles on external aggression are that the 4-point scaling combines diplomatic and military hostility at the highest scale position and also that the profiles are based on two different data collections.

The profiles of the 84 nations on external aggression, external amity, and internal political instability are given in Tables 1, 2, and 3.

Another method of assigning numerical values to countries for behavioral events is to use country scores on dimensions ascertained through factor analysis. Rummel and Tanter both factor-analyzed their data collection on external conflict and Rummel named the emergent dimensions war, diplomacy, and belligerency.[12] The war dimension consists of high loadings on the following variables: number killed in international conflict, wars, accusations, threats, military actions, protests, and mobilizations. The diplomatic dimension comprises nonviolent acts of hostility: expulsions and recalls of ambassadors, expulsions and recalls of lesser officials, and troop movements. The third dimension, belligerency, includes severence of diplomatic relations, negative sanctions, and antiforeign demonstrations. Country factor scores on each of these dimensions provide a measure of the extent to which each country is engaged in the set of behaviors designated by the factor.

The dimension of permissiveness-coerciveness of a political regime entails various notions of democratic institutions, civil liberties, and freedom of political opposition. To determine empirically the level of coerciveness or permissiveness of a government is not as straightforward a task as the collection of data on political unrest and internation hostility.[13] However, we have measured nations on this dimension by means of an ordinal rating of countries on a 6-point scale from most permissive to most coercive. Ratings were based on a detailed set of considerations which revolved around three basic questions: (a) To what degree are civil rights present and protected? (b) To what extent is political opposition tolerated and effective? (c) How democratic is the polity? [14]

Ratings were given to 84 countries for the fifteen-year period 1948-1962, assigning one scale value to each country for the entire time period. The ratings were made after consulting a minimum of five case studies per country.[15] The resultant scaling of countries places permissive Western democracies at point 1 and coercive totalitarian regimes at point 6 on the continuum. In between these two extremes, countries fall about equally into the four remaining scale positions.

Finally, the level of transactions occurring between and among nations was assessed in two ways: as political or diplomatic and as other nondiplomatic interaction. In both types of transactions, level is defined in terms of the number of countries with which a nation has a high frequency of interaction. Interaction with only one other country, even if highly frequent in occurrence and highly charged with either amity or hostility, does not yield a high transaction score. Another way of describing the transaction measure is to say that it represents each country's number of participations in different dyadic interactions.

Political-diplomatic transaction level is thus scored on the basis of participation in hostile and amicable acts between nations. The greater the number of countries with which a nation has amicable or hostile relations, above a certain base level, the higher its diplomatic transaction score. Nondiplomatic transactions could be measured in various ways. Deutsch has used the volume of mail exchanged between countries,[16] and the volume of foreign trade is another possible indicator. To these we have added the number of passenger flights between nations.[17] The number of countries with which a nation is connected by passenger flights, and the weekly frequency of these flights, are used as indicators to yield the nation's nondiplomatic transaction score.

Our ecological indicators are also of two types: combined indexes based on a variety of selected indicators and single indicators drawn from available sources.

Two of the combined indexes are based on a single set of ecological indicators, which are treated in different fashion to correspond to different theoretical concepts.[18]

The systemic frustration index was devised to represent the theoretical notion of systemic frustration, which in turn was interpreted as the ratio of social wants to social satisfactions within a society. Data were gathered on eight ecological indicators for the period 1948–1955. Two of these indicators were regarded as a means of spreading want formation within a society: literacy level and level of urbanization.[19] The remaining six indicators were taken in combination as a measure of level of social satisfaction: GNP per capita; caloric intake per person per day; number of newspapers and radios per 1,000 population; percent of population having telephones, and number of persons per physician. The combined coded score on these six indicators was divided by coded literacy or coded urbanization levels, whichever was higher. This ratio corresponded to the theoretical ratio:

$$\frac{\text{social satisfactions}}{\text{social wants}} = \text{systemic frustration}.$$

The modernity index was computed as the average score on the same eight indicators, converted to standard score form. This yielded a picture of each nation's level of attained development based on a variety of measures. In order to distinguish level of attained modernity, or levels of development within the sample, the distribution of countries on the modernity continuum was divided into three groups. The High Modern group consists of the 24 countries with the highest average scores; the Low Modern group comprises the 23 countries at the opposite end of the distribution with the lowest average scores, and the Mid-Modern range contains 37 countries falling between these two groups. The modernity groupings are given in Table 4.[20]

The rate of socioeconomic change index was based on nine ecological indicators gathered for the twenty-eight-year period, 1935–1962. The indicators are: national income per capita, standard of living, infant mortality, primary education, secondary education, literacy, radios and newspapers per 1,000 persons, and level of urbanization. Yearly percentage rate of change was calculated by the formula: maximum value − minimum value/minimum value/years, and coded change scores were combined to yield the overall index.[21]

The various single indicators used in this analysis are drawn primarily from the *World Handbook of Political and Social Indicators* and McClelland, *The Achieving Society*.[22] They may be organized into the following groups:

1. Demographic: Total population.
2.   Wealth: Area in square kilometers.
                   GNP per capita in U.S. dollars 1957.
                   GNP in millions U.S. dollars.
                   Trade as percentage of GNP.
3. Interaction: Foreign Mail per capita.
4.   Military: Military personnel as percentage of total population.
                   Defense expenditure as percentage of GNP.
5. Motivational: Need achievement score, 1925 and 1950.

This last measure perhaps needs some explanation. It is based on a coding of samples of stories in children's elementary school readers for the type of motivational themes expressed. Those countries in which a sample of stories indicates strong emphasis on striving, goal-and-task-orientation, success, and the like, receive a high need-achievement score. McClelland has scored 25 countries for need-achievement level in 1925 and 40 countries for need-achievement level in 1950. Through such scores, McClelland hopes to distinguish societies striving toward achievement, that is, modernity and development, from countries in which the population has lower aspirations.

We have, then, 27 variables with which to approach the question, does level of development affect the patterning of internation behavior? Twelve of these variables provide different measures of internation transaction. Among these are two transactional profiles of level of external aggression and one of level of external amity. These are based on total transactions for each country, yielding a total weighted country score as explained above. In addition, two measures of net aggression level are constructed by subtracting country rank position on the amity profile from rank position on the aggression profile. This net aggression level is calculated for total acts directed against the country (Net Aggression, Target), in which case it assesses the net international environment to which the country is subject. It is also calculated for total acts engaged in (Net Aggression, Initiator), indicating whether, on balance, the country is more hostile or more amicable, if all its actions are taken into account, regardless of target.

Furthermore, the study includes the three factor dimensions of Rummel: war (which includes some acts of diplomacy, such as accusations, threats, and protests), diplomacy, and belligerency (which is identified as an "arousal" or animosity dimension). There are also four measures of internation transaction level included in the analysis. Diplomatic transaction level measures the number of other countries toward which amicable or hostile behavior is exhibited. Nondiplomatic transaction level is determined in three ways: (a) the number of other countries with which direct passenger flight connections are maintained; (b) the total number of weekly flights to other countries; and (c) the volume of foreign mail received. The remaining fifteen variables may be regarded as potential predictors of these various forms of internation transaction. All the variables are listed in Table 5.

The 27 variables were intercorrelated for the sample of 84 nations (or for the maximum number of countries available on each variable). Also, the sample was divided along two dimensions. Level of development split the group into the three modernity groupings described above. In addition, five "major powers" of the world were identified, the U.S., the U.S.S.R., United Kingdom, France, and mainland China. Analyses were performed both including and excluding these major powers on the grounds that their pattern of internation transactions might differ from that of the lesser powers. Four of these major powers derived from the High Modern group of countries, the fifth from the Low Modern group. Thus, each correlation is given seven ways: (a) all 84 nations; (b), 84 nations without the major powers (84/WMP); (c) the High Modern group; (d) High Modern without the major powers (HiMod/WMP); (e) the Mid-Modern range (Mid-Mod) which has no major powers; (f) the Low Modern group; and (g) the Low Modern without major powers, i.e., without mainland China (LoMod/WMP).

These correlations are presented in Table 5. The table reveals the intercorrelations for the first ten measures of internation interaction only. Correlations above .4 are bracketed for ease of discussion. This is not to claim statistical significance, which will vary with the number of countries involved, but because a correlation of this size or larger was taken rather arbitrarily as indicative of a tendency worthy of discussion.[23] The number of countries entering into each correlation is given in parentheses beneath the coefficient.

A final point should be made before discussing the patterning revealed in Table 5. In breaking the overall sample into subgroups, the possibility of statistical artifacts is increased. Again, it is not our purpose to see how many statistically significant correlations may be obtained by this subdivision. Rather, our purpose is to see what seem to be the trends within the various levels of development.

Let us look first at the intercorrelations among the various measures of internation transactions, especially those which may serve as reliability checks for each other. The two scalings of external aggression, for example, should be highly correlated, although we must bear in mind that they cover a slightly different time period (1955–1960 and 1955–1961), interpret the intensity level of events differently, and, finally, are based on different data collections. Nevertheless, in column 2 of the first block of correlations in Table 5, we find that the correlation between the two scales is .52 for the sample of 72 nations scored on both and that it is above .40 for all subgroups except the LoMod/WMP, where it is .39.

Again, we would expect level of external aggression to correlate with net aggression initiated and find that it does so with a degree of association of .51 for the entire sample of 84 nations, if we use the 7-point external aggression scale. Reading down column 5 of the first block of correlations, we find that for all subgroupings, the relationship between these two is .42 or higher. Similarly, level of external aggression and country scores on Rummel's war dimension should be intercorrelated. We find this to be the case, again using the 7-point external aggression scale, with an r of .58 for the 71 countries scored on both measures. And in column 6 of the first block of correlations, the degree of association between these two measures is above .51 for all subgroups. This is reassuring, since, as has been mentioned, these two measures are based on different data collections.

It must also be pointed out that the 4-point scale of external aggression does not intercorrelate very highly with either net aggression initiated or with any of the three Rummel dimensions. In fact, it does not correlate well with any of the remaining eight measures of internation interaction, as may be seen by looking across the top row of the second block of correlations. The three highest correlations are .31 with Rummel's diplomatic dimension, .31 with level of diplomatic interaction, and .30 with the war dimension (Rummel). Although these correlations are lower than expected, they do at least provide a coherent picture in which the 4-point scaling of external aggression can be seen to include both military (war) and diplomatic acts. It is curious that this scale does not correlate more highly with Rummel's three dimensions, since it is based on the same data bank.

These are the reliability checks for internation transactions which are built into the correlation matrix, and they cover only the measures of external aggression. For the remainder of the internation transactional measures, we will look for patterning across the entire sample and within subsamples.

One relationship that emerges and complies with expectation is that external aggression expressed is highly related to amount of aggression received. We see this in two sets of correlations. In column 4 of the first block of correlations, we find that the relationship for the sample of 84 nations between Net Aggression, Target and total aggression expressed, on a 7-point scale, is .41 and that for all subgroups except the Low Modern it ranges from .43 to .52. For the Low Modern groups, the correlations are .27 and .28, suggesting that these countries are more apt to express aggression without being retaliated against or provoked. We see even stronger relationships between our measure of net aggression initiated and net aggression experienced (target). In column 5 of the fourth block of correlations, we find that for the entire sample of 84 nations the degree of association between these two is .65 and that it remains consistently high (the lowest r is .59) for all subgroupings. Again, however, the 4-point external aggression scale does not yield the same result. For the entire sample of 72 nations, the correlation to Net Aggression, Target, is only .10. In column 4 of the second block of correlations, we find no correlation higher than .15 for these two variables and for the Low Modern group of nations, we find a low inverse relationship.

If we continue to seek patterns of aggression, we may look for intercorrelations among Rummel's three dimensions of aggressive behavior at different developmental levels. Although we would not expect to find correlations between the dimensions for the entire sample of nations, for countries in the Mid-Modern range war and belligerency are intercorrelated (.56) and in the Low Modern groups diplomatic aggression and belligerency are correlated (.51 and .50 for Low Modern and Low Modern without the major power, respectively). Thus, belligerency, which implies animosity of feeling, apparently accompanies other forms of aggression in nonmodern countries. In the High Modern group, however, if anything, belligerency is negatively related to the other two types of aggressive behavior.

If we turn to amicable behavior and diplomatic and nondiplomatic transaction level, we find that patterning also appears in the data. For the entire sample of nations, external amity behavior correlates only to Net Aggression, Initiator, and here we find an inverse relationship of $-.48$ for all 84 countries and $-.51$ for all 84 without the major powers. This is a relationship certainly to be expected and may be regarded as a reliability check on the amity scoring. Within subgroupings, however, some interesting and unexpected patterns emerge which will be pursued further in other data treatments reported later in this paper. For High Modern and Low Modern countries, a strong positive relationship seems to obtain between external aggression and external amity behavior. This relationship does not occur in the Mid-Modern range of countries. If we look first at the 7-point aggression scale, we see that the relationship between aggression and amity is .57 for the High Modern group of countries. This coefficient drops to .38 when we exclude the major powers. For the Low Modern group of nations, the relationship is .36, whether or not we include mainland China. By contrast, within the Mid-Modern group of countries, there is no relationship ($r = -.02$). This patterning emerges even more strikingly if we use the 4-point aggression scale. Here the correlation is .55 for the High Modern group of countries and .41 without the major powers. The relationship is .48 for the Low Modern group, with or without mainland China. But for nations in the Mid-Modern range, the correlation is -.07.

In further corroboration of this patterning, if we examine columns 6, 7, and 8 of the third block of correlations, we find that for High Modern countries, including the major powers, there is a correlation of .48 between external amity and factor scores on Rummel's war dimension and .36 with his diplomatic aggression dimensions. (There is no correlation to the belligerency dimension: -.04). Excluding the major powers, these correlations are lowered; the association between amity and war is lost (.09), but that between amity and diplomatic aggression remains to some degree (.22). If we look at the Low Modern group of nations, the pattern is even more pronounced. There is a correlation of .33 between amity and war and one of .39 between amity and diplomatic aggression for the entire Low Modern group. When we omit mainland China, the relationship is even higher: .35 for war; .40 for diplomatic aggression. (The relationship between amity and belligerency is again low: .12.) For countries at the Mid-Modern position, however, there is no correlation between external amity and the three Rummel external conflict dimensions (war: .05; diplomacy: .08; belligerency: .06). This confirmation of the pattern between amity scores based on the Chambers data bank and aggression scores based on the Rummel-Tanter data bank gives some confidence in the finding.

What does it imply? Apparently both High Modern and Low Modern countries engage simultaneously in aggressive and amicable behaviors. The countries in the Mid-Modern range do not show this variety of pattern. We might suppose that the High Modern and Low Modern countries engage in a higher level of diplomatic, and perhaps also nondiplomatic, transaction. They are thus involved in more relations with more countries of the world, with their hostile interactions offset by amicable ones. Countries in the Mid-Modern range seem to be beset by more associations of a single type, which could be a reflection of their lower transaction level.

To evaluate this use of transaction level as a mediating explanatory variable, we may look at the correlations between diplomatic and nondiplomatic transactions and the various internation behaviors. The greatest number of high correlations occur between diplomatic, and also nondiplomatic, transaction levels and level of external amity. In columns 9 and 10 of the third block of correlations, we find that for the entire sample, there is a degree of association of .45 between amity and diplomatic transaction, and an association of .48 to nondiplomatic transaction measured in terms of passenger flights. These correlations remain fairly consistently high (ranging from .27 to .82) throughout all subgroupings. The implication is that at all developmental levels, interaction with a large number of countries is based on amity, not hostility.

To return to the high-aggression–high-amity pattern, however, we find that there is some degree of association for the entire sample of countries between level of external aggression and level of diplomatic and nondiplomatic transactions, although it is not so high as for amity. With the 7-point aggression scale, there is a correlation of .37 to diplomatic transaction and one of .23 to flights. The latter is considerably lowered, however, if we omit the major powers. With the 4-point external aggression scale, there is a correlation of .31 to diplomatic transaction, which is lowered to .29 by omitting the major powers. The correlations to flights are negligible. Similarly, there are correlations of .37 and .29, respectively, between Rummel's war dimension and diplomatic and nondiplomatic transactions for the entire sample of 71 countries. And the association between Rummel's diplomatic-aggression dimension and diplomatic-transaction level is .53, whereas it is .23 to flights. (The belligerency dimension does not correlate with transaction level.)

Thus, there is also some tendency for hostile relations to form the basis of a large number of interactions. If we look at the developmental levels, we find that it is the High Modern and Low Modern countries which fit this pattern, not the countries in the Mid-Modern range. With the 7-point aggression scale, there is a correlation of .60 between aggression and diplomatic transaction and an association of .57 to nondiplomatic transaction in the High Modern group of countries. These coefficients are somewhat lowered if we omit the major powers. For the Low Modern group, there is a correlation of .50 between aggression and diplomatic transaction, which is even higher if we omit mainland China. (The correlations to flights are .35 and .38.) In the Mid-Modern range, these correlations are near zero. A similar picture emerges if we use the 4-point aggression scale or Rummel's war or diplomatic-conflict dimensions. Furthermore, there is an inverse correlation for Mid-Modern countries between Net Aggression, Initiator, and level of transaction.

The patterning which appears, then, is that there are two groups of countries at either end of the modernity continuum which appear to experience a large number of both amicable and hostile interrelationships. Countries at the middle of the modernity continuum either tend to express hostility toward a small number of others or, if their diplomatic transaction level is high, to engage in amicable interchange. We will find, in further substantiation of this pattern, that countries in the Mid-Modern group have the highest net hostility score; their hostile interchanges are the least apt to be offset by amicable ones.

Before discussing these patterns further, we might give some consideration to possible predictor variables of international aggression and amity. For the entire sample of nations, the picture is not entirely promising. Among the better predictors of external aggression level are extent of foreign trade as a percentage of GNP and foreign mail received (inverse relationships), level of internal political instability, defense expenditures, and need achievement. Among the better predictors of external amity are defense expenditures (.23) and level of GNP (.34). Both of these coefficients drop considerably, however, if the major powers are omitted. Transaction level is better explained by the variables included in the analysis. In the first place, diplomatic and nondiplomatic transactions are correlated at all levels of development, and the coefficient is .56 for the entire sample of 84 countries. Also, both types of transactions are related to level of GNP and GNP per capita. Diplomatic transaction is also related to population and area, while passenger flights are a function of modernity. Thus transaction level seems to be a matter of wealth and size and, in the case of passenger flights, level of modernity.

If we examine the three developmental groupings separately, however, we find many more possible predictor variables. In modern countries, for instance, high levels of external aggression and external amity seem to be inversely related to foreign mail, foreign trade as a percentage of GNP, and to the level of need achievement in 1925, but they are positively related to military personnel and defense expenditures, population and area, and level of internal political instability. Many of these relationships still obtain even if we omit the major powers.

It is interesting to note that population and area are not consistently related to internation aggression or amity. At some levels of development and with some measures of internation behavior the relationships are positive; in other cases they are negative. Only between level of diplomatic interaction and population size do we find consistent positive relationships at all levels of development. (These correlations range in value from .40 to .93.) Another variable that needs explanation is foreign trade as a percentage of GNP. It appears to be one of the better predictors of internation behavior, showing a strong inverse relationship to all of our variables: aggression, amity, and transaction level. This indicator is really not a measure of volume of foreign trade, however, but rather of degree of economic dependence. The U.S. and Russia rank as the lowest two countries on this variable, Barbados and Libya as the highest.

Finally, an unexpected pattern in the data is the lack of any strong relationship between external aggression and either military personnel or defense expenditures. For the entire sample of nations, the war dimension correlates the best with these two measures of preparedness, .30 to military personnel and .32 to defense expenditure. When we examine the developmental groupings, we find the explanation for these low relationships. In the High Modern group of countries, the relationships are very high, especially if we include the major powers. The correlations are also positive for the Low Modern group of nations and, although not as high as for the modern group, show some reasonable degree of relationship. For the countries in the Mid-Modern group, however, we are more apt to find an inverse relationship between extent of external aggression and degree of preparedness. On the variable of Net Aggression, Initiator, where one might certainly expect military preparedness, we find instead a correlation of $-.24$ to military personnel and one of $-.14$ to defense expenditures. Only with Rummel's war dimension do we find a single substantial positive correlation within this modernity group, which is $r = .36$ to defense expenditures. Perhaps we must assume that the Mid-Modern countries engaging in hostilities are the ones least prepared to do so.

In brief summary of the correlation matrix, it seems that for countries at either end of the developmental continuum, external aggression is one aspect of a high transactional behavior pattern which also includes a large number of amicable interactions. For Mid-Modern countries, external aggression implies a low level of transaction and few amicable exchanges. This might be characterized as a relatively isolated "feuding" pattern, seemingly unrelated to preparedness for military adventure. Furthermore, external aggression cannot very well be "explained" in terms of any single related variable which will be equally applicable to transactional behavior across developmental levels, with the possible exception of internal political unrest. Within the High Modern group of countries, however, and especially for the major powers, all of the commonsense variables apply: wealth, size, population, and military preparedness. Some noncommonsense variables are also in evidence, such as level of political instability and level of need achievement in 1925 (inverse). Also, level of mail flow shows a high inverse relationship. External amity also shows a relationship to the same predictor variables for the High Modern group, which is not surprising since amity and hostility are part of the same transactional pattern for countries at this level of development.

Within the Low Modern group of countries, although the transactional pattern resembles that of the High Modern group, there are not many possible predictor variables. Size shows some relationship to external aggression. Need-achievement level in 1950 shows a high positive relation (.84) based on a very few cases ($N = 4$), and systemic frustration shows a high negative relationship ($-.73$), also based on few cases ($N = 9$). Foreign trade as a percentage of GNP shows a strong negative relationship.

For the Mid-Modern group, almost all of the correlations to possible predictors are negligible. Only with some measures of external aggression do we find positive correlations to both level of internal political unrest and level of need achievement in 1925 (the latter based on a very few cases). There are also some sizable negative correlations between external aggression and both population size and level of GNP.

A second set of findings provides information not available in the correlation matrix. This concerns the difference in average level of transactions, direction, and intensity among countries at different developmental levels. The findings are given in Table 6 for the three developmental levels including the major powers and in Table 7 with the major powers excluded.

If we scan the tables for highest average score on each transactional behavior, we note that the High Modern group of countries is lowest in scaled external-aggression level, even when the major powers are included in the analysis. The differences are striking with major powers excluded. Evidently, there is a sufficient number of peaceful modern countries to counterbalance the high aggression level of the leading powers. The High Modern also lead in amity transaction score but by very little. Countries in the Mid-Modern group are most frequently the targets, as well as the initiators, of net aggression. On Rummel's dimensions, if we leave the major powers in the sample, the High Modern lead on the war and diplomatic aggression dimensions; the Low Modern are the highest in belligerency. The pattern changes if we omit the major powers. Now the Low Modern excel in war, but by very little, and the Mid-Modern group leads in diplomatic conflict. Belligerency is still the domain of the Low Modern group. When it comes to transactional level, the High Modern group clearly leads in both diplomatic and nondiplomatic transactions, especially if the major powers are included. Excluding the major powers, diplomatic transaction level is about the same at the three levels of development, but internation passenger flights are still the province of nations at the highest level of development.

Also included in Tables 6 and 7 are average scores on internal political instability for the two time periods, 1955–1961 and 1948–1962. The High Modern group of countries are clearly the least afflicted with internal conflict in comparison with countries at both of the lower developmental levels, a finding which we have discussed elsewhere.[24] The difference between the Mid-Modern and the Low Modern groups is small on level of internal unrest, although the Mid-Modern are somewhat more beset with this form of conflict.

We may deduce from these tables that there are quite a few modern countries which are both externally peaceful and internally stable in contrast to the less developed groups of nations, which are more consistently beset with both types of conflict.

Certain transactional patterns have been discovered within the correlational matrix. These may be further elaborated, and the particular countries that fit each type may be identified. Table 8 gives a breakdown of countries by developmental level in terms of three major transactional variables: hostility, amity, and interaction level. Interaction level is a combined index based on both diplomatic and nondiplomatic (flights) interaction. The three transactional variables are divided at the median into High and Low levels.

We see that for the High Modern group of nations, two patterns account for 79 percent of countries. Within this 79 percent, countries either show a high-hostility, high-amity, high-interaction pattern or, at the opposite extreme, indicate a low-hostility, low-amity, low-interaction pattern. Only one country shows an excess of hostility over amity (in terms of an above-or-below the median split), and that is the Netherlands. Two countries show more amity than hostility, with higher interaction—Czechoslovakia and Canada. And two countries indicate low levels of hostility and amity with higher interaction—Belgium and Denmark. It should be pointed out that the combined index of diplomatic and nondiplomatic (passenger flights) transaction levels tends to alter the pattern of the modern countries from what it would be if we did not use passenger flights. Some modern countries, which are not very involved in diplomatic transactions, are nevertheless very high on transactions such as airline traffic. In this sense they are certainly very much a part of the world, although able to stand apart from the major conflicts and diplomatic involvements. Thus, if one substitutes passenger flights as the measure of transaction level, instead of the combined interaction index, there will be eight countries in the next-to-last cell (high interaction, low amity, low hostility).

Looking at both the Low Modern and the Mid-Modern groups of countries, we also find some tendency for nations to group themselves at either of the two extreme activity or withdrawal patterns. At the Mid-Modern level, 53 percent of countries fall into these two postures; in the Low Modern group, the level drops to 45 percent of countries. One other strong pattern, which has already been mentioned in discussing the correlation matrix, is revealed for the Mid-Modern group of countries. This is a higher level of hostile than amicable transactions, combined with a low level of interaction. This pattern emerges whether we use diplomatic or nondiplomatic transaction levels or the combined transaction index. These countries are not in high interaction with many other nations and, when they do interact, they are more apt to have a hostile than an amicable relationship. This "feuding" pattern accounts for almost one-quarter (22 percent) of the nations at this developmental level, whereas it is completely absent among High Modern nations and characterizes only two countries in the Low Modern group, China (Taiwan) and Haiti.

The Low Modern group of nations shows the greatest diversity of patterns; 18 percent are high on both hostility and amity but low in transaction level. This is explained, however, by the nondiplomatic transaction measure. These countries do not have direct passenger flight connections with many other nations. If one uses the diplomatic transaction measure only, all of these four nations move to the first cell, and we find ten Low Modern nations showing the high-hostility, high-amity, high-involvement pattern. We thus find that among countries lowest in economic development there is a large proportion of high participants in international affairs.

A transactional posture that is peculiar to nations at the low end of the developmental continuum is a higher level of amicable than hostile transactions with a low interaction level. Again, however, this picture is a function of the combined transaction index, not of diplomatic transactional level alone. If we substitute purely diplomatic transactions as our measure of interaction, three countries move to the left into the high-amity, low-hostility, high-interaction cell, indicating a supportive transactional posture. This pattern is not confined to this developmental level; it also characterizes two High Modern and three Mid-Modern nations.

We may thus distinguish four transactional postures in internation relations: the High Participant posture, the Withdrawal posture, the Feuding posture, and, to some degree, the Supportive posture. Do these postures depend upon developmental level? This is difficult to answer from the data and might be argued either way. Participants and Withdrawers are found at all levels of development, to an extent that we did not anticipate, at least not for the High Participant posture. Evidently, a low level of economic development does not prevent a nation from being a High Participant in international affairs in the sense of wielding considerable hostile and amicable weight. The one pattern which does seem to be tied to developmental level is what we have dubbed the Feuding posture. Why should this be the case? Returning to the correlation matrix, it does appear that aggression is a function of GNP and population, which are measures of international "power," in both High Modern and Low Modern countries. In the Mid-Modern group, however, the correlations to GNP and to population are both negative, using the 7-point aggression scale ($-.26$ and $-.23$, respectively). It appears to be the smaller countries that are engaging in the feuding. Also, whereas for High Modern countries external amity is also related to GNP and population ($r = .55$ and $.49$, respectively), this is not the case for the Low Modern group ($r = .06$ and $.05$). With Mid-Modern countries, however, there is a positive relationship, albeit a small one ($r = .21$ and $.22$) between external amity and the two measures of "power." We might hazard the interpretation that "power" may lead to both hostile and amicable relations among High Modern nations, whereas it leads to more amicable behavior at the Mid-Modern level and to more hostile behavior at the Low Modern level. On the other hand, the correlations are small on which to make such generalizations and the theoretical argument that is advanced below is not based on these considerations of wealth and size.

Since these data on internation transactions are descriptive of the world at a particular point in time, it is necessary to clarify the world situation between 1955 and 1961. Many conflicts of today were not then in existence. The Korean war had terminated and large-scale U.S. involvement in Vietnam had not begun. Thus, the U.S. was not involved in war. The U.S.S.R. was severely at odds with Hungary; the U.K., France, and Israel were attacking Egypt and Syria.

These patterns are given in Figures 1 and 2 which depict, in sociographic form, the hostile and amicable relations of the world during the time period. Only dyadic transactions based on a frequency in excess of fifteen interactions are included in the tables, for purposes of clarity of exposition. Total transactions occurring between dyads during the seven years are summed to yield average value, which will indicate either net hostility or net amity. A high net score on either affective dimension is distinguished from a low net score by a double versus a single line; also, frequency of interactions (above the base level, fifteen) are divided into high and low levels and distinguished by continuous and dotted lines.

In Figures 1 and 2 we find reflected the Cold War pattern of the world as well as those nations which attempt to bridge both camps and those which have their own private involvements relatively undisturbed by the major currents. While a great many patterns of interest can be gleaned from both international sociograms, the dominant pattern which emerges is the bipolarity of structure

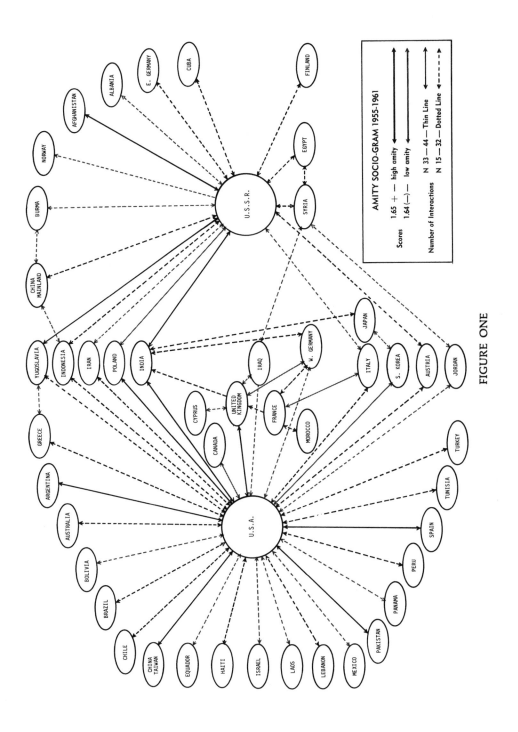

FIGURE ONE

AMITY SOCIO-GRAM 1955-1961

Scores   1.65 + — high amity
         1.64 (—) — low amity

Number of Interactions   N 33 — 44 — Thin Line
                         N 15 — 32 — Dotted Line

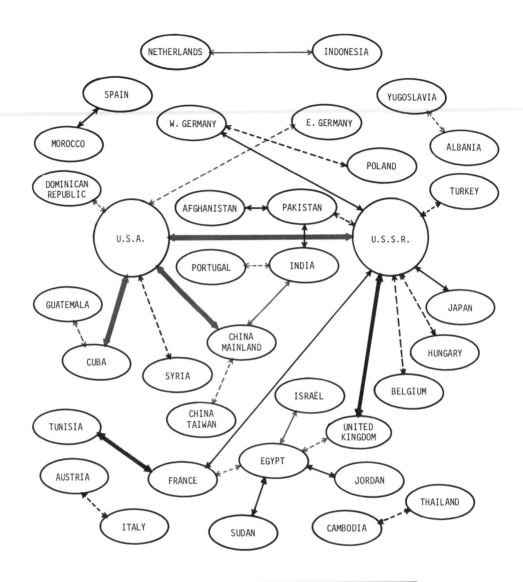

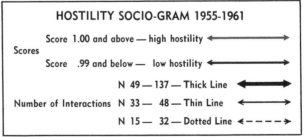

HOSTILITY SOCIO-GRAM 1955-1961

Scores

Score 1.00 and above — high hostility

Score .99 and below — low hostility

Number of Interactions

N 49 — 137 — Thick Line

N 33 — 48 — Thin Line

N 15 — 32 — Dotted Line

FIGURE TWO

produced by the weight of the United States and the Soviet Union. In this respect our data substantiate, on a quantitative level, the usual perception of international relations.

Beyond this structure, we also find in Figure 2 the hostilities between dyads which are reflected in the correlation matrix and the tables of transactional levels. Hostility between the Netherlands and Indonesia, Thailand and Cambodia, Tunisia and France, Spain and Morocco, Guatemala and Cuba, Afghanistan and Pakistan, Yugoslavia and Albania, Austria and Italy, China (mainland) and China (Taiwan), Portugal and India supplements the more far-reaching hostile transactional involvements of Egypt and especially of the two major powers, the U.S. and the U.S.S.R.

If the number of hostile dyads distressing the world seems to present a bleak portrait, however, we must stress that in sheer frequency, amicable dyadic interactions exceed hostile ones, 3 to 1. We have 295 internation dyadic interactions based on a frequency of fifteen or more transactions during the seven-year period. Of these, 219 yield a net amity score and 76 a net hostility score. Although the data are obviously not complete and do not provide an index to the total number of internation transactions occurring between dyads during the seven-year period, we have no reason to suspect systematic bias in reporting more amicable than hostile transactions. On the contrary, if there is bias, it lies in the opposite direction. Conflict is far more newsworthy than day-to-day peaceful interaction. Thus, we may have some confidence that the ratio is more or less correct and that there are more pairs of nations which, on balance, strike an amicable note than ones which are weighted toward hostility.

The findings reported are descriptive, and undoubtedly many more patterns could be unraveled in the data using other analyses and alternative perspectives. It is tempting to pursue the question as to why these patterns and relationships occur in international relations. Perhaps we could bring forth some theoretical insights, formulate hypotheses, and seek their substantiation in the empirical findings. For the present, we will focus on one empirical finding which appears in the global patterning and which is reported in Tables 6 and 7. This concerns the difference in level of external aggression characterizing the different levels of development. Can we offer an adequate explanation for this pattern?

The nonmodern nations (the Mid-Modern as well as the Low Modern) are more externally aggressive in their international behavior than is the High Modern group. This observation holds for the overall sample of countries and is especially striking when we omit the major powers from the sample. We may illustrate this relationship through another data treatment which also indicates country positions on modernity and external aggression. By dividing the sample of nations on the modernity continuum, we create a modern and a nonmodern group of nations. The same division may be made on the variable of external aggression, dividing the sample of nations at the median on the 4-point external aggression scale, into a peaceful and an aggressive group. If we then compare these broad modernity groupings for level of external aggression, we have a fourfold contingency table. (See Table 9.)

Although the relationship between development and external aggression is not overriding, there is apparent in the table a tendency for modern countries to be peaceful and for nonmodern nations to be externally aggressive. We may ask why this difference between modern and nonmodern nations should occur. The answer suggested lies along lines which we have explored in our previous research on internal political aggression.[25] Identifying internal conflict as systemic aggressive behavior, we applied the frustration-aggression hypothesis [26] to the problem.

Much has been written since 1939 regarding the validity of this hypothesis and many refinements in interpretation have been suggested.[27] Nevertheless, for the purpose of rough and preliminary investigation, the basic hypothesis as originally stated, with only slight modification, seemed applicable to the prediction of political aggression. Identifying political instability as a form of systemic aggression, we restated the hypothesis as follows: Systemic aggression is the result of systemic frustration.[28]

It is suggested that a similar theoretical framework is applicable to expressions of external hostility and aggression. Undoubtedly, individual items in the Rummel-Tanter data on external conflict denote aggressive events of various levels of intensity, as do our own data collections. With this view of external aggression as comprising a diverse set of behaviors of varying levels of hostility, it is plausible to seek the explanation of external systemic aggression in some of the sources of systemic frustration. When we add the variable of external systemic aggression, the systemic frustration–systemic aggression framework generates the following set of hypotheses:

1. The higher the level of systemic frustration within a polity, the higher the consequent level of systemic aggression, which may be expressed either in the form of internal political instability or in external conflict and hostility, or in both forms of aggression.

2. Sources of systemic frustration within a society identified in previous studies consist of: (a) the discrepancy between socioeconomic wants and socioeconomic satisfactions; (b) a high rate of change on socioeconomic indicators; and (c) the coerciveness level of the political regime.

3. Thus, the greater these three sources of systemic frustration, the higher the level of external as well as of internal aggression.

This formulation gains support if we remember that by and large the non-modern countries are more systemically frustrated than are the highly developed nations. Perhaps the low level of modernity itself is a source of frustration, either confounding other sources of frustration or contributing to them.

One point to be considered in these hypotheses is whether external aggression should be viewed as a form of displaced aggression. The notion of displaced aggression forms an integral portion of the frustration-aggression hypothesis. According to Dollard, *et al.*, if aggression against the agent perceived to be the source of frustration is inhibited due to a fear of punishment, the aggressive impulse may be vented on other substitute objects.[29] Translating the notion of displacement into political terms yields the proposition that when a regime is sufficiently coercive to inhibit acts of aggression against itself, this aggressive impulse on the part of the populace may be directed elsewhere, often against external targets. This proposition, that nations resort to external hostility in order to divert the attention of dissatisfied segments of the population, has its supporters.[30] And the proposition could be investigated empirically using data on internal and external conflict. It must be said, however, that in this study no attempt is made to investigate displacement of aggression from the internal to the external sphere. As a first foray into the area of international conflict using the frustration-aggression framework, it is merely claimed in the hypotheses stated above that both forms of systemic aggression, the internal and the external, co-vary with level of systemic frustration.

In order to investigate the hypotheses underlying this study, namely, that level of external aggression co-varies with level of systemic frustration, we may check back to the correlational matrix of Table 5. Frustration level may be described in terms of three of our indexes: relative socioeconomic deprivation (systemic frustration index), rate of change on selected socioeconomic indicators, and level of coerciveness or permissiveness of political regime. We know from our previous research that there is a relationship between our measures of systemic frustration and internal political instability.[31] The systemic frustration index, 1948–1955, is related to political instability with a correlation of .50 for instability measured in the 1955–1961 time period and $r = .58$ for the 1948–1962 time period. Rate of socioeconomic change, 1935–1962, is correlated .57 with instability, 1955–1961, and .68 for instability, 1948–1962. Level of coerciveness of the political regime is correlated .41 with instability, 1955–1961, and .51 with instability, 1948–1962. Actually, coerciveness is curvilinearly related to political unrest, with countries at the extreme coerciveness position (that is, countries lying at point 6 on the coerciveness scale), experiencing less political unrest than countries at mid-coerciveness positions 4 and 5. (The *eta* describing this relationship is .72, which is a significant improvement over the *r* obtained. $F = 14.02$, $p < .001$.)

If we look now at Table 5 to see what predictive value these three indexes have for level of external aggression, we find that there are only small positive correlations ranging from .20 to .30 between these measures and level of external aggression, measured on either a 7-point or a 4-point scale. Nor do these correlations increase within the various modernity subgroupings. As we have pointed out earlier, however, level of political unrest does show a stronger relationship to both scalings of external aggression. Also, the correlations between political instability and external aggression increase within particular modernity subgroupings.

As an alternative way of treating the data, each systemic frustration and systemic aggression index was divided close to or at the median, thus dividing the sample of nations into two approximately equal groups, one of high- and one of low-scoring nations on the variable measured. The relationship between these various indexes is given in Table 10. This and the following tables have the advantage that specific names of countries may be identified.

In Table 10, countries are characterized as frustrated if they were assigned a high score on at least two of the three indexes of systemic frustration. Similarly, countries are classed as satisfied if they scored low on two or more of these three frustration indexes. Furthermore, countries are divided into three groups with respect to the variables of systemic aggression: peaceful and stable countries, aggressive and unstable countries, and a mixed category combining peaceful-unstable and stable-aggressive countries.

The consistent relationship between the variables of systemic frustration and systemic aggression emerges in Table 10. Of eighteen stable, peaceful countries, fourteen are satisfied and only four deviate from the prediction. In the mixed category, countries are equally divided between those that are frustrated and those that are satisfied. And thirteen countries are characterized as frustrated and appear as both externally aggressive and politically unstable, whereas six countries go against the hypothesis. The Chi square for this relationship is 7.99, with a probability level of less than .02.

The strength of the relationship between external and internal aggression using the 4-point scaling of external aggression is indicated in Table 11. As may be seen in this table, of thirty-two stable countries, twenty-three (that is, almost three-quarters) are peaceful and only nine are externally aggressive. And of thirty-five unstable countries, twenty-three are externally aggressive, and the remainder are peaceful.

This finding is of particular interest, since it has been both denied and asserted by different researchers. Rummel, for example, as a result of factor-analyzing variables of internal and external conflict, asserts that the two dimensions are unrelated.[32] Tanter finds a very small relationship between the two.[33] Denton, using factor analysis, finds some relationship between level of civil strife and the occurrence of large-scale war.[34] And Haas finds that levels of domestic violence first increase and then decrease—several years before the onset of external conflict.[35] Most recently, Wilkenfeld intercorrelated country scores on Rummel's three dimensions of external conflict with scores on his three dimensions of internal conflict for countries falling within the different political groupings identified by Banks and Gregg [36] and found substantial intercorrelations within groupings.[37]

The moderately high correlation between political instability and external aggression, as well as the moderately strong relationship between systemic frustration and political instability, suggested yet another treatment of the data. An expanded table was constructed employing sixteen possible dichotomized combinations of the independent variable and four possible combinations of the two forms of systemic aggression. As may be noticed in Table 12, satisfaction-frustration, high change-low change, permissiveness-coerciveness, and modern-nonmodern in the columns, and stability-instability and peacefulness-aggression in the rows, are arranged in all possible combinations. The columns are ordered from highest satisfaction to highest frustration levels. Between these two extremes are countries satisfied on two or three, or frustrated on two or three of the four indexes. The center of the table separates the four satisfaction from the four frustration categories. Similarly, the rows of the table are ordered from the peaceful-stable category to the aggressive-unstable one.

The groupings of countries in the table supports the notion that syndromes may be identified in the present-day international arena. In the upper left-hand cell of Table 12, a potential nonaggression pattern may be identified. Here are ten highly developed modern countries (Canada, Denmark, Finland, Ireland, the Netherlands, New Zealand, Norway, Sweden, Switzerland, and Uruguay) which are at the same time satisfied on three measures of possible systemic frustration and which are also relatively peaceful and stable. These countries enjoy permissive political regimes, experience low rates of change on ecological variables, and have a small discrepancy between social want formation and social want satisfaction. As may be seen, this is the most populated cell in the table. There are seven additional countries distributed among the remaining cells of the two extreme left-hand columns, and none possesses a trait combination that would represent an extreme deviation from the alleged syndrome of six traits. The lower left-hand cell of the table remains empty; Belgium is peaceful but unstable, as is Italy (which is of mid-modern development). Australia, Israel, and West Germany are aggressive but stable, but Mexico and Pakistan are midmodern and low modern countries, respectively, which are both aggressive and unstable.

At the other extreme, in the lower right-hand cell of the table, are countries illustrative of a possible external-aggression syndrome. Of the twelve countries in the extreme right-hand column, six or 50 percent are collected in this cell: Egypt, Haiti, Iraq, Nicaragua, South Korea, and Venezuela. They register as frustrated on the same three measures of systemic frustration, are nonmodern, unstable, and externally aggressive. Again, as may be seen, this is the second most-populated cell in the table. Only El Salvador, a mid-modern country, is peaceful and stable despite being frustrated, coercive, and a high changer, constituting the extreme deviant from the external-aggression syndrome. It should be noted that there are no high modern countries in this group.

It may also be seen that countries which experience satisfaction on three measures, and frustration on only one, also fit generally the notion of the nonaggression syndrome, whereas countries frustrated on three indexes and satisfied on one only predominantly partake of the external-aggression syndrome. Thus, of eighteen peaceful, stable countries, eleven are satisfied on three or four indicators, and of nineteen aggressive, unstable countries, fourteen are frustrated on three or four measures (leaving five deviant countries).

Another finding concerns the deviant countries that are peaceful and unstable, or stable and aggressive, recorded in the two middle rows of the table. The combination of peacefulness and instability occurs fairly frequently, although not as frequently as the two syndrome combinations of peace and stability or external aggression and political instability. There are eleven countries in the sample which combine the pattern of external peace and internal instability and among these only Belgium is a highly developed modern country. Seven of these stem from the group of countries which are frustrated on three or four indexes.

On the other hand, the combination of internal stability and external aggression is rather rare, as was also seen in the larger sample of countries (see Table 11). Only five countries from the 53 in this table (Australia, Costa Rica, Israel, West Germany, and Yugoslavia) show this pattern. And these are all among the more highly developed countries (either high modern or among the more highly developed nations of the mid-modern group). This is in striking contrast to the previous pattern of peace and internal instability which favors the less developed countries. Looking at the marginals of the expanded table, this is the rarest combination that occurs and provides further evidence of the underlying relationship between internal and external aggression. It is also striking that in frustrated countries this pattern is almost nonexistent. Only one of the frustrated countries in the sample, Yugoslavia, is stable and externally aggressive.

It is in this respect that the external-aggression pattern finds an important interpretation. In the face of systemic frustration, although the impulse to external aggression seems by far less compelling than the impulse to internal instability, it has a greater probability of occurrence if the country is also unstable. It may be that instability is a catalyst or mediating variable for internation aggression. Systemic frustration, measured here as a combination of the discrepancy between wants and satisfactions, coerciveness, high change, and low modernity, may rather be considered the instigating variable to aggression. And if one considers internal and external aggression as two possible manifestations of the same aggressive impulse, then the relationship between social frustration and some form of political aggression is quite strong. Of twelve countries frustrated on all indicators, only one does not experience either internal or external aggression. And of twenty-five countries frustrated on three or four indicators, only four countries show this deviation.

The fact that other patterns of frustration-aggression are also evidenced in other cells of the table, however, points up the fact that there is less than perfect predictability of either external aggression or nonaggression. Nevertheless, the possibility for prediction of a nation's behavior in the international sphere is improved by knowing its level both of systemic frustration and of political instability.

On the basis of these findings, one might characterize the external-aggression pattern by saying that the nonmodern country which is sufficiently frustrated to be politically unstable has the strongest probability of also being externally aggressive. Conversely, the nonaggression syndrome seems to indicate that the modern satisfied country has the greatest probability of being both internally stable and externally nonaggressive. This finding is qualified, however, by the overriding demands of international relations in the case of major powers, which were excluded from the sample under investigation. The status of the major powers in the international political system seems to follow a pattern of behavior *sui generis*, although the fact that they come predominantly from the high modern group of nations does suggest the influence of level of development.

TABLE ONE

PROFILES: EXTERNAL AGGRESSION, 1955–1961, 7-POINT SCALE

1	2	3	4
			52 Iraq 4011
			50.5 Greece 4005
			50.5 East Germany 4005
			49 Poland 4005
			48 Yugoslavia 4005
			47 West Germany 4005
			46 Ghana 4004
			45 Venezuela 4004
			44 Austria 4003
			43 Domin. Republ. 4003
			3rd Quartile
			42 Guatemala 4003
			41 Chile 4002
			39.5 Un. So. Africa 4002
			39.5 Colombia 4002
			37 Mexico 4002
			37 Ecuador 4002
			37 Saudi Arabia 4002
			35 Uruguay 4002
			33.5 Iran 4002
			33.5 Panama 4002
			32 Cambodia 4002
			31 Norway 4001
		19 Japan 30053	29.5 Brazil 4001
		17.5 Libya 30021	29.5 Belgium 4001
		17.5 Canada 30021	28 Czechoslovakia 4001
		16 Bulgaria 30019	26.5 El Salvador 4001
		15 Denmark 30017	26.5 Peru 4001
		14 Italy 30015	25 Ethiopia 4001
		12.5 Switzerland 30014	23.5 Sweden 4001
		12.5 S. Korea 30014	23.5 Malaya 4001
		11 Romania 30010	22 Liberia 4010
		9.5 Cyprus 30009	**2nd Quartile**
3 Ceylon 10005	6 New Zeal. 20021	9.5 Philippines 30009	
2 Ireland 10001	5 Bolivia 20012	8 Finland 30007	21 Sudan 4000
1 Luxembourg 0	4 Laos 20004	7 Australia 30004	20 Iceland 4000
1st Quartile			

5	6	7

68	United States	50481			
67	China (Mainland)	50156			
66	Tunisia	50153			
65	Indonesia	50125			
64	Cuba	50107	82	Egypt	60219

4th Quartile

63	China (Taiwan)	50075	79	France	60156			
61.5	Turkey	50052	78	India	60140			
61.5	Argentina	50052	77	Jordan	60122			
60	Netherlands	50050	76	Syria	60117			
59	Lebanon	50044	75	Morocco	60104			
58	Thailand	50040	74	Pakistan	60068			
57	Burma	50037	72.5	Afghanis.	60047			
56	Honduras	50023	72.5	Nicaragua	60047			
55	Albania	50020	71	Spain	60040			
54	Haiti	50016	70	Costa Rica	60037	84	U.S.S.R.	70471
53	Paraguay	50015	69	Portugal	60027	83	Hungary	70401

81 Israel 60215
80 Un. King. 60194

TABLE TWO

PROFILES: EXTERNAL AMITY, 1955–1961

1	2	3	4
		78 U.S.S.R. 41035	
		77 West Germany 40493	
		76 India 40397	
		75 Japan 40365	
		74 Yugoslavia 40260	
		73 Poland 40292	
		72 Italy 40266	
		71 Indonesia 40260	
		70 Pakistan 40243	
		69 Iran 40231	
		68 Turkey 40210	
		67 Egypt 40207	
		66 Jordan 40202	
		65 Tunisia 40177	
		64 Morocco 40174	
		4th Quartile	
		63 Afghanistan 40172	
		62 East Germany 40170	
		61 Brazil 40166	
		60 Ghana 40163	
		59 Greece 40153	
		58 Burma 40150	
		57 Argentina 40146	
		56 Canada 40138	
		55 Czechoslovakia 40137	
		54 China (Mnland) 40130	
		53 Cuba 40127	
		51.5 Israel 40117	
		51.5 Ethiopia 40117	

Rank	Country	Score
84	United States	52000
83	Unit.Kingdom	50704
82	France	50423
81	Iraq	50236
80	Saudi Arabia	50130
79	Syria	50126

Rank	Country	Score
50	Austria	40109
49	Lebanon	40106
48	Mexico	40101
47	Hungary	40090
46	Finland	40088
45	Sudan	40087
43.5	Malaya	40086
43.5	Cambodia	40086

3rd Quartile

Rank	Country	Score
42	Peru	40075
40.5	Belgium	40074
40.5	Australia	40074
39	China (Taiwan)	40073
38	Ceylon	40071
37	Bulgaria	40070
36	Switzerland	40068
35	Thailand	40066
34	Cyprus	40063
33	Albania	40059
32	Libya	40058
31	Netherlands	40051
29.5	Philippines	40050
29.5	Guatemala	40050
28	Sweden	40044
26.5	Un. So. Africa	40042
26.5	Denmark	40042
25	Portugal	40039
24	Haiti	40038
23	Ecuador	40034
22	Venezuela	40033

2nd Quartile

Rank	Country	Score
21	Colombia	40031
20	Uruguay	40025
19	Ireland	40020

Rank	Country	Score
18	Spain	30192
17	New Zealand	30102
16	Romania	30097
15	Norway	30088
14	Chile	30073
13	Bolivia	30056
12	So. Korea	30046
11	Laos	30045
10	Nicaragua	30043
9	Iceland	30042
8	Panama	30035
7	Costa Rica	30034
6	El Salvador	30030
5	Paraguay	30028
4	Liberia	30027
3	Luxembourg	30017
2	Dom. Repub.	30014

1st Quartile

Rank	Country	Score
1	Honduras	20041

TABLE THREE

FREQUENCY DISTRIBUTION OF COUNTRIES IN TERMS OF THEIR DEGREE OF RELATIVE POLITICAL STABILITY, 1955–1961

(stability score shown for each country)

0	1	2	3	4	5	6
N. Zealand 000	Norway 104	W. Germany 217	Tunisia 328	France 499	India 599	Indonesia 699
	Netherlands 104	Czech. 212	G. Britain 325	U. of S. Africa 495	Argentina 599	Cuba 699
	Cambodia 104	Finland 211	Portugal 323	Haiti 478	Korea 596	Colombia 681
	Sweden 103	Romania 206	Uruguay 318	Poland 465	Venezuela 584	Laos 652
	Saudi Arabia 103	Ireland 202	Israel 317	Spain 463	Turkey 583	Hungary 652
	Iceland 103	Costa Rica 202	Canada 317	Dom. Rep. 463	Lebanon 581	
	Philippines 101		U.S. 316	Iran 459	Iraq 579	
	Luxembourg 101		Taiwan 314	Ceylon 454	Bolivia 556	
			Libya 309	Japan 453	Syria 554	
			Austria 309	Thailand 451	Peru 552	
			E. Germany 307	Mexico 451	Guatemala 546	
			Ethiopia 307	Ghana 451	Brazil 541	
			Denmark 306	Jordan 448	Honduras 535	
			Australia 306	Sudan 445	Cyprus 526	
			Switzer. 303	Morocco 443		
				Egypt 438		
				Pakistan 437		
				Italy 433		
				Belgium 432		
				Paraguay 431		
				U.S.S.R. 430		
				Nicaragua 430		
				Chile 427		
				Burma 427		
				Yugoslavia 422		
				Panama 422		
				Ecuador 422		
				China 422		
				El Salvador 421		
				Liberia 415		
				Malaya 413		
				Albania 412		
				Greece 409		
				Bulgaria 407		
				Afghanistan 404		

Stability ——— 0 ——— 1 ——— 2 ——— 3 ——— 4 ——— 5 ——— 6 Instability

TABLE FOUR

MODERNITY INDEX

	Country	Score	Country	Score	
	United States	2.54	Colombia	−.20	
	New Zealand	1.91	Lebanon	−.21	
	Switzerland	1.83	Mexico	−.21	
	Australia	1.71	Brazil	−.23	
	Sweden	1.70	Paraguay	−.26	
	Denmark	1.54	Peru	−.30	
↓	United Kingdom	1.51	Turkey	−.36	↓ Mid
High	Canada	1.49	Ecuador	−.37	Modern
Modern	Norway	1.41	El Salvador	−.40	↑
↑	Iceland	1.26	Nicaragua	−.40	
	Luxembourg	1.07	Ceylon	−.41	
	Belgium	.94	Guatemala	−.41	
	Ireland	.93	Dominican Repub.	−.46	
	Netherlands	.89	Honduras	−.46	
	Finland	.81	Egypt	−.47	
	France	.80	Korea	−.49	
	Austria	.61	Syria	−.49	
	W. Germany	.59	Thailand	−.49	
	Argentina	.57	Tunisia	−.49	
	E. Germany	.50	Morocco	−.50	
	Uruguay	.47	Philippines	−.50	
	Israel	.46	Burma	−.53	
	U.S.S.R.	.40	Taiwan	−.53	
	Czechoslovakia	.34	Jordan	−.54	
	Hungary	.24	Bolivia	−.56	
	Japan	.20	Iraq	−.57	
	Bulgaria	.19	Ethiopia	−.60	
	Poland	.19	Iran	−.62	
↓	Romania	.12	China	−.65	↓ Low
Mid	Italy	.11	Ghana	−.67	Modern
Modern	Cuba	.10	India	−.70	↑
	Chile	.07	Malaya	−.73	
	Costa Rica	.03	Haiti	−.74	
	Panama	.01	Libya	−.77	
	Spain	.00	Pakistan	−.87	
	Union of S. Africa	−.04	Afghanistan	−.97	
	Cyprus	−.05	Saudi Arabia	−.98	
	Greece	−.06	Indonesia	−1.13	
	Yugoslavia	−.09	Laos	−1.25	
	Albania	−.10	Sudan	−1.37	
	Venezuela	−.10	Cambodia	−1.46	
↓	Portugal	−.16	Liberia	−1.62	↓

TABLE FIVE

PRODUCT-MOMENT CORRELATIONS AMONG INTERNATION AND ECOLOGICAL VARIABLES

		1 Ext. Aggr. 7-pt.	2 Ext. Aggr. 4-pt.	3 Ext. Amity	4 Net Aggr. Target	5 Net Aggr. Initi.	6 War Dim.	7 Dipl. Dim.	8 Bellig. Dim.	9 Dipl. Inter.	10 Flights Countr.	11 Flights No.	12 For. Mail
	84		[.52] (72)	.24 (84)	[.41] (84)	[.51] (84)	[.58] (71)	.38 (71)	.30 (72)	.37 (84)	.23 (82)	.11 (82)	[−.47] (51)
	84 WMP		[.49] (67)	.15 (79)	[.43] (79)	[.55] (79)	[.51] (66)	.29 (66)	.21 (67)	.32 (79)	.09 (77)	−.07 (77)	[−.52] (48)
	HI MOD		[.60] (21)	[.57] (24)	[.43] (24)	[.42] (24)	[.72] (21)	[.54] (21)	−.03 (21)	[.60] (24)	[.57] (24)	.33 (24)	[−.67] (20)
1 Ext. Aggr. 7-pt. Scale	HI MOD WMP		[.44] (17)	.38 (20)	[.47] (20)	[.46] (20)	[.53] (17)	.23 (17)	.06 (17)	[.54] (20)	.35 (20)	.10 (20)	[−.67] (17)
	MID-MOD		[.47] (34)	−.02 (37)	[.52] (37)	[.66] (37)	[.53] (34)	.33 (34)	.17 (34)	.06 (37)	.02 (36)	−.05 (36)	−.01 (20)
	LO MOD		[.40] (17)	.36 (23)	.27 (23)	[.44] (23)	[.55] (16)	.21 (16)	.24 (17)	[.50] (23)	.35 (22)	[.40] (22)	−.27 (11)
	LO MOD WMP		.39 (16)	.36 (22)	.28 (22)	[.43] (22)	[.55] (15)	.24 (15)	.26 (16)	[.55] (22)	.38 (21)	[.43] (21)	−.27 (11)
	84			.20 (72)	.10 (72)	.26 (72)	.30 (70)	.31 (70)	.19 (70)	.31 (72)	.08 (71)	.08 (71)	−.33 (42)
	84 WMP			.12 (67)	.10 (67)	.28 (67)	.24 (65)	.27 (65)	.23 (65)	.29 (67)	−.05 (66)	−.08 (66)	−.35 (39)
	HI MOD			[.55] (21)	.15 (21)	.32 (21)	[.48] (20)	[.40] (20)	−.20 (20)	[.51] (21)	[.42] (21)	[.40] (21)	−.26 (17)
2 Ext. Aggr. 4-pt. Scale	HI MOD WMP			[.41] (17)	.12 (17)	.31 (17)	.33 (16)	.15 (16)	−.16 (17)	[.51] (17)	.16 (17)	.24 (17)	−.21 (14)
	MID-MOD			−.07 (34)	.13 (34)	.34 (34)	.24 (34)	.28 (34)	.24 (34)	.05 (34)	−.02 (34)	−.12 (34)	−.21 (19)
	LO MOD			[.48] (17)	−.13 (17)	−.05 (17)	.07 (16)	[.41] (16)	.33 (16)	[.47] (17)	.27 (16)	.26 (16)	[.45] (6)
	LO MOD WMP			[.48] (16)	−.12 (16)	−.09 (16)	.02 (15)	[.45] (15)	.37 (15)	[.48] (16)	.33 (15)	.30 (15)	[.45] (6)

13 Trade	14 Milit. Pers.	15 Defense Exp.	16 GNP	17 GNP p/cap.	18 Pop.	19 Area	20 Instab. 7-yr.	21 Instab. 15-yr.	22 Frustr.	23 Mod.	24 Coerc.	25 Change	26 NAch 1950	27 NAch 1925
−.38 (70)	.15 (82)	.28 (73)	.18 (84)	−.17 (84)	.24 (84)	.20 (84)	.28 (84)	.32 (82)	−.01 (61)	−.17 (84)	.27 (84)	.20 (78)	.28 (39)	[−.49] (23)
−.30 (65)	.09 (77)	.20 (68)	−.05 (79)	−.35 (79)	.19 (79)	−.07 (79)	.29 (79)	.37 (77)	.07 (58)	−.30 (79)	.32 (79)	.28 (73)	.29 (35)	[−.56] (19)
[−.59] (21)	[.59] (23)	[.78] (20)	.34 (24)	−.13 (24)	[.58] (24)	.39 (24)	[.52] (24)	[.53] (24)	.22 (21)	−.23 (24)	.29 (24)	.27 (24)	.17 (20)	[−.53] (18)
−.31 (17)	[.44] (19)	[.58] (16)	.13 (20)	−.37 (20)	.25 (20)	−.07 (20)	.37 (20)	[.54] (20)	.27 (18)	[−.41] (20)	.21 (20)	.13 (20)	.10 (16)	[−.63] (14)
−.05 (32)	−.04 (36)	.11 (31)	−.26 (37)	−.10 (37)	−.23 (37)	−.06 (37)	.06 (37)	.34 (36)	.20 (31)	−.08 (37)	.20 (37)	.04 (35)	.33 (15)	.33 (5)
−.51 (17)	.10 (23)	.21 (22)	.31 (23)	−.06 (23)	.32 (23)	.14 (23)	.11 (23)	−.06 (22)	[−.73] (9)	.18 (23)	.16 (23)	.13 (19)	[.84] (4)	(0)
[−.50] (16)	.11 (22)	.22 (21)	.37 (22)	.04 (22)	.39 (22)	.07 (22)	.11 (22)	−.10 (21)	[−.73] (9)	.17 (22)	.12 (22)	.12 (18)	[.84] (4)	(0)
[−.47] (60)	.11 (72)	.31 (64)	.18 (72)	−.17 (72)	.21 (72)	.21 (72)	[.43] (72)	.39 (72)	.25 (56)	−.22 (72)	.20 (72)	.25 (67)	.35 (36)	−.03 (22)
[−.42] (55)	.08 (67)	.26 (59)	−.002 (67)	−.34 (67)	.14 (67)	.10 (67)	[.45] (67)	[.42] (67)	.33 (53)	−.34 (67)	.24 (67)	.32 (62)	.34 (32)	−.004 (18)
[−.61] (18)	.26 (21)	[.53] (19)	.38 (21)	−.04 (21)	[.48] (21)	.38 (21)	[.60] (21)	[.45] (21)	.32 (19)	−.22 (21)	.23 (21)	.22 (21)	[.45] (19)	.05 (17)
[−.44] (14)	.05 (17)	.23 (15)	.30 (17)	−.29 (17)	.39 (17)	.23 (17)	[.53] (17)	[.44] (17)	[.40] (17)	[−.44] (16)	.21 (17)	.23 (17)	[.44] (15)	.21 (13)
−.17 (29)	.06 (34)	.20 (29)	−.21 (34)	.01 (34)	−.19 (34)	.04 (34)	[.43] (34)	.33 (34)	−.09 (29)	−.20 (34)	.06 (34)	−.03 (33)	.21 (13)	[.87] (5)
[−.68] (13)	.18 (17)	.39 (16)	.28 (17)	−.14 (17)	.28 (17)	.24 (17)	.21 (17)	.34 (17)	[−.78] (17)	[.53] (11)	.03 (17)	.18 (13)	[.90] (4)	(0)
[−.67] (12)	−.09 (22)	.06 (21)	.25 (16)	−.11 (16)	.25 (16)	.22 (16)	.21 (16)	.31 (16)	[−.78] (8)	[−.52] (16)	−.06 (16)	.15 (12)	[.90] (4)	(0)

		1 Ext. Aggr. 7-pt.	2 Ext. Aggr. 4-pt.	3 Ext. Amity	4 Net Aggr. Target	5 Net Aggr. Initi.	6 War Dim.	7 Dipl. Dim.	8 Bellig. Dim.	9 Dipl. Inter.	10 Flights Countr.	11 Flights No.	12 For. Mail
	84				−.20 (84)	[−.48] (84)	.28 (71)	.19 (71)	.09 (72)	[.45] (84)	[.48] (82)	[.41] (82)	−.04 (51)
	84 WMP				−.23 (79)	[−.51] (79)	.09 (66)	.09 (66)	.14 (67)	[.43] (79)	.32 (77)	.16 (77)	−.07 (48)
	HI MOD				.11 (24)	−.18 (24)	[.48] (21)	.36 (21)	−.04 (21)	[.60] (24)	[.82] (24)	[.72] (24)	−.27 (20)
3 Ext. Amity	HI MOD WMP				.10 (20)	−.29 (20)	.09 (17)	.22 (17)	.07 (17)	.27 (20)	[.62] (20)	.38 (20)	−.18 (17)
	MID-MOD				−.26 (37)	[−.57] (37)	.05 (34)	.08 (34)	.06 (34)	[.44] (37)	.33 (36)	.18 (36)	.25 (20)
	LO MOD				−.27 (23)	[−.41] (23)	.33 (16)	.39 (16)	.12 (17)	[.43] (23)	.30 (22)	.17 (22)	.27 (11)
	LO MOD WMP				−.27 (22)	[−.43] (22)	.35 (15)	[.40] (15)	.12 (16)	[.55] (22)	.31 (21)	.17 (21)	.27 (11)
	84					[.65] (84)	.23 (71)	.16 (71)	−.17 (72)	−.10 (84)	−.19 (82)	−.13 (82)	.005 (51)
	84 WMP					[.66] (79)	.27 (66)	.21 (66)	−.17 (67)	−.24 (79)	−.24 (77)	−.19 (77)	−.003 (48)
	HI MOD					[.61] (24)	[.42] (21)	.07 (21)	−.19 (21)	.01 (24)	.07 (24)	−.15 (24)	−.19 (20)
4 Net Aggr. Target	HI MOD WMP					[.59] (20)	[.47] (17)	.06 (17)	−.18 (17)	−.07 (20)	.04 (20)	−.26 (20)	−.21 (17)
	MID-MOD					[.68] (37)	.21 (34)	.38 (34)	−.14 (34)	−.37 (37)	−.39 (36)	−.26 (36)	.17 (20)
	LO MOD					[.63] (23)	.23 (16)	[−.41] (16)	−.26 (17)	−.08 (23)	−.23 (22)	−.02 (22)	[−.41] (11)
	LO MOD WMP					[.65] (22)	.25 (15)	[−.43] (15)	−.27 (16)	−.09 (22)	−.24 (21)	−.03 (21)	[−.41] (11)
	84						.17 (71)	.14 (71)	−.03 (72)	−.14 (84)	−.28 (82)	−.22 (82)	−.18 (51)
	84 WMP						.23 (66)	.20 (66)	−.03 (67)	−.31 (79)	−.31 (77)	−.26 (77)	−.19 (48)
	HI MOD						.38 (21)	.06 (21)	.04 (21)	.03 (24)	−.14 (24)	−.23 (24)	−.17 (20)
5 Net Aggr. Initia-tor	HI MOD WMP						[.47] (17)	.00 (17)	.05 (17)	.02 (20)	−.23 (20)	−.32 (20)	−.19 (17)
	MID-MOD						.19 (32)	.26 (34)	.00 (34)	[−.51] (37)	[−.41] (36)	−.36 (36)	−.11 (20)
	LO MOD						.12 (16)	−.25 (16)	.03 (17)	.02 (23)	−.31 (22)	−.06 (22)	[−.40] (11)
	LO MOD WMP						.06 (15)	−.21 (15)	.06 (16)	−.18 (22)	−.28 (21)	−.03 (21)	[−.40] (11)

13 Trade	14 Milit. Pers.	15 Defense Exp.	16 GNP	17 GNP p/cap.	18 Pop.	19 Area	20 Instab. 7-yr.	21 Instab. 15-yr.	22 Frustr.	23 Mod.	24 Coerc.	25 Change	26 NAch 1950	27 NAch 1925
−.20 (70)	.14 (82)	.23 (73)	.34 (84)	.18 (84)	.16 (84)	.19 (84)	.07 (84)	−.04 (82)	.14 (61)	.10 (84)	−.08 (84)	−.18 (78)	.10 (39)	.15 (23)
−.09 (65)	.06 (77)	.15 (68)	.18 (79)	−.03 (79)	.12 (79)	.15 (79)	.09 (79)	−.001 (77)	−.01 (58)	−.07 (79)	.10 (79)	−.06 (73)	.07 (35)	.22 (19)
[−.52] (21)	.32 (23)	[.54] (20)	[.55] (24)	.24 (24)	[.49] (24)	.21 (24)	[.61] (24)	.33 (24)	.21 (21)	.06 (24)	.10 (24)	.03 (24)	.12 (20)	.04 (18)
−.24 (17)	−.005 (19)	.06 (16)	.34 (20)	−.16 (20)	.37 (20)	.18 (20)	[.62] (20)	.37 (20)	.39 (18)	−.37 (20)	.17 (20)	.31 (20)	−.007 (16)	.19 (14)
.10 (32)	.12 (36)	.13 (31)	.21 (37)	.13 (37)	.22 (37)	.15 (37)	.27 (37)	.17 (36)	.09 (31)	.06 (37)	−.04 (37)	−.22 (35)	.12 (15)	−.21 (5)
[−.60] (17)	.02 (23)	.13 (22)	.06 (23)	.25 (23)	.05 (23)	.09 (23)	−.31 (23)	−.35 (22)	−.009 (9)	.31 (23)	.11 (23)	−.23 (19)	−.08 (4)	(0)
[−.61] (16)	.02 (22)	.13 (21)	.08 (22)	.25 (22)	.06 (22)	.17 (22)	−.31 (22)	−.36 (21)	−.009 (9)	.31 (22)	.12 (22)	−.23 (18)	−.08 (4)	(0)
.12 (70)	.06 (82)	.00 (73)	−.08 (84)	−.17 (84)	−.07 (84)	−.15 (84)	.16 (84)	.13 (82)	.06 (61)	−.11 (84)	.24 (84)	.11 (78)	.12 (39)	−.39 (23)
.12 (65)	.05 (77)	.00 (68)	−.31 (79)	−.19 (79)	−.09 (79)	−.28 (79)	.16 (79)	.13 (77)	.05 (58)	−.11 (79)	.25 (79)	.11 (73)	.11 (35)	−.38 (19)
.15 (21)	[.47] (23)	.12 (20)	−.10 (24)	[−.46] (24)	−.01 (24)	−.11 (24)	.21 (24)	.06 (24)	.18 (21)	−.35 (24)	−.01 (24)	.36 (24)	−.16 (20)	[−.53] (18)
.23 (17)	[.47] (19)	.13 (16)	[−.45] (20)	[−.52] (20)	−.34 (20)	−.36 (20)	.16 (20)	.03 (20)	.15 (18)	−.36 (20)	−.09 (20)	.37 (20)	−.18 (16)	−.51 (14)
.18 (32)	−.11 (36)	.00 (31)	[−.46] (37)	−.15 (37)	[−.48] (37)	−.36 (37)	.12 (37)	.28 (37)	−.001 (36)	−.20 (31)	[.40] (37)	.18 (37)	.29 (15)	.34 (5)
−.01 (17)	.11 (23)	.04 (22)	−.02 (23)	[−.62] (23)	.01 (23)	−.04 (23)	.12 (23)	−.05 (23)	−.23 (22)	−.16 (9)	.28 (23)	−.12 (19)	[.69] (4)	(0)
−.04 (16)	.11 (22)	.04 (21)	.005 (22)	[−.63] (22)	.05 (22)	−.06 (22)	.14 (22)	−.05 (22)	−.23 (21)	−.16 (9)	.32 (22)	−.12 (18)	[.69] (4)	(0)
.05 (70)	.04 (82)	−.03 (73)	−.12 (84)	−.22 (84)	−.03 (84)	−.14 (84)	.13 (84)	.21 (82)	.15 (61)	−.14 (84)	.24 (84)	.20 (78)	.23 (39)	[−.52] (23)
.05 (65)	.05 (77)	−.02 (68)	−.40 (79)	−.21 (79)	−.12 (79)	−.30 (79)	.13 (79)	.21 (77)	.13 (58)	−.12 (79)	.22 (79)	.18 (73)	.24 (35)	[−.53] (19)
.12 (21)	[.41] (23)	.20 (20)	−.10 (24)	−.37 (24)	−.004 (24)	−.11 (24)	−.04 (24)	.03 (24)	.12 (21)	−.26 (24)	.02 (24)	.22 (24)	.04 (20)	[−.53] (18)
.21 (17)	[.42] (19)	.28 (16)	[−.47] (20)	[−.40] (20)	−.35 (20)	[−.43] (20)	−.11 (20)	.01 (20)	.01 (18)	−.22 (20)	−.07 (20)	.14 (20)	.03 (16)	[−.52] (14)
.11 (32)	−.24 (36)	−.14 (31)	[−.61] (37)	−.20 (37)	[−.57] (37)	−.24 (37)	−.09 (37)	.17 (36)	−.07 (31)	−.22 (37)	.24 (37)	.17 (35)	.31 (15)	[.52] (5)
−.05 (17)	.32 (23)	.20 (22)	.24 (23)	−.23 (23)	.26 (23)	.06 (23)	.24 (23)	.14 (22)	−.15 (9)	−.04 (23)	.26 (23)	.07 (19)	[.88] (4)	(0)
.02 (16)	.34 (22)	.23 (21)	.09 (22)	−.21 (22)	.12 (22)	−.36 (22)	.24 (22)	.09 (21)	−.15 (9)	−.07 (22)	.18 (22)	.04 (18)	[.88] (4)	(0)

		1 Ext. Aggr. 7-pt.	2 ·Ext. Aggr. 4-pt.	3 Ext. Amity	4 Net Aggr. Target	5 Net Aggr. Initi.	6 War Dim.	7 Dipl. Dim.	8 Bellig. Dim.	9 Dipl. Inter.	10 Flights Countr.	11 Flights No.	12 For. Mail
	84							.20 (71)	.18 (71)	.37 (71)	.29 (70)	.23 (70)	.02 (41)
	84 WMP							.13 (66)	.31 (66)	.31 (66)	.02 (65)	−.11 (65)	−.06 (38)
	HI MOD							.18 (21)	−.11 (21)	.38 (21)	.39 (21)	.25 (21)	−.08 (17)
6 War Dimen- sion	HI MOD WMP							−.15 (17)	−.06 (17)	[.41] (17)	−.06 (17)	−.19 (17)	−.04 (14)
	MID- MOD							.30 (34)	[.56] (34)	.27 (34)	.11 (34)	−.02 (34)	−.13 (19)
	LO MOD							−.14 (16)	.22 (16)	[.41] (16)	−.12 (15)	−.004 (15)	[.67] (5)
	LO MOD WMP							−.09 (15)	.27 (15)	.32 (15)	−.07 (14)	.04 (14)	[.67] (5)
	84							.03 (71)	[.53] (71)	.23 (70)	.11 (70)	−.22 (41)	
	84 WMP							.07 (66)	.18 (66)	.05 (65)	−.10 (65)	−.23 (38)	
	HI MOD							−.15 (21)	[.74] (21)	.36 (21)	.12 (21)	−.34 (17)	
7 Diplo- matic Dimen- sion	HI MOD WMP							−.15 (17)	.08 (17)	.16 (17)	−.15 (17)	−.28 (14)	
	MID- MOD							−.02 (34)	.13 (34)	.01 (34)	−.05 (34)	−.05 (19)	
	LO MOD							[.51] (16)	.35 (16)	.32 (15)	.24 (15)	[.58] (5)	
	LO MOD WMP							[.50] (15)	[.63] (15)	.29 (14)	.21 (14)	[.58] (5)	
	84							−.001 (72)	−.02 (71)	−.09 (71)	−.20 (42)		
	84 WMP							.20 (67)	.02 (66)	−.06 (66)	−.20 (39)		
	HI MOD							−.14 (21)	−.19 (21)	−.12 (21)	−.08 (17)		
8 Bellig- erency Dimen- sion	HI MOD WMP							−.24 (17)	−.17 (17)	−.09 (17)	−.11 (14)		
	MID- MOD							.23 (34)	.22 (34)	.07 (34)	−.15 (19)		
	LO MOD							.13 (17)	.18 (16)	.21 (16)	[.67] (6)		
	LO MOD WMP							.29 (16)	.15 (15)	.19 (15)	[.67] (6)		

13 Trade	14 Milit. Pers.	15 Defense Exp.	16 GNP	17 GNP p/cap.	18 Pop.	19 Area	20 Instab. 7-yr.	21 Instab. 15-yr.	22 Frustr.	23 Mod.	24 Coerc.	25 Change	26 NAch 1950	27 NAch 1925
−.17 (59)	.30 (71)	.32 (63)	.10 (71)	.06 (71)	.12 (71)	.19 (71)	.06 (71)	−.01 (71)	−.06 (56)	.07 (71)	.07 (71)	−.03 (66)	.06 (36)	−.11 (22)
−.03 (54)	.17 (66)	.26 (58)	−.10 (66)	−.08 (66)	.01 (66)	−.05 (66)	.06 (66)	.07 (66)	.08 (53)	−.10 (66)	.15 (66)	.07 (61)	.04 (32)	−.06 (18)
[−.48] (18)	[.74] (21)	[.60] (19)	.06 (21)	−.14 (21)	.32 (21)	.22 (21)	.38 (21)	.16 (21)	.32 (19)	−.19 (21)	.10 (21)	.24 (21)	.21 (19)	−.20 (17)
−.33 (14)	[.80] (17)	[.63] (15)	−.18 (17)	−.04 (14)	−.18 (17)	←.09 (17)	.11 (17)	.13 (17)	.39 (16)	−.26 (17)	−.05 (17)	.07 (17)	.21 (15)	.12 (13)
.12 (29)	−.12 (34)	.36 (25)	−.03 (34)	−.01 (34)	−.01 (34)	−.04 (34)	.11 (34)	.22 (34)	.15 (29)	−.03 (34)	.29 (34)	.10 (33)	−.23 (13)	[.47] (5)
−.15 (12)	.24 (16)	.33 (15)	.21 (16)	−.23 (16)	.25 (16)	.29 (16)	−.19 (16)	−.39 (16)	−.36 (8)	.08 (16)	.29 (16)	.09 (12)	[.82] (4)	(0)
−.004 (11)	.27 (15)	.38 (14)	−.01 (15)	−.19 (15)	.05 (15)	.11 (15)	−.21 (15)	[−.50] (15)	−.36 (8)	.04 (15)	.17 (15)	.03 (11)	[.82] (4)	(0)
−.12 (59)	.16 (71)	.31 (63)	[.41] (71)	.17 (71)	.11 (71)	[.43] (71)	.27 (71)	.14 (71)	.05 (56)	.12 (71)	.23 (71)	.13 (66)	.24 (36)	.00 (22)
.06 (54)	.07 (66)	.17 (58)	−.05 (66)	−.06 (66)	.02 (66)	.01 (66)	.36 (66)	.24 (66)	.17 (53)	−.06 (66)	.33 (66)	.25 (61)	.31 (32)	−.02 (18)
[−.56] (18)	.22 (21)	[.67] (19)	[.61] (21)	.17 (21)	[.80] (21)	[.77] (21)	[.47] (21)	[.41] (21)	−.16 (19)	.07 (21)	.38 (21)	.29 (21)	.26 (19)	−.03 (17)
−.10 (14)	.05 (17)	−.03 (15)	.03 (17)	−.14 (17)	.16 (17)	.27 (17)	[.59] (17)	[.52] (17)	.03 (16)	−.17 (17)	[.41] (17)	.13 (17)	.31 (15)	.06 (13)
.28 (29)	−.06 (34)	.15 (29)	−.19 (34)	.24 (34)	−.22 (34)	−.19 (34)	.16 (34)	−.04 (34)	.25 (29)	−.16 (34)	.30 (34)	.35 (33)	.34 (13)	.11 (5)
−.05 (12)	[.56] (16)	[.55] (15)	.00 (16)	.15 (16)	−.01 (16)	−.09 (16)	[.46] (16)	.14 (16)	−.08 (8)	.34 (16)	−.09 (16)	.25 (12)	−.04 (4)	(0)
−.12 (11)	[.56] (15)	[.55] (14)	.27 (15)	.12 (15)	.26 (15)	.22 (15)	[.47] (15)	.19 (15)	−.08 (8)	.37 (15)	.02 (15)	.29 (11)	−.04 (4)	(0)
.03 (60)	−.09 (72)	.25 (64)	−.07 (62)	−.16 (72)	.04 (72)	−.05 (72)	.09 (72)	.06 (71)	.13 (56)	−.18 (72)	−.01 (72)	.15 (67)	.04 (36)	.13 (22)
−.01 (55)	−.07 (67)	.30 (59)	−.06 (67)	−.15 (67)	.16 (67)	−.003 (67)	.09 (67)	.06 (67)	.11 (66)	−.18 (53)	−.01 (67)	.14 (67)	.06 (62)	.13 (18)
.06 (18)	−.002 (21)	.05 (19)	−.07 (21)	.16 (21)	−.10 (21)	−.08 (21)	−.30 (21)	−.19 (21)	−.24 (19)	.24 (21)	−.19 (21)	−.14 (21)	−.10 (19)	.21 (17)
−.04 (14)	.06 (17)	.32 (15)	−.003 (17)	.28 (17)	−.08 (17)	−.05 (17)	−.29 (17)	−.18 (17)	−.26 (16)	.35 (17)	−.21 (17)	−.27 (17)	−.08 (15)	.21 (13)
.04 (29)	−.15 (34)	.36 (29)	−.09 (34)	−.18 (34)	.01 (34)	.07 (34)	−.02 (34)	.09 (34)	.14 (29)	−.17 (34)	−.01 (34)	−.02 (33)	−.32 (13)	[.47] (5)
.08 (13)	.15 (17)	.19 (16)	−.08 (17)	.24 (17)	−.06 (17)	−.17 (17)	.21 (17)	−.02 (16)	−.26 (8)	.22 (17)	−.22 (17)	−.24 (13)	[.70] (4)	(0)
.03 (12)	.14 (16)	.19 (15)	.06 (16)	.22 (16)	.10 (16)	−.13 (16)	.21 (16)	.02 (15)	−.26 (8)	.24 (16)	−.18 (16)	−.22 (12)	[.70] (4)	(0)

TABLE FIVE (*Continued*)

		1 Ext. Aggr. 7-pt.	2 Ext. Aggr. 4-pt.	3 Ext. Amity	4 Net Aggr. Target	5 Net Aggr. Initi.	6 War Dim.	7 Dipl. Dim.	8 Bellig. Dim.	9 Dipl. Inter.	10 Flights Countr.	11 Flights No.	12 For. Mail
	84										[.56] (82)	[.57] (82)	−.15 (51)
	84 WMP										[.43] (77)	.31 (77)	−.36 (48)
	HI MOD										[.61] (24)	[.57] (24)	−.30 (20)
9 Diplomatic Interaction	HI MOD WMP										.35 (20)	[.52] (20)	[−.40] (17)
	MID-MOD										[.54] (36)	.37 (36)	−.21 (20)
	LO MOD										[.44] (22)	[.43] (22)	[−.51] (11)
	LO MOD WMP										[.71] (21)	[.68] (21)	[−.51] (11)
	84											[.83] (82)	.15 (50)
	84 WMP											[.78] (77)	.17 (47)
	HI MOD											[.84] (24)	−.12 (20)
10 Flights No. of Countries	HI MOD WMP											[.74] (20)	.06 (17)
	MID-MOD											[.87] (36)	[.56] (19)
	LO MOD											[.86] (22)	−.39 (11)
	LO MOD WMP											[.85] (21)	−.39 (11)

13 Trade	14 Milit. Pers.	15 Defense Exp.	16 GNP	17 GNP p/cap.	18 Pop.	19 Area	20 Instab. 7-yr.	21 Instab. 15-yr.	22 Frustr.	23 Mod.	24 Coerc.	25 Change	26 NAch 1950	27 NAch 1925
[−.42]	.20	.37	[.86]	.38	[.43]	[.60]	.03	−.003	−.16	.28	−.05	−.14	.13	.00
(70)	(82)	(73)	(84)	(84)	(84)	(84)	(84)	(82)	(61)	(84)	(84)	(78)	(39)	(23)
−.38	.20	.29	[.45]	−.16	[.40]	.05	.21	.17	.17	−.15	.16	.11	.27	−.28
(65)	(77)	(68)	(79)	(79)	(79)	(79)	(79)	(77)	(58)	(79)	(79)	(73)	(35)	(19)
[−.68]	[.40]	[.86]	[.89]	.39	[.93]	[.63]	.29	.25	−.07	.24	.13	.07	.19	−.07
(21)	(23)	(20)	(24)	(24)	(24)	(24)	(24)	(24)	(21)	(24)	(24)	(24)	(29)	(18)
[−.48]	.34	[.45]	[.60]	−.30	[.74]	−.002	.26	[.46]	[.55]	[−.55]	[.42]	.06	[.42]	−.16
(17)	(19)	(16)	(20)	(20)	(20)	(20)	(20)	(20)	(18)	(20)	(20)	(20)	(16)	(14)
−.31	.39	[.48]	[.47]	.11	[.46]	.01	.06	−.04	.10	.21	.06	−.09	.004	[−.87]
(32)	(36)	(31)	(37)	(37)	(37)	(37)	(37)	(36)	(31)	(37)	(37)	(35)	(15)	(5)
[−.50]	−.06	.15	[.78]	−.15	[.78]	[.73]	.25	.17	−.27	.22	.11	.16	[.71]	
(17)	(23)	(22)	(23)	(23)	(23)	(23)	(23)	(22)	(9)	(23)	(23)	(19)	(4)	(0)
[−.42]	−.02	.26	[.56]	[−.51]	[.57]	[.43]	.32	.006	−.27	.20	−.26	.11	[.71]	
(16)	(22)	(21)	(22)	(11)	(22)	(22)	(22)	(21)	(9)	(22)	(22)	(18)	(4)	(0)
−.26	.12	.08	[.51]	[.51]	.17	.21	−.05	−.20	−.39	[.47]	−.38	[−.43]	−.10	−.23
(68)	(81)	(72)	(82)	(82)	(82)	(82)	(82)	(81)	(61)	(82)	(82)	(78)	(39)	(23)
−.15	−.02	−.10	[.61]	.33	.28	.10	−.06	−.16	−.31	.32	−.34	−.34	−.21	−.38
(63)	(76)	(67)	(77)	(77)	(77)	(77)	(77)	(76)	(58)	(77)	(77)	(73)	(35)	(19)
−.35	.32	[.58]	[.57]	.32	[.55]	.19	[.44]	.20	.002	.16	−.05	−.14	−.08	−.29
(21)	(23)	(20)	(24)	(24)	(24)	(24)	(24)	(24)	(21)	(24)	(24)	(24)	(20)	(18)
.14	−.01	.21	[.54]	.05	[.59]	−.05	.29	.11	.02	−.12	−.03	−.14	−.33	−.36
(17)	(19)	(16)	(20)	(20)	(20)	(20)	(20)	(20)	(18)	(20)	(20)	(20)	(16)	(14)
−.36	.12	.16	[.59]	.30	[.53]	.11	−.02	−.14	−.25	.27	−.32	−.24	−.14	[−.93]
(31)	(36)	(31)	(36)	(36)	(36)	(36)	(36)	(36)	(31)	(36)	(36)	(35)	(15)	(5)
[−.48]	−.26	−.17	.24	−.01	.22	.11	.16	−.04	.20	.06	[−.44]	−.08	.27	
(16)	(22)	(21)	(22)	(22)	(22)	(22)	(22)	(21)	(9)	(22)	(22)	(19)	(4)	(0)
[−.57]	−.27	−.18	[.65]	−.03	[.63]	[.59]	.16	−.01	−.20	.08	[−.42]	−.06	.27	
(15)	(21)	(20)	(21)	(21)	(21)	(21)	(21)	(20)	(9)	(21)	(21)	(18)	(4)	(0)

VARIABLE CODE NUMBERS

1. External Aggression 7-pt. Scale
2. External Aggression 4-pt. Scale
3. External Amity 5-pt. Scale
4. Net Aggression, Target
5. Net Aggression, Initiator
6. War Dimension (Rummel)
7. Diplomatic Dimension (Rummel)
8. Belligerency Dimension (Rummel)
9. Diplomatic Interaction, No. of Countries
10. Passenger Flights, No. of Countries
11. Passenger Flights, Total per week
12. Foreign Mail Sent per Capita
13. Foreign Trade as Percentage of GNP
14. Military Personnel as Percentage of Total Pop.
15. Defense Expenditure as Percentage of GNP
16. GNP, 1957, US $
17. GNP per Capita, 1957, US $
18. Total Population 1961
19. Area in Square Kilometers
20. Political Instability, 1955–1961
21. Political Instability, 1948–1962
22. Systemic Frustration, 1948–1955
23. Level of Attained Modernity, 1948–1955
24. Permissiveness—Coerciveness of Political Regime
25. Rate of Socioeconomic Change, 1935–1962
26. Need Achievement Level 1950
27. Need Achievement Level 1925

MEAN VALUES OF INTERNATION TRANSACTIONAL VARIABLES
INCLUDING MAJOR POWERS

	High Modern	Mid-Modern	Low Modern	
External Aggression 7-pt. Scale	3997	4431	4439	$\overline{X}$
	(1641)	(1213)	(1203)	SD
	(24)	(37)	(23)	N
External Aggression 4-pt. Scale	3099	3426	3653	
	(1231)	(924)	(800)	
	(21)	(34)	(17)	
External Amity 5-pt. Scale	39842	37133	39705	
	(5639)	(5661)	(4678)	
	(24)	(37)	(23)	
Net Aggression, Target	976	1037	965	
	(175)	(277)	(244)	
	(24)	(37)	(23)	
Net Aggression, Initiator	927.5	1086	931	
	(188)	(303)	(186)	
	(24)	(37)	(23)	
War Dimension (Rummel)	242	152	164	
	(330)	(196)	(97)	
	(21)	(34)	(16)	
Diplomatic Dimension (Rummel)	221	218	159	
	(193)	(133)	(92)	
	(21)	(34)	(16)	
Belligerency Dimension (Rummel)	172	187	284	
	(44)	(84)	(226)	
	(21)	(34)	(17)	
Diplomatic Interaction, No. of Countries	11	5	6	
	(18)	(4)	(4)	
	(24)	(37)	(23)	
Passenger Flights, No. of Countries	29	16	12	
	(18)	(12)	(8.5)	
	(24)	(36)	(22)	
Passenger Flights, Total per Week	716	189.5	82	
	(795)	(254)	(124)	
	(24)	(36)	(22)	
Political Instability, 1955–1961	268	472	416	
	(138)	(108)	(155)	
	(24)	(37)	(23)	
Political Instability, 1948–1962	2.8.396	4.4.563	4.1.467	
	(1.1.569)	(6.669)	(1.1.929)	
	(24)	(36)	(22)	

MEAN VALUES OF INTERNATION TRANSACTIONAL VARIABLES EXCLUDING MAJOR POWERS

	High Modern	Mid-Modern	Low Modern	
External Aggression 7-pt. Scale	3532	4431	4407	$\overline{X}$
	(1351)	(1213)	(1220)	SD
	(20)	(37)	(22)	N
External Aggression 4-pt. Scale	2808	3426	3619	
	(1191)	(924)	(812)	
	(17)	(34)	(16)	
External Amity 5-pt. Scale	38102	37133	39686	
	(4021)	(5661)	(4782)	
	(20)	(37)	(22)	
Net Aggression, Target	968	1037	967	
	(188.5)	(277)	(250)	
	(20)	(37)	(22)	
Net Aggression, Initiator	921	1086	922	
	(202)	(303)	(185)	
	(20)	(37)	(22)	
War Dimension (*Rummel*)	135	152	157	
	(210)	(196)	(96)	
	(17)	(34)	(15)	
Diplomatic Dimension (*Rummel*)	168	218	163	
	(122)	(133)	(93)	
	(17)	(34)	(15)	
Belligerency Dimension (*Rummel*)	175	187	292	
	(49)	(84)	(231)	
	(17)	(34)	(16)	
Diplomatic Interaction, No. of Countries	4	5	5.5	
	(4)	(4)	(3)	
	(20)	(37)	(22)	
Passenger Flights, No. of Countries	23	16	12	
	(14)	(12)	(9)	
	(20)	(36)	(21)	
Passenger Flights, Total per Week	507	189.5	86	
	(553)	(254)	(126)	
	(20)	(36)	(21)	
Political Instability, 1955–1961	244	472	416	
	(134)	(108)	(159)	
	(120)	(37)	(22)	
Political Instability, 1948–1962	2.7.293	4.4.563	4.0.819	
	(1.1.819)	(6.669)	(1.1.825)	
	(20)	(36)	(21)	

TABLE EIGHT

COMBINED LEVELS OF EXTERNAL HOSTILITY, AMITY, AND INTERACTION

	Hi Inter. Hi Amity Hi Hostility	Low Inter. Hi Amity Hi Hostility	Hi Inter. Hostil. > Amity	Low Inter. Hostil. > Amity	Hi Inter. Amity > Hostil.	Low Inter. Amity > Hostil.	Hi Inter. Low Amity Low Hostility	Low Inter. Low Amity Low Hostility	Totals
High Modern	Argent. Austria E. Germany France Israel U.K. U.S. U.S.S.R. W. Germany		Netherlands		Canada Czechosl.		Belgium Denmark	Australia Finland Iceland Ireland Luxembourg New Zealand Norway Sweden Switzerland Uruguay	
	9	0	1	0	2	0	2	10	24
Mid-Modern	Egypt Greece Lebanon Poland Syria Turkey Yugosl.	Cuba Hungary Tunisia	Spain Thailand	Albania Costa Rica Dom. Rep. Honduras Paraguay Portugal Nicaragua Venezuela	Brazil Italy Japan	Mexico		Bulgaria Ceylon Chile Colombia Ecuador El Salv. Guatemala Panama Peru S. Korea Romania U. of S. Africa	
	7	3	2	8	3	1	0	12	36
Low Modern	Burma China (M) India Indonesia Iraq Pakistan	Afghan. Ghana Jordan Morocco		China (T) Haiti	Iran	Cambodia Ethiopia Malaya Saudi Arabia Sudan		Bolivia Laos Libya Philipp.	
	6	4	0	2	1	5	0	4	22
Totals	22	7	3	10	6	6	2	24	82

TABLE NINE

RELATIONSHIP BETWEEN MODERNITY AND EXTERNAL AGGRESSION
(4-POINT SCALE)

	Level of Modernity				
	Hi Mod (−.16 through −2.54)		Lo Mod (−1.62 through −.20)		
Peaceful (0000–4014)	Belgium Canada Denmark Finland Greece Ireland Italy Japan Netherlands New Zealand	Norway Sweden Bulgaria Czechoslovakia Poland Portugal Romania Spain Switzerland Uruguay 20	Brazil Ceylon Paraguay Philippines Afghanistan Bolivia Colombia Dominican Republic Ecuador	El Salvador Ethiopia Liberia Peru Saudi Arabia Thailand 15	35
Aggressive (4015–4516)	Australia Chile Costa Rica Israel West Germany Albania Argentina Cuba East Germany	Hungary U. of S. Africa Yugoslavia 12	Burma Cambodia India Mexico Pakistan Turkey Egypt Guatemala Haiti Honduras	Indonesia Iran Iraq Jordan Lebanon Nicaragua Paraguay South Korea Taiwan Venezuela 20	32
		32		35	67

Chi Square = 1.86
   $p = .18$

TABLE TEN

RELATIONSHIP BETWEEN INDEXES OF SOCIOECONOMIC FRUSTRATION, COERCION, RATE OF CHANGE, AND LEVELS OF EXTERNAL AGGRESSION, POLITICAL INSTABILITY

Level of Aggression	Level of Frustration				Totals
	Satisfied on Two or Three Indexes		Frustrated on Two or Three Indexes		
Peaceful (0000–4014) Stable (000–422)	Bulgaria Canada Czechoslovakia Denmark Finland Greece Ireland	Netherlands New Zealand Norway Philippines Sweden Switzerland Uruguay 14	Ecuador El Salvador Panama Portugal	4	18
Mixed (Stable–Aggressive, Peaceful–Unstable)	Australia Belgium Brazil Costa Rica	Israel Italy Spain West Germany 8	Bolivia Ceylon Colombia Dom. Republ.	Japan Peru Thailand Yugo-slavia 8	16
Aggressive (4014–4516) Unstable (423–699)	Argentina Chile Cuba	Mexico Pakistan U. of S. Africa 6	Egypt Guatemala Haiti India Indonesia Iran Iraq	Lebanon Nicaragua Paraguay S. Korea Turkey Venezuela 13	19
Totals		28		25	53

Chi Square = 7.99
$p = <.02$

TABLE ELEVEN

RELATIONSHIP BETWEEN POLITICAL STABILITY AND EXTERNAL AGGRESSION

Level of External Aggression	Level of Political Instability			Totals
	Stability (000–422)		Instability (423–699)	
Peaceful (0000–4014)	Afghanistan Netherlands Bulgaria New Zealand Canada Norway Czechoslovakia Panama Denmark Philippines Ecuador Portugal El Salvador Romania Ethiopia Saudi Arabia Finland Sweden Greece Switzerland Ireland Uruguay Liberia	23	Belgium Bolivia Brazil Ceylon Colombia Dom. Rep. Italy Japan Peru Poland Spain Thailand 12	35
Aggressive (4015–4516)	Albania Australia Cambodia Costa Rica East Germany Israel Taiwan West Germany Yugoslavia	9	Argentina Iraq Burma Jordan Chile Lebanon Cuba Mexico Egypt Nicaragua Guatemala Pakistan Haiti Paraguay Honduras S. Korea Hungary Turkey India U. of S. Africa Indonesia Venezuela Iran 23	32
Totals		32	35	67

Chi Square = 7.10
$p = <.01$

RELATIONSHIP BETWEEN THE SOURCES OF SYSTEMIC FRUSTRATION, POLITICAL STABILITY, EXTERNAL AGGRESSION

	Satisfied (3.25–4.75) Permissive (1–3) Low Change (1.22–2.57) Modern (2.54–.34)	Satisfied Permissive Low Change Nonmodern (.24–1.16)	Satisfied Permissive High Change (2.60+) Modern	Satisfied Permissive High Change Nonmodern	Satisfied Coercive (4–6) Low Change Modern	Satisfied Coercive Low Change Nonmodern	Frustrated (1.5–3.0) Permissive Low Change Modern
Peaceful (0000–4014) Stable (000–422)	Canada Denmark Finland Ireland Nether. Norway Sweden Switz. Uruguay New. Zea. 10				Czech.	Bulgaria	
	10	0	0	0	1	1	0
Aggressive (4015–4516) Stable	Austral. Israel W.Germ. 3			Costa Rica			
	3	0	0	1	0	0	0
Peaceful Unstable (423–699)	Belgium	Italy		Brazil		Spain	
	1	1	0	1	0	1	0
Aggressive Unstable		Mexico Pakist.			Argentina	U. of S. Afr. Cuba	
	0	2	0	0	1	2	0
Totals	14	3	0	2	2	4	0

Frustrated Permissive Low Change Nonmodern	Satisfied Coercive High Change Modern	Satisfied Coercive High Change Nonmodern	Frustrated Permissive High Change Modern	Frustrated Permissive High Change Nonmodern	Frustrated Coercive Low Change Modern	Frustrated Coercive Low Change Nonmodern	Frustrated Coercive High Change Modern	Frustrated Coercive High Change Nonmodern	Totals
Greece Philip.		Portugal		Panama		Ecuador		El Salv.	
2	0	1	0	1	0	1	0	1	18
								Yugosl.	
0	0	0	0	0	0	0	0	1	5
		Colombia		Ceylon Japan				Bolivia Dom. Rep. Peru Thail.	
0	0	1	0	2	0	0	0	4	11
Chile		Indonesia Iran Lebanon		India Turkey		Guatem. Paragu.		Egypt Haiti Iraq Nicara. S. Kor. Venez.	
1	0	3	0	2	0	2	0	6	19
3	0	5	0	5	0	3	0	12	53

NOTES

[1] Research for this paper has been partially supported by National Science Foundation Grant No. GS-1417.

[2] Rudolph J. Rummel, "Dimensions of Conflict Behavior Within and Between Nations," *General Systems*, VIII (1963), 1–50, and Raymond Tanter, "Dimensions of Conflict Within and Between Nations, 1958–60," *The Journal of Conflict Resolution*, X (March 1966), 41–64. We gratefully acknowledge the generosity of these researchers for making their data bank on external conflict available to us. Rummel is now embarking on a far more elaborate collection of external-conflict data, using a more comprehensive code format. See Rudolph J. Rummel, "Foreign Conflict Behavior Code Sheet," *World Politics*, XVIII (Jan. 1966), 283–96.

[3] The data were collected from five sources: *The New York Times Index, New International Yearbook, Keesing's Contemporary Archives, Facts on File*, and *Britannica Book of the Year*.

[4] John Stuart Chambers, Jr., "Hostility and Amity in International Relations: A Transactional Study" (unpublished M.A. thesis, San Diego State College, 1966). The source for the data was *Deadline Data on World Affairs*.

[5] Ivo K. and Rosalind L. Feierabend, "Aggressive Behaviors Within Polities, 1948–1962: A Cross-National Study," *Journal of Conflict Resolution*, X (Sept. 1966), 249–71. Also, Ivo K. and Rosalind L. Feierabend, *Cross-National Data Bank of Political Instability Events (Code Index)* (San Diego State College: Public Affairs Research Institute, 1965); Francis W. Hoole, "Political Stability and Instability Within Nations: A Cross-National Study" (unpublished M.A. thesis, San Diego State College, 1964); and Betty A. Nesvold, "Modernity, Social Frustration and Stability of Political Systems: A Cross-National Study" (unpublished M.A. thesis, San Diego State College, 1964).

[6] *Deadline Data on World Affairs* and *Britannica Book of the Year*.

[7] The data collection has just been updated from the same sources for the 1962–1966 time period.

[8] See Feierabend and Feierabend, "Aggressive Behaviors Within Polities," and Nesvold, "Modernity, Social Frustration and Stability of Political Systems," for the scaling of political instability. See Ivo K. and Rosalind L. Feierabend, "The Relationship of Systemic Frustration, Political Coercion, International Tension and Political Instability: A Cross-National Study," paper presented at the Annual Meeting of the American Psychological Association, New York City, Sept. 1966, and Frank W. Scanland, III, "International Conflict and Internal Frustration: A Cross-Polity Study" (unpublished M.A. thesis, San Diego State College, 1966), for the 4-point scaling of external aggression. See Chambers, "Hostility and Amity," for the 7-point scaling of external aggression and the external amity scale.

[9] The judgmental method of attitude scaling was first devised by L. L. Thurstone, "Theory of Attitude Measurement," *Psychological Bulletin*, XXXVI (1929), 222–41. The degree of consensual validation obtained for the political instability scale was $r = .87$, using a group of seven judges.

[10] The 7-point scaling of external aggression (Feierabend, Feierabend, and Chambers scale) is described in Chambers, "Hostility and Amity."

[11] See n. 8, above.

[12] Rummel, "Dimensions of Conflict Behavior"; and Tanter, "Dimensions of Conflict, 1958–60."

[13] Other researchers have also broached the difficult task of measuring structural variables in cross-national data. In Arthur S. Banks and Robert B. Textor, *A Cross Polity Survey* (Cambridge, Mass., 1963), countries are divided into groups on a number of political variables, and in Arthur S. Banks and Phillip M. Gregg, "Grouping Political Systems: Q-Factor Analysis of a Cross-Polity Survey," *The American Behavioral Scientist*, IX (Nov. 1965), 3–6, countries are aligned in groups that reflect political structure. Phillips Cotwright, "National Political Development: Measurement and Analysis," *American Sociological Review*, XXVIII (April 1963), 253–64, scores countries yearly for level of political development, 1928–1961, on such categories as extent of party representation and elective character of executive. The Yale Political Data Program has undertaken a collection of variables on political structures for the

projected *Second World Handbook of Political and Social Indicators* and we are currently collecting yearly data on political structures related to the notion of permissiveness-coerciveness for 84 countries for 20 years, 1945–1965.

[14] For the detailed set of criteria used, see Feierabend and Feierabend, "The Relationship of Systemic Frustration, Political Coercion, International Tension and Political Instability: A Cross-National Study," and Jennifer G. Walton, "Correlates of Coerciveness and Permissiveness of National Political Systems: A Cross-National Study" (unpublished M.A. thesis, San Diego State College, 1965).

[15] See Walton, "Coerciveness and Permissiveness," Appendix B, pp. 98–148, for bibliography.

[16] See Karl W. Deutsch, "International Communication: The Media and Flows," *Public Opinion Quarterly*, XX (Spring 1956), 143–60.

[17] Grateful acknowledgment is extended to James N. Bierman who collected the interactional data on passenger flights from the *Official Airline Guide*, World-Wide Timetable Edition (Chicago, 1967).

[18] For the theoretical foundation, see Feierabend and Feierabend, "Aggressive Behaviors Within Polities," and "Systemic Conditions of Political Aggression: An Application of Frustration-Aggression Theory," manuscript awarded the Socio-Psychological Prize of the American Association for the Advancement of Science, Dec. 1966. See also Ted Gurr, *New Error Compensated Measures for Comparing Nations* ("Research Monograph" No. 25, Princeton University, Center of International Studies, May 1966).

[19] The selection of these indicators corresponds to such mechanisms as "exposure to modernity" discussed, for example, in Karl W. Deutsch, "Social Mobilization and Political Development," *American Political Science Review*, LV (Sept. 1961), 493–514, or to the mechanisms discussed in Daniel Lerner, *The Passing of Traditional Society* (Glencoe, Ill., 1958).

[20] The indicators themselves are intercorrelated and the ranking of level of development yielded by using the eight in combination is highly correlated to the ranking of countries into stages of development, based on GNP per capita only, which is found in Russett, *et al.*, *World Handbook of Political and Social Indicators* (New Haven, 1964), 294–98. We may compare the composition of our three modernity groupings with the five levels of development distinguished in the *World Handbook*. Our High Modern group includes all the 14 countries in the *World Handbook's* Group V, "High Mass-Consumption" societies, as well as 10 more countries which fall at the top of Group IV in the *World Handbook*, "Industrial Revolution" societies. Thus Finland, Israel, Czechoslovakia, Austria, U.S.S.R., East Germany, Iceland, Ireland, Argentina, and Uruguay are also included in our High Modern group, along with the very advanced Western societies such as the U.S., Canada, and Switzerland. Our Low Modern group of 23 nations includes countries from Levels I and II in the *World Handbook*, "Traditional Primitive" societies and "Traditional Civilizations," as well as countries which fall in the lower half of Level III, "Transitional" societies. Finally, our Mid-Modern group bridges Levels III and IV in the *World Handbook*, combining countries from the upper half of Level III with countries falling in the lower half of Level IV.

[21] See Feierabend and Feierabend, "Aggressive Behaviors Within Polities," and Wallace W. Conroe, "Cross-National Analysis of the Impact of Modernization upon Political Stability" (unpublished M.A. thesis, San Diego State College, 1965).

[22] David C. McClelland, *The Achieving Society* (Princeton, 1961).

[23] A significance level of .05 or better is yielded by the following correlations for the indicated number of cases.

N	r	N	r	N	r
12	.50	25	.34	50	.24
15	.45	30	.31	60	.22
20	.38	40	.27	70	.20

[24] Feierabend and Feierabend, "Aggressive Behaviors Within Polities."

[25] Ivo K. Feierabend, Rosalind L. Feierabend, and Betty A. Nesvold, "Correlates of Political Stability," paper delivered at the Annual Meeting of the American Political Science Association, New York City, Sept. 1963.

[26] John Dollard, *et al.*, *Frustration and Aggression* (New Haven, 1939).

[27] Some recent important works on the nature of aggression and its relation to frustration are those by Leonard Berkowitz, *Aggression: A Social Psychological Analysis* (New York, 1962) and "The Concept of Aggressive Drive: Some Additional Considerations," in *Advances*

in Experimental Social Psychology, ed. L. Berkowitz, Vol. II (New York, 1965); Arnold H. Buss, *The Psychology of Aggression* (New York, 1961); Elton B. McNeil, "Psychology and Aggression," *Journal of Conflict Resolution*, III (1959), 195–293; and J. D. Carthy and F. J. Ebling, eds., *The Natural History of Aggression* (New York, 1964). For a theoretical framework specifically applicable to political violence see Ted Gurr, "The Genesis of Violence: A Multivariate Theory of the Preconditions of Civil Strife" (unpublished Ph.D. dissertation, New York University, 1965).

[28] The frustration-aggression sequence was originally postulated in terms of individual behavior, although the adaptation of the sequence to the behavior of groups was foreseen by the authors. See, for example, the following statements: "Although frustration as such can occur only to an individual organism, any given frustrating condition may occur to several individuals simultaneously. In such a case, a 'group' is viewed distributively rather than as a collective thing." Dollard, *et al.*, *Frustration and Aggression*, 13. See also Gurr, "The Genesis of Violence."

[29] *Frustration and Aggression*, 39–54. More recent formulations have added the psychological concept of gradients of generalization to the notion of displacement, pointing out that the object that is most similar to the perceived frustrating agent will be the most satisfying one onto which to displace aggression. On the other hand, the stronger the inhibiting fear inspired by the perceived agent of frustration, the more this fear will also generalize to highly similar objects. Thus, in displacing aggression, the frustrated individual must balance two gradients of generalization. In more recent work Berkowitz has questioned this formulation, which depicts aggression as a drive propelling the individual in search of a target on which to release his impulse. Berkowitz's research suggests that targets (stimulus objects) actually may serve to elicit aggressive impulses. (See "The Concept of Aggressive Drive.")

[30] See, for example, Sigmund Neumann's discussion in Taylor Cole, ed., *European Political Systems* (New York, 1959).

[31] Feierabend and Feierabend, "Aggressive Behaviors within Polities." See also Ted Gurr with Charles Ruttenberg, *The Conditions of Civil Violence: First Tests of a Causal Model* (Research Monograph No. 28, Center of International Studies, Princeton University, April 1967).

[32] Rummel, "Dimensions of Conflict Behavior."

[33] Tanter, "Dimensions of Conflict, 1958–60."

[34] F. H. Denton, "Some Regularities in International Conflict, 1820–1949," *Background*, IX (1966).

[35] Michael Haas, "Some Societal Correlates of International Political Behavior" (unpublished Ph.D. dissertation, Stanford University, 1964).

[36] Banks and Gregg, "Grouping Political Systems."

[37] Jonathan Wilkenfeld, "Domestic and Foreign Conflict Behavior of Nations," *Journal of Peace Research*, I (1968), 56–70.

CHAPTER SIX

LEVELS OF POLITICAL DEVELOPMENT & INTERSTATE CONFLICT IN SOUTH ASIA

LLOYD JENSEN

MOST RESEARCH on the relationship between development and foreign policy has focused on the question of how the foreign policy of one of the larger states, usually the United States, can facilitate modernization in the less developed area.[1] Little attention has been given to the link between the level of development of a state and how it behaves in the international system, in spite of the fact that such a link is just as crucial in determining the goals and purposes of development. Does internal development, for example, tend to induce international conflict, or might it play an ameliorative role?

The notion of national development is a complex one, involving as it does a multiplicity of meanings. Not only can one conceive of different sectors of development such as economic, political, technological, and social, but within each sector there appears to be an unlimited number of criteria and definitions.

Perhaps the critical problem for the developing areas in their fledgling attempts to become modernized is that of political development. It might be argued that all other forms of development hinge on political development. Without political stability and the development of national unity, economic, social, technological, and military development will be difficult if not impossible to achieve. Governments forced to use their resources primarily to preserve themselves and confronted frequently with the costs of internal conflict will find the path to development difficult at best.

Most studies that have systematically probed the relationship between internal political development and foreign policy behavior have been based upon gross data analysis in which large numbers of countries are examined in an effort to determine the underlying dimensions of their domestic and foreign behaviors.[2] In a nonquantitative fashion, Richard Rosecrance has also examined on a longitudinal basis the relationship between internal political development and foreign conflict in his study of nine international systems since 1740.[3] Conclusions with respect to the relationships between internal instability and external aggressiveness in the various studies are strikingly different; Rosecrance sees a positive relationship whereas the other studies indicate a negative one.

This study purports to evaluate this relationship in still another way by examining the effects of national political development upon the rivalry of India and Pakistan since independence. A case study was decided upon because of its manageability and because it afforded the opportunity to examine a conflict situation on a longitudinal basis rather than a cross-sectional one. The question is whether the same state tends to behave in different ways as its development evolves. Although a case study detracts from one's ability to generalize to a larger population of states, it allows one to analyze a situation in greater depth in order to ascertain the nuances involved. It also enables one to examine the fruitfulness of certain research techniques which can then be extended to additional case studies.

The selection of the Indo-Pakistani conflict was motivated by the availability of adequate primary and secondary sources and by the fact that the conflict between the two has been the overriding foreign policy issue for both parties. One writer has gone so far as to assert that "almost every action of Pakistan can be interpreted as being motivated by fear of India." [4] Although India has had broader foreign policy interests, particularly in terms of Nehru's attempts to play a mediating role in the Cold War, its conflict relations with Pakistan provide a fairly useful index of its aggressive behavior. The exception to this general rule might be India's conflict with China, in which case India was clearly on the defensive, and the Indian invasion of Goa in 1961.

The analysis quite properly could be extended to other all-consuming dyadic relationships such as Arab-Israeli or even United States-Soviet relations. In some respects, the developing states such as India and Pakistan provide a much more interesting case study since they are so deeply involved in the process of political modernization and consequently hypotheses concerning the effects of rapid developmental change upon interstate relations can be readily tested on the basis of recent experiences. On the other hand, the data sources are generally not as good as those for the more developed states.

In view of the multiple meanings given the term "political development," one needs to be precise about its definition. Essentially, most of the definitions boil down to notions of complexity, efficiency and effectiveness, stability, national unity, and competitiveness and responsiveness. Since political development means so many different things it becomes difficult if not impossible to develop hypotheses linking the abstract notion of development to foreign policy styles. Instead, one must be satisfied with hypotheses concerning individual aspects of the developmental process. For example, if one regards development as primarily the growth of more complex political structures, he might examine the hypothesis which holds that with such a change foreign policy becomes less dependent upon the idiosyncratic notions of a ruler, becoming at once both more stable and more dependent upon governmental structures and roles.[5] With increased effectiveness and efficiency in the formation of foreign policy, one might predict less penetration from the outside as well as more respect for the foreign policy of a state.

The image of a highly efficient and effective British foreign policy has tended to bolster the power position of the United Kingdom, a factor that is often added to explain calculations of British capabilities. Such hypotheses are difficult to test in the short term since development of this sort involves a very gradual process of nation-building. With minimal fluctuation, it becomes difficult to ascertain what features of political development help in explaining the myriad fluctuations that one finds in foreign policy behavior. Why do states engage in violent conflict with each other in one period and not in another? Obviously, external events provide the basic explanation, but to what extent might internal development be a contributing factor to conflict?

It has been suggested that democracies with their tolerance for competitive structures and beliefs in the peaceful settlement of disputes project these notions to their behavior at the interstate level. The evidence, however, does not support this contention, for democracies appear to be no more peace-loving in their behavior than are their more dictatorial counterparts.[6] Rather than accounting for variance in foreign policy choices, the salience of democracy as a measure of the relationship between political development and foreign policy would seem to be more relevant to questions concerning the speed of decision-making and the ability to obtain internal compliance once a decision is made. Similarity of values along a democratic dimension seems to be neither a necessary nor a sufficient reason for alignment, as democracies have frequently aligned with authoritarian regimes because of power considerations.

Some of the limitations of the above measures of political development appear to be relatively unresponsive to changes in the short run; thus, it was decided to concentrate upon political stability and expressions of national unity as indicators of the level of political development. By using political stability and national unity as yardsticks of development, one is able to get around the value-laden notion of what type of political regime is best. This is particularly a problem for those who use democracy as their major criterion of political development. Ascribing primary consideration to political stability as the main indicator is not to say that all internal conflict is dysfunctional, for some conflict has been found by Coser, Simmel, and others to integrate and stabilize social relationships.[7] It is not argued that internal political stability ought to be viewed as the central notion of national development, for even those regimes with a highly underdeveloped political structure may be highly stable. Nevertheless, stability is central to the notion of development, for without it development in all areas will be affected adversely.

The research strategy used in examining the link between external political instability and foreign policy involved in the first instance a systematic search of chronicles of events in order to obtain as complete a picture as possible of internal Indian and Pakistani politics as well as their efforts at cooperation and conflict at the interstate level. The basic sources utilized for this purpose included the *New York Times Index* and *Deadline Data on World Affairs,* supplemented by such other chronicles as the *Annual Register of World Events* and *Asian Recorder.* Secondary materials were also useful as a corroborative source of evidence, suggesting again the vital importance of the area specialist in synthesizing vast amounts of data.

The essential purpose of the exercise was to examine the patterns of internal and external behavior in Indo-Pakistani relations. Despite the collection of individual events, no effort is made to sum them into indexes of internal political instability or external conflict propensities. Such an accounting is too premature given the nature of information concerning developing regions. First and foremost, one must expect gaps and errors in the reporting of events from these regions. The severity of riots and demonstrations, for example, is very much related to whether Pakistan or India is reporting. There is even a determined effort to quash reporting of riots because of their epidemic tendencies. Reportage of a communal riot in India induces retaliation in Pakistan as well as spreading riots throughout India. Foreign reporters are frequently not allowed to go to the scene of either internal or external turmoil in developing regions, and their continued tenure in these countries frequently depends upon their willingness to withhold information that the regime would prefer not to have transmitted. Editorial policies, competition with other events on any given day, and the limited number of objective foreign reporters also affect the reporting of events.

Given the reservations concerning the completeness and authenticity of the data involved, it is suggested that less powerful statistical techniques should be utilized. In the study of the developing nations, particularly when analyzing events, perhaps we can do no better than to establish rough rank orders in which it is possible to assert that more of variable x appeared in year 1 than in year 2. Evidence for these evaluations can come both from the chronicles of events and from assessments of scholars in the field who have been able to probe more deeply into a particular period and place in time.

Before presenting data concerning the ranking of internal political instability during the post-independence period in India and Pakistan, it is necessary to explain more exactly what sorts of data were important in making the evaluations. In essence, it might be argued that the most important measure of internal instability is that of the perception of the decision-making elite. What is crucial is whether or not these elites perceive their power position as being threatened. Subjective information of this sort is extremely difficult to obtain. Indeed, a content analysis of pronouncements of the ruling elite may do little to enlighten us on this score, for it is quite probable that at the very times in which the elite feels most insecure, it will publicly state that it has considerable support and that there is little danger of internal decay. If one were to develop a perceptual measure based upon content analysis, such a measure may have to be related to the propensity to make strong statements concerning the degree of stability which a given elite argues that it enjoys.

Given the very serious problems of measuring the perceptions, researchers often retreat to more objective indicators of political instability. Most obvious among these are violent changes of government through revolution and coup. Political instability is also indicated by the frequency of governmental crises and changes of government. Next in importance might be indicators of internal turmoil and displeasure directed toward the governing elite in the form of riots and demonstrations. Indirectly, one might even argue that indicators of severe economic instability tend to correspond with periods of political instability. If polling techniques tapping public support of governmental regimes were more sophisticated and employed more frequently in the developing areas, one might obtain additional evidence for ranking the degree of instability, but unfortunately reliable polls are not available since polling is in its infancy in this area. Another piece of information that might affect elite perceptions of stability is the matter of holding elections. Even though loss of power may not be contemplated, the ruling elite desires to maximize its power by obtaining as many seats as possible for its given party or political faction. As a result, foreign policy issues frequently assume renewed importance during election years. Conflict patterns with other states also serve an educational function in behalf of national identity.

In probing for the above sorts of indicators, rough rankings can be given to the twenty years since independence in terms of relative instability. Although certain years have obviously experienced greater instability than other years, it would be difficult to rank each of the years precisely, given the inadequacy of the data. The difficulties involved are reduced, and, it is hoped, the accuracy of the estimate increased, if one ranks the years in terms of quartiles rather than on an individual rank order. An attempt at such a ranking for India and Pakistan is found in Tables 1 and 2. In interpreting the tables, it is important to note that these are based only upon relative instability and are therefore noncomparable for India and Pakistan. On the whole, India has been the much more stable state politically.

The following discussion is designed to give the reader an impression of why certain years were ranked in the various quartiles. Only the key events and evaluations are included.

In India, the years 1947 and 1948 would have to be included among the most unstable politically. The new government was seeking to build support for the symbols of the nation-state, confronted as it was with mass migration and the spilling of blood following partition. The year 1948, in particular, showed great instability with Gandhi's assassination and a similar plot to kill Nehru. The year marked the beginning of a communist-led revolt in Hyderabad and was also a time of considerable economic difficulty throughout India. The period 1964 through 1966 must also be included in the first quartile, for it was a period of extensive change in the top leadership. Nehru died in May 1964, creating the problem of a search for a successor. Two months later demonstrations against the Congress party were initiated in a number of the larger Indian towns, followed by continuing nationwide demonstrations over what has been labeled the most serious food crisis since independence.[8] The following year saw minimal improvement in the food situation. Prime Minister Shastri's position was perhaps a little more secure, but the general trend toward decentralization of power into the hands of regional interests continued. A serious internal crisis arose in Jammu and Kashmir, parts of which had been incorporated into India. The year 1966 was likewise a year of considerable instability as Mrs. Indira Gandhi succeeded Shastri following the latter's death in January. The new prime minister was greeted with a censure motion in February and an extensive series of leftist-inspired strikes and demonstrations in such places as Kerala, Calcutta, and Bombay.

Among the least stable years in India in the second quartile is 1963, during which the increasing power of regional interests, at the expense of the central government, inspired the enactment of an antisecession act. Events during the year led one author to assert that Nehru's political position was weaker than it had been in previous years.[9] Also included are 1950 and 1958, years in which Nehru threatened to resign. In 1950 his popularity had been reduced to what at that time was considered a new low,[10] and in 1958 Nehru had been concerned about what he believed to be a deterioration of support within the Parliament. The outcries of opposition to any consideration of resignation suggest that his position was not excessively unstable.

One might also expect a lessening of a sense of security on the part of elites during election years, particularly if there is a threat of decreasing support. Thus, the second and third national elections in 1957 and 1962, respectively, were central to the decision to place these years in the second quartile. Concern about the outcome of the elections was perhaps well founded, for in 1957 a communist victory was achieved in the state of Kerala. The third national elections resulted in a new polarization of Left and Right, which made Nehru's position more precarious.

Turning to the third quartile in Table 1, it should be noted that most of the years were included because of extensive political demonstrations and riots. This was true of events in 1949, particularly around Calcutta where the Congress party was defeated. A critical food shortage was reported in 1951, and the following year saw the first general elections during which the Congress party fared better than was the case in subsequent elections. The years 1956 and 1960 were also included in this quartile because of the frequency of politically motivated riots which were among the worst since independence. Yet, the stability of a political system is not only a function of the frequency of rioting, for, if this were the case, recent developments could be said to reveal the United States as one of the least stable states in the world. In the absence of other more extreme indicators, however, riots do provide some basis for ranking stability. The sharp increase of rioting in 1956 is well documented by data from the Dimensionality of Nations project, in which only two riots were coded for India in 1955, as contrasted with twenty-nine riots in 1956, and only eight in 1957.[11] An extensive series of riots in 1960 led Nehru to label the events as the most "ghastly and deplorable happenings in India in the past fifteen years."[12]

The years represented in the fourth quartile were placed there because data suggesting instability were minimal or lacking. Such was particularly the case with the years 1953 and 1954. During 1955 there were intensified pressures for an independent Sikh state, but these events appeared to have had minimal impact upon the central government. The years 1959 and 1961 saw some local disturbances, but these developments were minor when compared to other years. Nehru apparently felt strong enough politically to take over the communist-controlled Kerala government in 1959.

Turning to the assessments of the relative political instability in Pakistan as shown in Table 2, more persuasive evidence of frequent political instability may be found. As a result, evaluations can be based to a greater extent upon crucial indicators of instability such as coups, cabinet instability, political arrests, and the like. This is all to the good, since the minor events in Pakistan are not as fully reported as in India; there are greater restrictions on the press in Pakistan and, moreover, Pakistan is smaller in population and has less impact in world affairs, a fact that is clearly reflected in the coverage of the world press.

The obvious starting point for inclusion in the first quartile is the year 1958, during which the deputy speaker in East Pakistan was killed, political upsets occurred in both provincial capitals, and dissident tribal chieftains declared their independence from Pakistan. Following those turbulent first nine months, Ayub Khan took over the reins of government and martial law was declared. As a new state, Pakistan was also confronted with problems of obtaining popular support following partition. In 1948 there was both a ministerial and a food crisis.

Refugees from India were forming an aggrieved political bloc, and Mohammad Ali Jinnah, who was instrumental in bringing Pakistan to independence, died during that year. The year 1951 was included in the first quartile, for it marked the assassination of Prime Minister Liaquat Ali as well as the discovery of an abortive communist coup. A state of emergency, the dissolution of the Constituent Assembly, extensive rioting, balance-of-payments problems, and statements to the effect that East Pakistan wished to become an independent state combined to make the year 1954 a turbulent one worthy of inclusion in the first quartile.

The common feature of the years included in the second quartile is that of parliamentary crises either at the national or provincial level. In 1949 parliamentary government was suspended in West Punjab, and in 1953 Pakistan's prime minister was dismissed amid problems of civil violence in the Punjab and riots in Lahore. Accusations of plots directed against the government were also prominent. The years 1955–1957 witnessed the resignation of four prime ministers. In 1956 a parliamentary crisis arose in East Pakistan and during the following year the constitution was suspended in West Pakistan.

The third and fourth quartiles primarily include years in which Ayub Khan controlled the government of Pakistan. Even so, all was not calm. The frequency of political arrests, particularly in 1962 and 1966, suggests a sense of insecurity on the part of the elite. There were major riots and demonstrations against the policies of President Ayub during 1962 and 1964. In 1965 Ayub asserted that external dangers did not concern him so much as internal ones.[13] A general strike demanding East Pakistani autonomy during the following year apparently went to such lengths that the President declared the government ready to accept the consequences of civil war if necessary.[14] The year 1952 was included in the third quartile because of some fairly serious economic problems created by food shortages and price hikes three times the normal rate.

The final quartile involved relatively minor incidents of instability, at least in terms of the Pakistani experience. During 1950 small riots occurred, but problems for Liaquat Ali's government seemed minimal in contrast to other years. Ayub Khan appeared to be in firm control of the government in 1959 during which time he initiated an austerity program. Events during the early sixties involving occasional arrests of political opponents suggested that perhaps all was not well with the Pakistani government. Nevertheless, the degree of stability achieved provided a sharp contrast with earlier events in Pakistan.

Problems of data gaps as well as inaccuracies also plague attempts to quantify interstate relations but perhaps to a less significant degree than in the case of internal events, for by definition interstate relations affect other states, making it more difficult to hide external conflict behavior.

Just as there is a hierarchy of importance among various behaviors representing internal political instability, external aggressive moves may be ranked ranging from the extreme of war to protests and demonstrations directed against a foreign regime. Along this continuum are such events as border skirmishes, economic and political sanctions, and threats. Using techniques similar to those employed above, quartiles of aggressive interstate behavior were established for India and Pakistan, as shown in Table 3.

Instead of providing separate aggressive measure for India and Pakistan, a single estimate was assigned to indicate the relative rank of the interstate conflict. This procedure evades the problem of attempting to assess blame for external aggressiveness, a move that was felt to be most desirable in view of the charges and countercharges and differing interpretations of events.

In assessing the level of interstate conflict behavior, all major conflict issues between the two states have been examined, including the Kashmir conflict, the Indus River conflict, and the evacuee problem as well as disputes along the Indo-Pakistani border.

The first quartile consists primarily of years in which open hostilities and violence occurred between the two states. Violence, mass emigrations, and the Kashmir war arising soon after partition make 1947 and 1948 the bloodiest years in Indo-Pakistani relations. The year of 1956 was likewise a year of considerable violence along the border, and relations were strained to the breaking point as Kashmir was made an integral part of India. Prime Minister Nehru also announced that U.S. aid had completely changed the Kashmir situation and India would no longer allow a plebiscite.[15] Further strains were placed upon relations between the two states in 1964–1965 following a detente between China and Pakistan. Open fighting occurred in Kashmir, and deaths numbered in the hundreds. Fighting between Indian and Pakistani forces in the Rann of Kutch area was clearly the most violent encounter since 1948.

Although the level of violence was perhaps lower during the years represented by the second quartile, animosity and conflict remained at a high level. Although a cease-fire was achieved in January 1949, there were reports of continued violations. Josef Korbel, who served on the U.N. investigation team in Kashmir, noted that, although there were several hundred reports of violations in the armistice, these reports proved with but few exceptions to be "unfounded or of a civilian, non-military nature."[16] Relations deteriorated during the year as the two engaged in a bitter economic war involving an official cessation of trade. Pakistani officials also complained on several occasions that India had shut off canal water which was essential to the continued existence of Pakistan. The year 1951 was included not so much because of border violence but rather because of a growing concentration of the Indian army near Kashmir. Korbel argued that during the summer of 1951 India and Pakistan reached the very brink of all-out war.[17] The year 1955 was reported to have marked the first serious breach of the 1949 Kashmir cease-fire agreement. Some 15,000 Pakistani volunteers threatened to march across the Kashmiri cease-fire line, and demonstrations were held in Pakistan calling for a "holy war" with India. The years 1962 and 1963 showed a further deterioration in relations, partially prompted by increased cooperation between Red China and Pakistan prior to Red China's invasion of territories held by India. During the course of 1962 several border clashes between Indian and Pakistani troops were reported as well as troop movements. In June of that year the first Security Council debates in four years were held on the Kashmir issue. The severity of relations in 1963 is suggested by one assessment which called the year the lowest ebb in Indian-Pakistani relations since partition.[18] This view is corroborated by a content analysis of *Dawn*, a semiofficial newspaper in Pakistan, in which it was found that during 1963 a record of 307 daily issues carried at least one front-page item connoting Indian aggressive designs. This figure averaged twice the level of the early days of martial law.[19]

The third quartile includes the years 1952 and 1958, which witnessed various border clashes. Pakistan, for example, in 1952 accused India of 594 breaches of the cease-fire pact.[20] Clashes in 1958 were centered primarily on the border between India and East Pakistan. Most serious perhaps was the Pakistani accusation that India had cut off Pakistan's water supply, damaging more than two million acres of crops. These two years were not assigned to the higher quartile, for there were moments of hope. In 1952 the two states signed a pact fixing the boundary between East and West Bengal and also signed a one-year trade agreement. A Prime Minister's Conference in 1958 settled most of the outstanding issues with respect to both the eastern and western frontier regions.[21]

Relations between India and Pakistan were somewhat exacerbated by the U.S.-Pakistani alliance of 1954. The Security Council was again asked by Pakistan to settle the dispute between India and Pakistan, but there was little evidence of violence. When Jammu and Kashmir formally became part of India in 1957, relations between India and Pakistan took a turn for the worse. Indian threats of cutting all supplies of canal waters by 1962 did little to inspire trust, nor did the creation of a new Pakistani political party designed to "liberate" Kashmir help matters. The year 1961 was included in the third quartile primarily because of the magnitude of the threats issued on each side. Nehru labeled Ayub

Khan a "warmonger" and was reported strengthening Indian forces on the Kashmir border.[22]

Events during the years included in the fourth quartile proved to be somewhat milder, and some success was achieved in settling certain basic differences. Chief among the agreements was that reached at Tashkent in January 1966, which brought with it a cessation of hostilities and normalization of relations between India and Pakistan. According to the Tashkent agreement, the issue of Kashmir was to be shelved until more crucial matters were settled.[23] Consensus was reached in April 1950 on the protection of religious minorities and on the restoration of trade. In 1953 another trade agreement removing discriminatory pricing was reached, and the two states were reported near agreement on a partition plan for Kashmir—a plan which appears to have been stifled by the U.S.-Pakistani alliance.[24] Also included in the fourth quartile are the years 1959 and 1960, when Ayub Khan demonstrated considerable moderation on the issue of Indo-Pakistani relations. During 1959 a one-year agreement was reached on the Indus River, a trade treaty was signed, consensus was obtained on four out of five disputed areas on the western borders, and security regulations were established to prevent clashes between border units. During 1960 a preliminary agreement was reached on financial problems dating from pre-independence, and further delineation of the western borders was achieved. Finally, the Indus River treaty was signed, ending twelve years of conflict over the issue.

Having examined the relative degree of internal political instability and interstate conflict in Indo-Pakistani relations, we can now study the relationship between these variables. Table 4 summarizes the quartile rankings established for internal instability in Pakistan and India as well as rankings for degree of interstate conflict.

With the data in Table 4 it is possible to shed some light on the proposition found so frequently in writings on South Asia to the effect that both India and Pakistan have utilized their external differences to divert attention from internal problems.[25] If the proposition were an accurate description, a high ranking on internal instability might be expected to show a similarly high ranking on interstate conflict and vice versa. Such, of course, assumes that the interstate conflict was not so overpowering that it considerably bolstered internal cohesion. Certain internal differences, for example, were forgotten in India in late 1962, given the preoccupation with the invasion of Indian territories by Communist China.

The quartile rankings suggest a number of instances where high instability in one or the other of the two states [26] was correlated with high interstate conflict. This was particularly true of the years 1947 and 1948, during which time it was difficult to separate the internal situation from the external one because of the extensive interstate mobility and bloodshed involving Moslems and Hindus following independence. Similar first-quartile rankings were found in 1964 and 1965. On the other hand, low rankings on both indicators were involved in the period 1959 through 1961. A simple Chi-square test suggests, however, that the relationship is not statistically significant. There are several reasons why this may be the case. In the first place, if the internal situation is too unstable, the natural reaction might be one of preoccupation with internal problems rather than attempts to divert one's internal instability with foreign adventurism. Engaging in conflict with foreign states always raises the risk that the already weak social and political fabric might collapse under pressure. If one were to rate the least stable years as far as Pakistan is concerned, 1954 and 1958 would have to be included. Although India on the whole has been much more stable than Pakistan, the one year that stands out in terms of uncertainty in the stability of the governing elite is 1966, a year that ranked in the fourth quartile in interstate conflict. Thus, very high instability in either the internal or external environment may tend to disrupt the positive link between internal instability and interstate conflict.

A second intervening factor which might tend to undermine the strength of the relationship is that of inputs from the international environment. Hostility is often simply a reaction to hostile moves by other states, having little or no relation to internal conditions. Furthermore, other actors in the international system such as China, the United States, the Soviet Union, and even the United Nations have also had some influence upon the course of events. Pressures from outside powers may serve to ameliorate conflict as shown by U.N. cease-fire resolutions and the good offices of the Soviet Union at Tashkent in 1966. Military alignment and support from the outside might also serve to exacerbate relations between India and Pakistan as the U.S.-Pakistani alliance did. Yet, since alignment with the outside world has been considerably more stable than have fluctuations in conflict behavior, one must examine other factors to explain the basis of the Indian and Pakistani conflict.

Finally, the lack of correlation between internal instability and interstate conflict may merely illustrate that external conflict is an effective integrator of national society. In this instance, one is getting into the very difficult issue of causal relationships. Since the rankings for the two variables were based upon a large series of events, which fluctuated widely in a given year, it is virtually impossible to provide conclusive evidence of a causal sort. Nor was the predictive capability of the hypothesis improved by lagging interstate conflict a year behind internal instability.

Further evidence suggesting that perhaps the internal political situation has some relationship to interstate conflict patterns can be found in terms of state reaction to negotiation and compromise. Internal political instability in itself may make negotiation more difficult, thus failing to moderate conflict patterns. It is almost taken as a truism that states do not favor negotiations just prior to the conduct of an election unless such negotiations are absolutely essential or a quick diplomatic victory is anticipated. There is always the threat of a long series of negotiations during which time rumors of appeasement can be circulated. Furthermore, compromise is difficult when the state is politically unstable. One student of the subject has suggested that since Ayub Khan's and Pandit Nehru's political positions grew weaker in their respective countries in 1963, concessions could hardly be expected during a set of negotiations forced upon them by pressures from the United States and the United Kingdom.[27] Indeed, the years of greatest progress in settling Indian and Pakistani differences tended to be those in which internal political instability was scored lowest. Among these years would be 1950, during which an agreement was reached ending a complete deadlock on trade and another providing for the protection of religious minorities. The period 1959 through 1961 was perhaps the most notable of all, for during these years agreement was reached on trade differences, the delineation of the western borders, funds left by refugees, the prepartition public debt, the use of the Indus River, and security regulations to prevent clashes between border units.

The problems of controlling for other variables when using a single case study make it difficult to assess just how important the internal political situation is as a determinant of foreign policy. Nevertheless, our examination of internal and external conflict patterns in South Asia allow us to suggest certain conditions under which internal political instability is more likely to induce foreign adventurism.

The utility of diversionary tactics for enhancing national unity is dependent first of all upon the nature of existing loyalties within a state. External agressiveness may serve only to split further a weak political and social fabric. Such is certainly a problem in South Asia with the large minority religious and linguistic groups in each state. In view of the heterogeneous nature of the populations in these states, internal conflict of a communal sort between Hindu and Moslem is highly associated with the level of conflict in Indian-Pakistani relations. It is perhaps not by accident that the most significant Hindu-Moslem communal riots occurred in the years corresponding to the greatest conflict between Pakistan and India. The years 1947 and 1948 witnessed virtually a blood bath of communal violence, and 1964 was reported to have been the most serious Hindu-Moslem crisis since independence. All three years were placed in the first quartile of interstate conflict.

Further evidence of the relationship between internal political instability and interstate conflict is suggested by the wave of communal rioting that erupted in September 1965 after Pakistan sent in regular troops to back Azad Kashmir (that portion of Kashmir supporting Pakistan) in its conflict with India.

A precise correlation between communal violence and interstate conflict is impossible, given the fabrication and withholding of information by the Indian and Pakistani governments. Nevertheless, the evidence suggests that this aspect of internal instability probably represents the highest correlation with interstate conflict. Indeed, when parts of a population identify to a certain degree with a foreign belligerent, the line between the internal and the external becomes exceedingly blurred. Minority groups during periods of conflict tend to be viewed as fifth columns. Still unanswered is whether internal communal conflict induces external conflict or the reverse. Perhaps these two are inseparable as each feeds upon the other.

The close relationship between communal violence and interstate conflict would appear to create real incentives for a government to minimize interstate conflict for the sake of domestic tranquillity, but this may not be that simple to accomplish. As in the case of India and Pakistan, the governments of both states have been accused of taking a soft position on the issue of the Indo-Pakistani conflict. For example, the Tashkent agreement of 1966 brought protests from groups in both states.

The utility of interstate conflict for overcoming internal problems is dependent upon whether the external conflict is salient for all important segments of the population. The Kashmir conflict, for example, has had limited utility in uniting East and West Pakistan, for the former simply has not been as concerned about the issue as has West Pakistan, which borders on the disputed territory. If a conflict is to be completely unifying, it must be perceived as a threat of all units of a state. If such is not the case, the conflict may be disintegrative; some groups may see the attention being given to a situation as excessive, leading to the neglect of internal problems they see as having greater importance. The charges leveled against the United States, that it is neglecting the Negro while concentrating upon the war in Vietnam, is a case in point.

Whether or not a government will seek to take advantage of external conflicts to produce internal unity and stability will also depend upon whether it can minimize internal turmoil by dealing directly with the economic and social problems creating the turmoil or whether it feels it has to take advantage of the short-run advantages of interstate conflict. In view of the slow rate of economic progress and the high internal political instability in Pakistan during the 1950's, it has been argued that Pakistan had the greater need for utilizing external conflict to hold together "a spiritless body politic."[28] The relative position of India and Pakistan in terms of economic growth has now reversed itself in the 1960's, with the Indian economy showing a certain sluggishness and that of Pakistan demonstrating an average annual increase of GNP of 5.5 percent between 1960 and 1965.[29] The slow economic progress, coupled with the growing strength of regionalism in India, may create increased incentives for the elite to attempt to gain short-term advantages by emphasis upon foreign diversion.

Slow economic progress might affect Indian attitudes toward Pakistan and Kashmir in yet another way. It has been suggested that during periods of severe economic crisis the Indian people are more likely to turn to right-wing religious parties than toward the Communists.[30] With increased power in the hands of religious conservatives, negotiation with Pakistan becomes more problematical and pressures toward increased conflict are created.

The above by no means exhausts the many links between national political development and interstate conflict between India and Pakistan. For example, one might raise questions concerning the effect of political maturation upon interstate conflict. Will succeeding generations not involved in the bloody independence movement be less volatile than current elites who jealously guard each small parcel of land? What effect will India's efforts and possible successes toward secularization have upon Indian and Pakistani relations? Daily developments in the political field continue to have an impact, but our interest has been directed primarily toward the effects of internal political stability and national unity upon conflict behavior in South Asia.

Evidence has been collected suggesting that at best there is only a weak relationship between internal instability and Indo-Pakistani conflict behavior. The relationship between internal and external conflict is perhaps most pronounced in the case of communal rioting, which tends to blur the division between the two environments. The utility of interstate conflict for diversionary purposes is dependent upon whether or not the external threat can unify the population as a whole or whether it merely integrates the majority, while widening the breach with the minority. The utilization of interstate conflict for diversionary purposes will also depend upon the level of economic progress and whether or not an elite feels it necessary to take advantage of the short-term unifying capabilities of external conflict.

A secondary purpose of this research has been to suggest a systematic way of looking at the relationship between internal and external events, minimizing as much as possible the distorting effects of data of dubious validity, which is particularly a problem in this area of the world because of the incompleteness and not infrequent falsification of news reporting. The attempt has been to combine the rigor of quantification with the more subjective evaluation of the expert as found in a perusal of the secondary literature on the subject.

More case studies of this sort, however, would be necessary to determine the exact relationship between internal political instability and interstate conflict. Sometimes there seems to be a relationship and sometimes not. The goal ought to be one of ascertaining the specific conditions under which political elites are more likely to favor short-run foreign adventurism over the long-term internal development in their quest for political stability.

TABLE ONE

RELATIVE INTERNAL POLITICAL INSTABILITY IN INDIA
SINCE INDEPENDENCE

First Quartile	Second Quartile	Third Quartile	Fourth Quartile
1947	1950	1949	1953
1948	1957	1951	1954
1964	1958	1952	1955
1965	1962	1956	1959
1966	1963	1960	1961

TABLE TWO

RELATIVE INTERNAL POLITICAL INSTABILITY IN PAKISTAN
SINCE INDEPENDENCE

First Quartile	Second Quartile	Third Quartile	Fourth Quartile
1947	1949	1952	1950
1948	1953	1962	1959
1951	1955	1964	1960
1954	1956	1965	1961
1958	1957	1966	1963

TABLE THREE

INTERSTATE CONFLICT BETWEEN INDIA AND PAKISTAN

First Quartile	Second Quartile	Third Quartile	Fourth Quartile
1947	1949	1952	1950
1948	1951	1954	1953
1956	1955	1957	1959
1964	1962	1958	1960
1965	1963	1961	1966

TABLE FOUR

QUARTILE RANKINGS ON INTERNAL INSTABILITY AND INTERSTATE CONFLICT

Year	Internal Instability India	Internal Instability Pakistan	Interstate Conflict	Year	Internal Instability India	Internal Instability Pakistan	Interstate Conflict
1947	1	1	1	1957	2	2	3
1948	1	1	1	1958	2	1	3
1949	3	2	2	1959	4	4	4
1950	2	4	4	1960	3	4	4
1951	3	1	2	1961	4	4	3
1952	3	3	3	1962	2	3	2
1953	4	2	3	1963	2	4	2
1954	4	1	4	1964	1	3	1
1955	4	2	2	1965	1	3	1
1956	3	2	1	1966	1	3	4

NOTES

[1] My special thanks go to Ronald Aulgur for assistance in data collection.

[2] Rudolph J. Rummel, "Dimensions of Conflict Behavior Within and Between Nations," *General Systems: Yearbook of the Society for General Systems Research*, VIII (1963), 1–50; and Raymond Tanter, "Dimensions of Conflict Behavior Within and Between Nations, 1958–1960," *Journal of Conflict Resolution*, X (March 1966), 41–64.

[3] *Action and Reaction in World Politics* (Boston, 1963).

[4] Khalid Bin Sayeed, "Pakistan's Foreign Policy: An Analysis of Pakistani Fears and Interests," *Asian Survey*, IV (March 1964), 746.

[5] James N. Rosenau, "Pre-Theories and Theories of Foreign Policy," in *Approaches to Comparative and International Politics*, ed. R. Barry Farrell (Evanston, 1966), 47.

[6] See the findings of Ivor Thomas, "War and Its Causes, 1815–1914," in *War and Democracy*, ed. E. F. M. Durbin and George Catlin (London, 1938); Lewis F. Richardson, *Statistics of Deadly Quarrels* (Chicago, 1960), 176; and Quincy Wright, *A Study of War* (Chicago, 1942), 221.

[7] George Simmel, *Conflict and the Web of Group Affiliations*, trans. K. H. Wolff and R. Bendix (Glencoe, Ill., 1955); Lewis Coser and Half Dahrendorf, *Class and Class Conflict in Industrial Society* (Stanford, Calif., 1959).

[8] John Hohenberg, *Between Two Worlds: Politics, Press, and Public Opinion in Asian-American Relations* (New York, 1967), 338.

[9] Karl Von Vorys, *Political Development in Pakistan* (Princeton, 1965), 168.

[10] New York *Times*, Aug. 9, 1950.

[11] Rudolph J. Rummel, *Dimensions of Conflict Behavior Within and Between Nations* (Evanston: Department of Political Science, Northwestern University), 79.

[12] *Annual Register of World Events*, 1960.

[13] *Deadline Data on World Affairs*, March 23, 1965.

[14] *Ibid.*, March 20, 1966.

[15] New York *Times*, April 3, 1956.

[16] *Danger in Kashmir* (Princeton, 1954), 162.

[17] *Ibid.*, 184.

[18] Margaret W. Fisher, "India in 1963: A Year of Travail," *Asian Survey*, IV (March 1964), 737–45.

[19] Von Vorys, *Political Development in Pakistan*, 167.

[20] New York *Times*, March 15, 1952.

[21] *Deadline Data on World Affairs*, Sept. 9, 1958.

[22] *Ibid.*, July 19, 1961.

[23] Alastair Lamb, *The Kashmir Problem* (New York, 1966).

[24] New York *Times*, March 5, 1953.

[25] Writers subscribing to this point of view have included Selig Harrison, "Troubled India and Her Neighbors," *Foreign Affairs*, XLIII (Jan. 1965), 320; Von Vorys, *Political Development in Pakistan*, 170; and Leicester Webb, "Pakistan's Political Future," *Futuribles*, I (1963), 318; and Lamb, *The Kashmir Problem*, 138.

[26] Since conflict tends to be reciprocal, political instability in only one state is sufficient, assuming the hypothesis is correct, to induce a high level of interstate conflict.

[27] Von Vorys, *Political Development in Pakistan*, 168.

[28] Harrison, "Troubled India and Her Neighbors," 320.

[29] Edward S. Mason, *Economic Development in India and Pakistan* (Cambridge, Mass.: Harvard University Center for International Affairs, 1966), 2.

[30] Philip G. Altback, "The Indian Political Scene on the Eve of the 1967 Elections," *Orbis*, X (Fall 1966), 891.

CHAPTER SEVEN

AMERICAN INFLUENCE IN DEVELOPED & UNDERDEVELOPED COUNTRIES

———

RUPERT EMERSON

To BE A GREAT POWER, and even more a super power, is to be concerned with what goes on in every corner of the globe. To be concerned is to seek to influence the turn of events wherever possible in order to secure a favorable outcome, or at least to forestall an unfavorable one. With the shrinking of time and space for both peaceful and belligerent purposes in the contemporary world and with the transition to independence of almost all the colonial territories, the interest of the super powers more literally embraces every corner of the globe than was feasible at any previous time, even though the potential addition to their strength which the multitude of lesser states might bring is in almost every instance of minimal significance.

The United States has accepted the necessity of dealing with a greater or less degree of intimacy with all the countries of the world; or, as its hostile critics would phrase it, it has reached out imperialistically, or perhaps neocolonially, to impose itself on as much of the world as it can lay hands on. Whatever version may be accepted, the United States finds itself involved in the affairs of a large number of countries and peoples at all levels of development from the most advanced to the most backward. In these circumstances it becomes a matter of consequence to explore the opportunities and limitations which stem from the level of development of the countries that the United States seeks to influence.

A first necessity is to secure some measure of agreement as to the countries which, for the purposes of this paper, the United States seeks to influence. A plausible answer in view of America's global role as a super power would be to say that the United States seeks to influence all countries without exception. In a sense this is undoubtedly a valid approach, but for the present purpose I suggest that we eliminate from consideration those states that must be considered implacably hostile to the United States, where "influence" ceases to have any appreciable element of friendly persuasion and cannot in any ordinary course of events be carried on within the framework of the more familiar channels of diplomacy and interstate relations. To put the matter in the bluntest terms, those countries that regard the United States as the enemy and are usually so regarded in return, are here held to fall outside any generally acceptable use of the term "influence." Pointing a gun or a nuclear bomb may be one way of exerting influence, but it is not the way that is contemplated here.

Even where guns or bombs are not immediately involved, the range of influence is sharply limited where the rulers of a country assume a basic incompatibility between their view of the world and that of the United States and seek, wherever possible, to close their doors to any penetration of American influence. Thus, to take two cases at one extreme end of the spectrum, the influence which the United States exerted on North Vietnam through devastating the country by continuous bombing is not considered here, nor are the embittered exchanges with China. In both instances, and other similar ones, there are undoubtedly also behind-the-scenes fragments of a more normal intercourse, but they are slight and currently sadly inconsequential. Other reasonably clear cases would be the relationship, or lack of it, between the United States and Castro's Cuba, Albania, North Korea, or East Germany. Obviously, a number of borderline cases can be brought in to complicate the issues, including even the Soviet Union itself, insofar as Moscow and Washington have accepted a kind of reciprocal relationship in which the possibility of discovering some common purposes is not excluded and an advance for one is not inevitably regarded as a defeat for the other. A case more nearly approaching the midpoint between the usual amicable or indifferent intercourse between states and the assumption of fundamental cleavage between them appears in the relations between the United States and Yugoslavia.

One other situation that is excluded from consideration here, although some mention is made of it later in another connection, is the colonial relationship. A country that possesses colonies has, by definition, the right to exercise its sovereign authority over them, so long as the colonial relationship exists. However much it may in fact rely upon influence (in the sense of persuasion of one sort or another) to accomplish its purposes, the ruling power has the right to command when it chooses to exercise it. Thus, the Virgin Islands, Guam, and American Samoa are directly under American colonial jurisdiction; Okinawa appears to be effectively no less so despite its more uncertain legal status; and in the Trust Territory of the Pacific, the United States exercises a somewhat more limited colonial control. Legally it may be that Puerto Rico lingers as a territory wholly subject to American sovereignty, but the compact creating the Commonwealth established a unique kind of relationship which the American Congress would be highly unlikely to override unilaterally.

Lastly, no attempt is made to deal with the vast topic of the kind of influence the United States exerts in the world by its mere existence and the extent of its wealth and power. Whether it acts or does not act, whether it intends to influence or to stand aside, the United States is inescapably a major factor in the world's affairs, affecting both the developed and the underdeveloped alike. This paper is confined essentially to conscious and deliberate efforts on the part of the

United States to influence other countries, although this does not, of course, in any way imply that the results achieved were those intended.

The first proposition I would advance concerns the primacy of politics. The basic political posture of countries, which in large measure determines the kind of outside influences they are prepared to tolerate, is determined by political and ideological considerations in which their level of development appears to play no role. Thus, without any change in level of development a coup or governmental overturn may reverse the political alignment of a country; influences to which it was formerly open may be ended or curtailed and another source or sources of influence may be substituted. No doubt it is also true, although it is more difficult to find concrete examples, that changes in level of development can take place which have no major bearing on political alignments or readiness to accept the intrusion of influence from outside sources.

Illustrations of this general proposition abound. Three of particular concern to the United States and representing different levels of development may be cited. Cuba was closely bound to the United States and wide open to American influence and capital until Castro took over. At the outset certainly no change in level of development was involved, and as the new regime progressed, the deterioration of the Cuban economy would, under other circumstances, have led to closer ties to the United States, but the ideological and political orientation of Castro and American hostility to him led to his opening the doors to the communist camp.

Because of its magnitude and the shock it gave Americans, the most striking case is that of China, which had been regarded as a grateful protégé and firm friend of the United States until Mao Tse-tung took command of all mainland China and denounced America as the leader of imperialist exploitation and oppression. As in the Cuban case, what had changed was not China's level of development but the fundamental political outlook of its rulers.

The third example, moving toward the top of the scale of development, is that of France. In the later phases of World War II, in the Marshall Plan, and in the common framework of NATO, France was closely linked to the United States. Since his return to power, Charles de Gaulle has moved France further and further away from the American orbit and has taken a number of steps to curtail the extent of American influence, including barring Britain from the Common Market in part because of her too close association with the United States.

If a fourth and lesser example, taken from close to the bottom of the development scale, is desired, it might be that of Congo (Brazzaville), where the amicable if casual relations with the United States were reversed when Fulbert Youlou was overthrown and his successors moved to the left, leading to withdrawal of the American diplomatic mission in 1965 after several unpleasant incidents.

These all happen to be examples of reversals of posture that told against the United States. Two that worked in the other direction are the coup which left Kwane Nkrumah in exile from Ghana while the government was taken over by military and police leaders friendly to the United States and the West in general, and the long-drawn-out process by which Sukarno was eased from power in Indonesia, again being replaced largely by the military who wanted no part of his ties to China and to the Indonesian Communist party. In neither instance was there any overt shift to alignment with the United States, but in both cases denunciations of the United States came to an end and doors that were being closed were opened again.

In the contemporary scene it can usually be taken for granted that the coming to power of a left-wing regime will bring with it efforts to curb the influence of the United States, regarded by the left as the ringleader of the capitalist-imperialist forces. The overthrow of such a regime has the reverse effect of restoring the United States to grace, although it is by no means necessarily the case that only left-wing regimes are hostile to the United States.

It is perhaps also in order to suggest that particularly in the less developed countries the determination of the basic political alignment of a country is likely to be the work of the few at the top or of the single leader, in whose hands effective governmental decision-making rests. The reversal of that determination through a coup or a revolution is likely to be carried out by an equally tiny segment of the society with equally little in the way of positive popular approval or disapproval other than passive acquiescence, even though the new regime, like the old, can produce popular demonstrations in its support. Such regimes, lacking any broad base, are obviously unstable and their hold on power is precarious. Most frequently a change in alignment, with the consequent shift in the outside influences to which a government is prepared to give access, follows the overturn of the established government, as in Ghana or Cuba, but it may also be the result of other circumstances, as, for example, in the turning away of Pakistan from the United States when the Chinese attack brought forth a flow of American arms and aid to India.

What lies behind such reversals of basic political alignment is usually difficult to determine and seems in many instances to represent little, if anything, more than one ruling potentate or oligarchy's replacing another, be it military or civilian. We live in an age that appears to breed regimes headed by single leaders, who are often unduly flattered by outsiders as being endowed with charisma, but who vanish from power leaving few who mourn their disappearance. Almost invariably they and their followers are charged both with failure to achieve development and with corruption, nepotism, and similar sins. Particularly where the military take over, there is likely to be a public demonstration of disgust with politics and politicians, regarded as self-serving and incompetent.

The elimination from consideration of countries that deliberately exclude American influence makes it possible to undertake a more meaningful examination of the question as to whether American influence prospers best in developed or in underdeveloped countries.

It would be idle to expect a single answer to satisfy the intricacies of such a question, both because the many states with which the United States is dealing differ strikingly among themselves and because the results the United States seeks and the methods it employs in pursuit of them vary greatly. Certain characteristic differences distinguish the developed from the underdeveloped countries, but even within each category what evokes a friendly response from one may antagonize another. Furthermore, there can be no doubt that, particularly in connection with more overtly political matters, the extent to which American influence can make itself felt is determined far less by degree of development than by political attachments and attitudes; i.e., a neutralist country benevolent to the East can be presumed to be less receptive to American influence than one benevolent to the West. As a crude example, one South Vietnamese may see American intervention as salvation, while another, adhering to the Viet Cong, regards it as imperialist oppression. The primacy of politics again makes itself evident.

The various kinds of influence the United States seeks to exert in the world can be broken down in a number of ways, but they overlap and criss-cross each other in such fashion as to guarantee that no scheme of classification can be regarded as wholly satisfactory. This is particularly true if one attempts to come at the problem through an analysis of the purposes of American efforts to influence other countries. The motivations of American policy are likely to be both multiple and obscure, subject to radically different interpretations. If foreign aid programs, both economic and military, may be taken as both significant expressions of American policy and important channels of influence, the dilemmas involved in assessing the motives that lie behind them are immediately evident.[1] (The situation is, of course, complicated by the fact that aid programs serve different purposes in different times and places, and the different phases of an aid program even within a single country may serve different purposes.) Where the hostile interpreter can portray them as a means of moving toward world domination by corrupting governments and factions and establishing neocolonial supremacy over satellites, the friendly witness will see them as serving the long-term interests at once of the United States and the rest of the free world by aiding in the development of stable, democratic, economically advancing countries, whose independence is safeguarded. American backers of such programs can defend them in such various and conflicting ways as that they are essentially indispensable instruments in the Cold War, that they are wise and prudent methods of dealing with the problems of the underdeveloped countries, which also promise to provide fruitful fields for American trade and investment, or that they represent generous recognition by the United States that the internationally underprivileged should share in the wealth of the affluent and be assisted in rising to take their own place in the modern world. These and a number of other variant defenses have been regularly put forward by the administration, in Congress, and elsewhere. The assumption is indeed plausible that all of them play some role in shaping American policy and in winning support for foreign assistance. The frequently heard plea that it is necessary to devise some single and logically consistent motivation for the aid programs ignores the diversity of views which enter significantly into the shaping of American foreign policy.

The assumption of a diversity of purpose, however, makes it more difficult to assess the relative success or failure of American influence abroad. What is the yardstick for measurement: the vehemence and reliability of the anticommunism that is achieved, the establishment and maintenance of stable democratic government, or the extent of the climb up the ladder of economic development? In any country the answers to these three questions may give very different results.

Given the primacy of Cold War considerations for so many aspects of American policy, it is almost inescapable to take as the overall goal in the political realm the desire to influence countries to collaborate with and accept the lead of the United States in the global struggle against the oft-depicted dangers of communist imperialism. If countries cannot be forced to climb on the anticommunist bandwagon, it is at least desired to keep them safely out of the enemy camp—a matter that becomes increasingly complex as the communist world breaks up within itself and loses its monolithic unity.

Whether or not one can buy friends remains a debated issue. There is, I am inclined to suggest, verbal agreement that it cannot be done and that it has some tinge of immorality about it, but it would also appear to be an operative belief that foreign assistance programs in fact have the buying of friends as one of their major purposes. To use a somewhat more neutral term, if they fail to "make" friends, it is generally felt that there is something wrong with them. It is affirmed from time to time that gratitude is not to be expected in the relations between states, but when gratitude is lacking, Americans are likely to have at least a wistful sense that they are being short-changed. Certainly it is evident that neither need nor ability to develop successfully is an adequate criterion for the granting of American aid. Both need and ability can be countered by lining up on the wrong side of the fence; and loud dismay is sure to be voiced in influential circles in the United States if aid recipients such as Nasser or Nkrumah publicly criticize American policy.

The more applied and specific political uses of influence are far too numerous and scattered to allow more than an indication of a few possibilities, such as persuading other countries to maintain armed forces at given levels of strength and availability, to grant rights for bases, to limit or end trade with communist countries, to block mainland China's representation in the United Nations, and generally to insure that they vote right on U.N. issues (although it does not appear that the offer or withdrawal of aid has been used to influence votes on specific issues).

Another range of political uses involves the bolstering up of friendly governments in time of need, as in the summer of 1967 in sending military transport planes to the Congo to assist in putting down a revolt, or the delicate and difficult task of promoting democracy, which AID has recently been instructed to undertake. The latter step rests on the double assumption that democracy is a superior form of government and that peoples so governed are likely to be friendly and congenial to the United States. For similar reasons, American influence has often been brought into play against a takeover by military regimes in Latin America, although the military overthrow of a leftist government, as in Indonesia or Ghana, is likely to be taken calmly by Washington. Despite an avowed affection for democracy, in many instances the United States has refrained from throwing its weight into the scales against authoritarian or dictatorial governments, accepting instead their affirmations of opposition to communism and thus tending to line the United States up with the right wing in Asia, Latin America, and elsewhere. Washington is inescapably in trouble in trying to weigh the gains hoped for from the ultimate strengthening of democracy in countries which have been assisted to stability and well-being as against the immediate gains to be derived from backing authoritarian and perhaps reactionary regimes whose anticommunist credentials are impeccable.

Commentators have also from time to time pointed out the dilemma involved in American enthusiasm, on the one hand, for democracy and social and economic development, including such measures as land reform, which are prone to disrupt the existing order, and, on the other hand, the fear of losing to revolutionary forces who may see their destiny linked to the Communists.[2] During the Cold War the latter fear has often brought American influence into play on the side of the status quo, even though it has also been recognized that failure to reform and develop leaves an attractive field open to the left.

For the most part, these uses of influence are self-regarding in the sense that they serve what is seen as directly an American interest. A number of other uses of influence, of significance primarily in relation to the less developed countries, may properly be held to be other-regarding in that their essential purpose is to establish the conditions which the American authorities see as necessary for the effective use of American aid. Similar conditions, often more rigid and more rigorously insisted upon, have been laid down by the International Bank and Monetary Fund. These may range from specific administrative acts which will clear the way for some particular project or involve acceptance of such rules of the game as those laid down for handling counterpart funds to a basic overhaul of the political-administrative structure in order to create the preconditions for development. Pressures for actions of this kind directly serve the American interest only insofar as they improve the prospects for development, which is, for whatever reason, regarded as constituting an American interest. Uses of influence that perhaps fall in between the self- and the other-regarding categories are the injunction that private enterprise should be promoted, and, further over in the self-regarding column, the disfavor with which nationalization and expropriation are regarded, although part of the argument for such an attitude is based on the conviction that moves toward socialism inhibit rather than advance development.

Given the diffuseness and uncertainty of the criteria to be applied, what is the verdict on the success or failure of American influence when in the case of two countries more or less equally in the good graces of the United States and sharing in the American bounty, country A maintains a reasonable facsimile of constitutional democratic government, is making praiseworthy headway in economic development, but is insistent on following a policy of nonalignment favorable to the East and indulging in at least ritual denunciations of the United States from time to time; whereas country B has an authoritarian and arbitrary government, absorbs American aid with no visibly significant effect on either development or the general standard of living, but gives ardent political and military support to American anticommunist activities?

In general terms it can be said that the opportunity open to the United States is greater in the more developed than in the less developed countries for the simple reason that the advanced countries are better organized, more capable of achieving what they set out to do, and able to produce greater economic and military strength. By definition they are abreast of the modern world and able to command much of the new-found power that is one of the distinguishing features of modernity, whereas the underdeveloped are still only wistfully eyeing that power. But, as I have already suggested, whether the United States can enlist the more advanced countries in its cause depends not upon their degree of advancement but on their political decision as to where they line up in the world. Without attempting to work out meticulously accurate gradations of development, it seems appropriate to assume that Germany, Italy, and Japan were to be listed in the ranks of the developed at the time of World War II, but they obviously offered no sphere in which American influence might operate except strictly on their own terms. Much the same can be said of the Soviet Union, with only minor qualifications and adjustments, throughout the half-century of its existence.

Where the political circumstances allow or encourage it, the magnitude of the collaboration that can be achieved between the advanced countries runs well ahead of what can be expected between the advanced and the underdeveloped. One important element is that where only the advanced are involved, there is a much greater degree of equality and reciprocity of influence, as contrasted with an almost wholly one-way flow of influence from the advanced to the developing country. Advancement also brings with it a multiplication of interests, employments, agencies, organizations, and the like, which make possible the contact between societies over a much wider range than is possible for the underdeveloped countries whose social, political, and economic structure is less intricately evolved.

The most successful of large-scale postwar American ventures was undoubtedly the series of steps taken in relation to Europe, of which the two most striking manifestations were the Marshall Plan and the Atlantic alliance embodied in NATO, which also led to the creation of the western European supranational functional organizations. Although the European powers had wills and voices of their own, American influence reached an expansive plateau which was higher and more extensive than any attained before or since. A number of factors may be picked out as the essential conditions of the successes which were then achieved. (a) The level of development of the countries principally concerned was relatively similar. All had a firsthand acquaintance with the modern world and several were outstanding leaders in it. This made possible a degree of high-level collaboration that is not possible where the advanced-underdeveloped relationship is involved. (b) However difficult it may be to pin down, a sense of common European identity, to which the United States was by no means wholly a stranger, eased the process of bringing sovereign states within a common framework and made it seem a natural rather than an externally forced and artificial device. The pulls and strains were real enough, but an underlying sense of traditional unity gave new institutions an emotional support. (c) The European countries were all in varying degree war-devastated and in grave need of outside aid to set their economies in motion again. The United States was the one country that could furnish such aid on a large enough scale to turn the trick and could also furnish the necessary leadership to get Europe rolling. (d) They all came to be moved by a common belief, varying in its bearing and intensity, that their security was threatened by the Soviet Union, which had absorbed the Baltic countries, established its East European satellites, reached out menacingly toward Greece and Turkey, and forced Czechoslovakia into its subordinate entourage. It is highly likely that no driving force is as impressive as a felt threat to national security; and in the postwar years not only did the threat seem real, but the United States with its economic and military strength, including atomic power, was the one available safeguard.

It need scarcely be added that as these conditions changed, the centrality of the United States was constantly lessened and the scope and weight of its influence began to fade. To mention only two items, the success of the Marshall Plan meant that European economies could stand on their own feet, and the end of the Stalin era in addition to other developing conditions in the U.S.S.R. made it far more difficult to conceive of the threat of a communist military attack on western Europe as a real danger. Precisely those conditions which had most enhanced American influence underwent drastic change. Britain, with some hesitation and uncertainties due perhaps to recollections of a greatness so recently vanished, decided to remain largely within the sphere of American influence, although it also sought to join the Europe of the Six, while de Gaulle appeared as the increasingly ardent champion of a national France and of a nationally organized Europe which would as far as possible insulate itself against American influence.

What kind of balance sheet can be drawn up? It remains the fact that the advanced countries can contribute much more to the realization of American purposes than can the underdeveloped—always granted they are prepared to make the contribution, as some are and some are not. One type of leverage the United States has in a number of the advanced countries, but obviously not in the advanced communist countries, is that American private finance and industry penetrate very deeply and widely. With rare exceptions, the underdeveloped countries have not proved attractive enough to the private investor to draw in large amounts of American capital or encourage the establishment of branch plants. The smallness of the market, the instability of governments, the fear of nationalization, the restrictions on the repatriation of profits, all combine to limit the interest of potential American investors except in a few extractive industries and particularly in the search for and the marketing of oil and its derivatives. The advanced countries, in contrast, have experienced a growing flood of American investments and, like Canada, become more and more aware of the vast economic power of the United States which threatens to dominate them. Any spectacular increase in the American involvement in the economy of another country is almost certain to rouse nationalist hostilities which may lead to restrictive or punitive measures intended to preserve or restore domestic control over the economic life of the country. When American economic expansion is combined with what is regarded as an undue extension of American political influence, and cultural influence as well, a nationalist reaction can be expected to erupt.

It is a plausible approximation of the facts to see the position of the developed and the underdeveloped countries in relation to the United States as the reverse of each other. The wealth and strength of the advanced countries both limit American attempts to influence them and make their potential support of American policies and actions highly valuable, whereas the poverty and weakness of the underdeveloped make access to them easier because of their greater need for what the affluent can provide them, but poverty and weakness also mean that their political and military specific gravity is minimal.

On the face of it, it might be thought that the lack of wealth and strength would make the underdeveloped more susceptible to external influence, and particularly to that of the United States as the major overall donor of foreign aid, but the record does not bear this out. Much of what has just been said about the advanced countries in reference to their hostility to American or other domination applies more or less equally to their less developed brethren. In fact, the wariness and suspicions of the less developed may be more acute than those of the advanced countries because so many of them have recently emerged from a detested colonialism whose return they dread. The neocolonialism against which the Left warns the new countries is closely akin to the kind of economic subordination, slipping all too easily into *de facto* political subordination, to which China, much of Latin America, and a few other countries have been subjected in the era of Western imperialism. How real the dangers of a return to colonialism or of a spread of neocolonialism may be at the present time is open to argument, but in the eyes of many of the ex-colonial peoples the dangers are real indeed; they consequently set limits to any attempt to exert external influence, limits that can be ignored only at the outsider's peril. Thus, the tying of political or military strings tó foreign aid is notoriously resented and can on occasion be disastrous, as in the case of the effort to draw Indonesia into alignment with the free world.[3]

On several counts it is inevitably an unsatisfactory task to seek to draw up a catalog of the successes and failures of American efforts to influence other countries. In many instances, the raw materials on which judgment must be based are lacking because it has not appeared on the public record what goals, if any, the United States set itself nor what methods were used to achieve them. Thus, it is often left as a matter of surmise whether Washington intervened or not, and in what fashion. By its enemies, if by no means always by its friends, the CIA is given credit for many exploits and upheavals abroad. It is likely that the CIA can achieve more with less effort in the underdeveloped than in the developed countries because of the instability of their political institutions and the small number of politically active persons who must be dealt with; but the ratio of fact to rumor remains almost wholly obscure. Nor is it possible to discern with any precision what the state of affairs would have been if the United States had kept its hands entirely off this or that situation in which it is credited with either a bulls-eye or a miss.

On the most general and superficial grounds it can be argued that American influence has been exerted successfully among the underdeveloped countries since so many have retained a nonalignment benevolent to the West, so few have joined the communist ranks, and some among those who seemed tempted to swing all the way to the left have moved back to something more nearly approaching a middle-of-the-road position. But in trying to allocate praise or blame for such an outcome, we can render only a most inconclusive verdict when our knowledge of the underlying facts is so limited and when we can do no more than make an instructed guess as to what the world would look like today if the United States had let the underdeveloped countries follow their own sweet pleasure.

Certainly any assumption that, since the United States is a super power in a world in which many of its fellow states are pygmies, it can accomplish what it pleases is far off the mark. As powers armed with the most modern and sophisticated weapons have found themselves baffled by guerrilla warfare, so the United States has been baffled by its inability to keep puny third-world governments in line under modern conditions even though it seems to have completely the upper hand. The two most striking examples which come immediately to mind are South Korea and South Vietnam, each of which has managed to maintain a surprising and often distressing freedom of movement despite the fact that both presumably owe their continued existence to the United States, which also contributes a substantial part of their support and has stationed overwhelming military force within their boundaries. A few well-known examples will illustrate the laxity of American influence or control. Syngman Rhee and Ngo Dinh Diem were both able to consolidate dictatorial regimes that became so obnoxious to their people that they were overthrown by violent uprisings. In the case of Diem the United States is said to have signaled its readiness to see his regime disposed of by suspending the vital commodity import program to Vietnam in October 1963, shortly before his ouster and assassination, but an intolerable situation had already been allowed to build up. In both instances the former leaders were followed by military regimes, in the Korean case at least neither of American choice nor to American pleasure. In the operation of these governments the United States obviously has a powerful influence and can exert some ultimate control, but much of what happens appears to be outside the American orbit. An extraordinary, but far from unique, sample is furnished by the tragicomic goings-on surrounding the Vietnamese elections of September 1967. That the elections were held at all, however, is a product of American pressure, which also played a significant and probably determining role in the transition in Korea from outright military rule to quasi-civilian rule under a new constitution following the election of General Park Chung-hee as president in 1963.

On June 11, 1967, the New York *Times* carried a Saigon dispatch by Jonathan Randal which reported American disaffection with the weaknesses of the Army of the Republic of Vietnam (ARVN) and the disinclination of General Westmoreland and his predecessors to come to a showdown with top Vietnamese military commanders over the removal of poor ARVN field commanders. "Since the American generals refuse to insist on unified command—on the ground such a step would validate enemy charges that the United States has taken over control of its 'puppet troops'—bad ARVN leaders enjoy virtual immunity from removal."

Ten days later, on June 21, the *Times* carried another Saigon dispatch which cited the dependence of the Vietnamese economy, military forces, and government on the United States and proceeded to quote "a ranking American official" who stated that "we really have almost no leverage over these people." The maneuvering of Premier Ky, the imposition of an unconstitutional censorship, and the campaigning ahead of the specified time were brought out in the story and were followed later by the banning of candidates whose voice deserved to be heard. The correspondent added, "These developments have deeply distressed the U.S. Embassy, because they conflict with the picture of the elections that the United States had hoped to be able to show the world. They also bode ill for rallying the South Vietnamese public behind the eventual victor. But embassy officials refused even to contemplate punitive steps against Marshal Ky." [4]

The curious counterpart of the ability of the Viet Cong and North Vietnamese forces to hold the American military at bay is the ability of Ky in South Vietnam and Park in South Korea to play their own game in their own fashions. Ky and his fellow generals are in power on American sufferance, but it is a sufferance Washington would find painful and costly to terminate. The men who should by all past reckoning be American puppets turn out in fact to have an identity of their own.

Apart from American inexperience in such matters, an element that seems to me of central significance in the contemporary scene is that "all past reckoning" has by now lost much of its validity. The colonial era has vanished, and the crude but forceful means of dealing with recalcitrant regimes of which an advanced power disapproves can no longer be brought into play. A few decades ago, if full-scale colonial rule were not established in countries that made themselves annoying in the fashion of Korea or Vietnam, at least blockades, bombardments, or temporary occupations probably involving the displacement and exiling of independent-minded political figures would have taken care of the situation.[5] Such measures are no longer available even though Washington did, in the special circumstances of the Caribbean, turn the clock back by its military intervention in the Dominican Republic. If remedies and sanctions of a colonial type cannot be brought into play, outlawed by the revolution in world opinion, by the principles of the free world which the United States claims to lead, and by traditional American anticolonialism, then the local regimes of the third world are given a freedom that the imperialist era denied them.

There are, I assume, few who would contemplate a return to the highhanded methods of imperialism and the strict controls of colonialism, but an embarrassing dilemma remains. In Korea and even more in Vietnam the United States has effectively, be it for good or for ill, taken on responsibilities and advocated reforms that require colonial-style control if they are really to be lived up to and put through; but colonialism has been repudiated.[6] The question: if the United States has committed itself to programs that can only be carried out in a colonial situation, should it pull back and re-evaluate the dilemma it has created for itself? Is "influence" enough to accomplish what the United States has found itself involved in? In a monumental way the United States has imposed itself on the Vietnamese society, distorting the pre-existing culture and internal balance of forces and opening the way to almost unlimited corruption of the society

224 RUPERT EMERSON

in various senses, but it does not accept the responsibility colonial governments assumed for what were often lesser interventions in the affairs of other peoples. To put it in part in personal terms: what has been the effect of allowing General Ky to represent to the world an American-controlled Vietnam, or, alternatively, could the United States afford to take the steps that would be needed to keep Ky in line or to replace him by a more acceptable and trustworthy, subservient leader? For a traditionally anticolonial power to take on the substance of colonial responsibilities in an era of anticolonialism is to assume an unconscionable burden of grief and pain. A credibility gap of even global dimensions inevitably divides proclaimed American intentions and what is actually done on the spot.

Korea and Vietnam are extreme cases of American influence in underdeveloped countries, examples which one can hope will not be repeated. In many other areas the United States, far less deeply involved, has tried to make its influence felt through manipulation of foreign aid and by other means drawn from the older, established diplomatic cupboard.

The relationship in theory and practice of foreign assistance to the foreign policy of the donor country has been constantly under review and debate. Among the many questions that may be raised, one of central importance may be phrased as follows: where the avowed goal of foreign aid is economic and social development, is it legitimate—and effective—to use it as an instrument for short-run political goals? One of the most realistic or, perhaps more accurately, hardboiled versions of an answer is contained in an article written by Hans Morgenthau a half dozen years ago in which he made it his basic assumption that foreign aid is politically motivated and is to be evaluated as a weapon in the political armory.[7] He saw development as only one of a number of uses of foreign aid, and one that is often more of a front than a reality, a buying of political advantage under the pretense that economic development is the goal. Reduced to its simplest terms, it was his contention that "much of what goes by the name of foreign aid, today is in the nature of bribes." If one seeks a more elaborate version, including a quick look at some of the history of international bribery, George Liska, in a book on American policy explicitly inspired by Professor Morgenthau, elaborates on the thesis that "the object of foreign aid, both economic and military, is to create a condition that would induce or consolidate a relationship which in turn would generate desirable acts."[8]

Although a good case can perhaps be made for the proposition that foreign aid should not be used for political purposes, it is surely beyond argument that it has consistently been so used, and I cannot see the faintest reason to doubt that such uses will continue. I have suggested earlier that it is among the expectations of those who appropriate the necessary funds, as well as of many others, that foreign aid should both win general favor for the United States and, as occasion offers, secure particular benefits. Undoubtedly it is a blunt and clumsy instrument, ill-designed for bringing political pressure, but it has its obvious utility, particularly as some of the more direct and forceful measures of the past, including forthright bribery, have been outlawed by the change in international mores and in the makeup of the international community.

In some instances, particularly where military or military-related assistance was involved, the grant of aid was clearly and immediately linked to the benefits received. Thus, George Liska, writing of the aid programs of the late 1950's, listed: "First, military facilities and assets, such as bases and installations: in Spain, Greece, Turkey, Taiwan, the Philippines, and South Korea in return for defense support; in Libya, Morocco, and Ethiopia in return for special assistance; and in Saudi Arabia in return for sale of military equipment under Section 106 of the Mutual Security Act and economic assistance for projects of mutual benefit in the field of air and naval transport. Or a country may receive aid for its armed forces, as do Greece, Turkey, Taiwan, Pakistan, Thailand, the Philippines, the Republic of Korea, Vietnam, Cambodia, and Laos. Second, the donor may acquire an alliance commitment or another form of desirable international behavior. Turkey is a good example." [9]

The most interesting and perhaps the most difficult aspect to examine is the extent to which political results can be achieved, results that appear to make a significant change in the position which the country concerned would otherwise have adopted. It is the sound conclusion of Edward S. Mason, one of the most experienced of the practitioners of and commentators on foreign aid, that the chief lesson to be learned "from the two decades of post-war experience is that aid is not a very effective political instrument, at least for short-term objectives. Aid can help countries whose political stance we approve of grow stronger and the withholding of aid can inflict some degree of damage on the economies of countries pursuing political objectives of which we disapprove. But the help bestowed or the damage inflicted is not likely to induce significant change in the political objectives pursued by these countries." [10]

The primacy of politics again asserts itself. In marginal cases aid can save a government when it might otherwise go under or the denial of aid in special circumstances may give the final push to a regime that is tottering on the brink. It can be persuasive where there is already a readiness to listen sympathetically, and a government somewhat casually wavering between one decision or another, as in relation to a vote on a U.N. resolution of no great concern to that country, may be swung in the direction Washington desires. On the other hand, aid cannot be expected to reverse strongly held political positions.

The hope that foreign aid might influence countries in a large variety of directions has been a constant one in Congress, reflected over and over again in the relevant legislation and evidently intended primarily for the less developed countries. Thus, there have been legislative pleas not only for the achievement of economic development but also for social justice, a more equitable distribution of wealth, and maximum participation on the part of the people in developing countries in democratic institutions. The administering authorities have also been instructed to take into account in providing development loans and technical assistance the degree to which the recipient country is making progress toward respect for the rule of law, freedom of expression, and recognition of the importance of individual freedom, initiative, and private enterprise. The 1963 AID Program Guidance Manual set as the political goals of the aid program "a community of free nations cooperating on matters of mutual concern, basing their political systems on consent and progressing in economic welfare and social justice."[11]

In more specific relation to international politics, American foreign assistance has been tied to efforts to promote the security of the free world, to back the Korean war, to stop trade with Cuba and North Vietnam, and to promote the development of regional institutions in several parts of the world. Other devices have been utilized to try to induce or compel more advanced countries to observe the American ban on intercourse with the "enemy." It is, regrettably, doubtful that these various injunctions have been successful.

The need of the less developed for aid and their yearning for development are in the ordinary course of events not great enough to induce them to reverse deep-seated political convictions nor to abandon their socialist inclinations in favor of a private-enterprise system they view with grave suspicion. In most instances, neither their political sophistication nor their existing institutions lend themselves conveniently to the substance of democracy, stable constitutionalism, or individual freedom.

A far larger number of specific political goals have been pursued than can be mentioned here, but a few outstanding cases of success and failure may serve to illustrate the problem. It should be remarked, incidentally, that for the external observer failures are generally more easily accessible and recognizable than successes, except in the general sense, already mentioned, that the so-called free world has suffered little attrition since the great and major loss of China.

The use of foreign aid as an instrument to influence major policies of countries of the third world appears to have scored few triumphs, at least where it ran counter to what it is plausible to think the country would have done in any event. This comment is based in part upon what appears to be the widely accepted view that the removal from power of Sukarno in Indonesia and of Nkrumah in Ghana is not to be attributed to American machinations but was brought about essentially by internal forces and disaffections. Furthermore, American attempts to keep Sukarno and Nkrumah in line during their years of power through manipulation of foreign aid and other devices were, on the whole, clear failures, although Nkrumah demonstrated a distinctive agility in publicly denouncing the United States and all its works while in fact maintaining friendly relations with American agencies and private economic interests, particularly those having any concern with the Volta Dam and activities subsidiary to it. As one sample of this agility, ten days after the publication of a book by Nkrumah in which the Peace Corps was damned as only one phase of a "huge ideological plan for invading the so-called Third World," the Ghana government requested that almost double the number of Peace Corps teachers be sent to replace those whose terms were expiring.[12] When Sukarno embarked on his policy of "confrontation" of Malaysia, American and other aid programs were virtually wholly abandoned,[13] but the confrontation continued until Sukarno was eased out of power.

A detailed study of the vagaries and effects of the American manipulation of military and economic assistance for India and Pakistan would be revealing as a study of what can, and even more of what cannot, be done. Professor Mason concludes from his survey of American relations with the two Asian countries that all three seriously overestimated the political leverage to be derived from foreign assistance and that "the very large amount of economic assistance provided to India and Pakistan has, to date, given the United States a very small amount of influence on political attitudes and behavior in those countries." [14] As in other parts of the world, the United States cherished the peculiar belief that it could provide arms for a country to be used solely for defense against the proper enemy, the communist powers, and not against its actual enemy, its neighbor. In fact, neither India nor Pakistan was prepared to heed the advice of the United States. The Kashmir controversy remains as much a fighting issue between the two countries as ever and open warfare has broken out between them, with Pakistan deeply offended by the fact that its ally, the United States, moved speedily to the military assistance of India when attacked by China. Perhaps the American curtailment of aid to both India and Pakistan when hostilities broke out between them had some effect in hastening the adoption of a cease-fire, but, however it is calculated, the American record of political influence successfully exerted in the subcontinent is very slight. On the face of it, it is folly to assume that a country of the size of India, or of Pakistan for that matter, can be diverted from its own major purposes by turning on or turning off the stream of aid, although both have been persuaded to adopt major economic measures regarded as necessary for development.

The conclusions to be drawn from the cases cited are further borne out by relations between the United States and Nasser in the U.A.R. The net effect of American influence seems to be of the same order as that described for India and Pakistan: a series of efforts to persuade Nasser to mend his ways have achieved substantially nothing whatsoever except bad feeling. The most dramatic event was, of course, the decision of Secretary of State Dulles to withdraw from support of the Aswan Dam project, which led directly to the ruinous Suez crisis of 1956 and to the assumption by the Soviet Union of responsibility for Aswan with a consequent drop in the standing of the United States. An equal lack of success has attended the American effort to bring down President Duvalier in Haiti, where aid was cut off in 1962. In the neighboring Dominican Republic aid was deliberately manipulated for political purposes on several occasions and did in fact achieve certain specific goals after the fall of Trujillo, but as the situation deteriorated Washington concluded that it could secure its broader objectives only through a military occupation.[15] It was, of course, grossly improbable that after its long span of dictatorial rule the country could be transformed into a functioning democracy in a couple of years. The same proposition was, incidentally, presumably even more true of Vietnam in view of its political history and its decades of ruinous warfare. The long history of American attempts to influence the turn of political development in Latin America has often been examined and is on the whole a chastening demonstration of the immense difficulty of securing in another country the kind of political outcome that is sought. The ambitious slate of reforms called for in the Alliance for Progress has also been ignored on too many occasions.[16]

Although it is obviously debatable whether it was either justifiable or desirable, the American intervention in British Guiana (later Guyana) achieved at least for the time being the desired result. In collaboration with the British (to what extent were they themselves operating under American pressure?), Washington succeeded in ousting Cheddi Jagan, who leaned too far to the left, and substituted for him the more acceptable and amenable Forbes Burnham, under whose auspices the country moved to independence. Among other devices the United States, having kept up a small-scale aid program when Jagan was in power in order to keep its foot in the door, in 1965 extended more than $5 million in aid to the Burnham government, whose total budget was some $45 million, which enabled Burnham, among other things, to build roads into the Indian-inhabited areas, where Jagan's strength lay, and to maintain the subsidized rice price at the level set by Jagan for the predominantly Indian rice growers.

Benjamin Higgins has contended that the motto most clearly established by the foreign aid experience would seem to be that "the feeding hand shall be bitten." That the feeding hand shall be loved or earn meaningful gratitude is improbable, but to predict that it shall be bitten reaches extravagantly beyond what the record justifies. In point of fact, a number of countries continue complacently or even enthusiastically to receive aid and demonstrate no particular desire to bite.

Two different unfortunate side effects accompanying aid are, however, well established and work to curtail the influence of the donor. The first is that once a pattern of granting assistance has been established, particularly in the case of the underdeveloped country whose need is inexhaustible, the recipients assume that it will be continued, and they regard any cessation or significant curtailment as an insult and intervention in domestic affairs—as it often is when the purpose is to inspire some action or inaction on the part of the recipient. In addition to the prevalent belief, for which a strong case can be made, that the internationally underprivileged have a right to share in the wealth and skills of the affluent, there develops a further belief that a particular country has a right to the continuance of specific aid programs of which they have been the beneficiaries. Nasser vigorously expressed his indignation when American aid was curtailed, and Indian authorities, with greater justification, have resented delays in completing arrangements for the delivery of food under Public Law 480. Under such circumstances it becomes an open question whether the delays and vexations accompanying American aid are not sometimes greater than the satisfactions the aid is supposed to provide.[17]

A second unfortunate side effect is that the grant of aid, most notably in the military sphere, may have the result of prejudicing the relations of the donor with neighbors or rivals of the recipient and may, on the insistence of the recipient, make it impossible to extend aid to such neighbors or rivals. That this is no new phenomenon is well illustrated by George Liska, who has surveyed the severe limitations imposed on French policy before World War I because of the extensive politically motivated French investment in Russia.[18] A particularly poignant contemporary example, already referred to in another context, is the bad feeling between India and Pakistan, which makes aid to either immediately suspect in the eyes of the other and which was exacerbated when Pakistan became an ally of the United States. Similar situations exist in the relations between Israel and the Arab states, and between Ethiopia and Somalia. In the latter instance, the American military and other aid to Ethiopia, in good part designed as recompense for the important American communications center at Asmara, has worked to alienate Somalia, which has been offered and has accepted substantial aid from communist sources. These countries thus secure a kind of reverse influence over the donor, who may be debarred from embracing other countries that would otherwise be open to its influence.

Such unintended political consequences of foreign aid must add up to an impressive total. Whether economic or military or some mix of the two, aid in any substantial quantity cannot help but have a bearing on both the internal and international political relationships of the aided countries. Given the instability of governments in the third world and the usual thinness of their domestic political base, the injection of aid in one or another fashion or its later withdrawal may have a decisive impact on the ability of a government to survive and perhaps on the dominance of a particular faction within the government.[19]

A frequent complaint against American aid policies and practices is that they involve too much meddling in the political life of other countries, but John D. Montgomery has argued that Americans, setting off from a doctrine of nonintervention in the affairs of other people, have been more deceived by assertions of the nonpolitical character of foreign aid than have the leaders of the underdeveloped countries. He went on to complain, "The noninterventionist dogma has been strictly followed to the point that the working out of the aid program has discouraged democratic forces in the host country and has restrained the expression of concern in cases where undemocratic forces have harvested the principal benefits of aid. . . . The view that the American presence is divorced from the politics of a recipient nation and from the social progress of its people has contributed to the shallowness of much of the public and private debate over issues of foreign aid."[20]

It is to be feared that the United States is in the position of being damned if it does and damned if it doesn't. On a visit early in 1967 to east Africa I was impressed by the frequency and vehemency of the complaint that the United States was sticking its fingers into far too many African matters and trying to push African states and peoples around. In many parts of the world one can hear the grievance that the United States is meddling too much in other people's affairs, but at the same time it is held against the United States that it is prepared to work on friendly terms with oppressive and dictatorial governments and lend them its support rather than to seek their overthrow. In some part, of course, the explanation is that American power and wealth open this country to attack by all concerned, but a real dilemma exists for which it is difficult to conceive any universally satisfactory answer: nonintervention remains a doctrine to which peoples are still generally inclined to subscribe and which has obvious merit, and yet intervention for good cause, to promote freedom and advancement and overcome evil, also has its attractions. Condemnation of the United States for the way in which it has used or abused its influence is likely to come from the Left which, as has been seen, tends to assume an anti-American position from the outset. Regrettably, the charge that Washington has been prepared to collaborate with and bolster up governments of the Right has enough substance to make defense of the American position difficult. In the eyes of much of the third world, the United States has also prejudiced its position by its negative attitude toward anticolonialist resolutions in U.N. and by its reluctance at the United Nations Conference on Trade and Development, to consider new approaches to the problems of development and international trade which even its NATO colleagues were prepared to examine sympathetically.

Our primary attention has been given to the use of American influence to achieve political objectives involving other countries. Another large sphere mentioned earlier is the use of influence to achieve reforms in aid-receiving countries, the purpose of which is to make American and other economic assistance more effective and to speed and strengthen the processes of development. In this sphere much of what has already been said as to the expectation of resistance to alien pressures is obviously relevant. It is, however, difficult to compare the limitations and opportunities stemming from the level of development because the problems which the highly developed and the underdeveloped present differ so greatly from each other. The Marshall Plan could achieve its success because all the foundations of development, including the existence of highly skilled personnel of all kinds, had already been laid, and efficient, specialized, and sophisticated governments were available to oversee the proceedings. When questions of economic, administrative, legal, or judicial reform were brought up, the European countries were equipped with experts who were familiar with the issues and who could through the machineries of the Organization of European Economic Cooperation collaborate to arrive at high level common understandings.

On the other hand, it is precisely the nature of underdevelopment that, in principle, all that has just been said of the advanced countries is at best only meagerly applicable to the countries just starting to develop.[21] The opportunities open to American influence are far greater in the sense that so much more needs to be accomplished if development is to be carried through; but the stumbling blocks are increasingly evident as the years go by. The limitations the harsh facts of underdeveloped life impose are disheartening. A few countries like India possess highly trained men who can carry on a fruitful dialogue with American and other experts and help them implement the resulting programs; a few like Tunisia have the effective political and administrative systems that are the indispensable prerequisites of development; a few like the major oil-producing countries have resources that provide a surplus above subsistence for development; and most of the African countries are free of the pressure of population which constantly encroaches on advancement elsewhere; but such bright spots are still far outweighed by the limitations inherent in the condition of under-development. The grave shortcomings of the Alliance for Progress demonstrate the difficulties blocking the path to reform because of national resistance to external intervention and because the ruling elements who control the inward flow of aid are naturally resistant to change that threatens their power and privilege.

Even where there is full readiness to work with the United States and generally accept its advice, American success in effectively influencing under-developed countries is drastically limited by the inability of governments to carry through reforms of procedures which they have endorsed and accepted. Leaving aside the effect of corruption, which, it has been plausibly argued, may on occasion promote rather than impede development, the issue concerns the incompetence of the administrative structures to perform the functions they are supposed to perform. Characteristically, bureaucracies are swollen far beyond what makes sense and at the same time the large array of often seriously under-paid government employees is unable or unwilling to take the necessary decisions. The multiplicity of official endorsements can receive the final sanction that makes them operative only when the cabinet minister or the head of government has himself acted; and it is only at that point that the perhaps impossible task begins of translating words on paper into administrative acts throughout the country.

None of this, of course, is intended either to question the need for aid of all available and appropriate kinds, nor to deny that valuable specific results have already been achieved and that more are undoubtedly to come. Even though spectacular breakthroughs may be lacking, the cumulative effect of years of exposure to foreign experts, the need to justify official policies and programs to the donor countries or international agencies, the working of a number of pilot projects and plants, the building up of some of the indispensable infrastructure —these must surely bring about changes that gradually open the door to a more sustained and widely embracing development. The prospects for significant development are essentially long range—at the present growth rate it would take India 137 years to catch up with Japan's present economic level [22]—and immediate showy gains are likely to be more illusory than real.

One vital element that is still missing is that the donor governments and peoples will have the patience to wait out the gradualness of advance and suffer through the inevitable shortfalls and failures. As has already become evident, donors may increasingly refuse to face up to the needs of the world's underprivileged. A quite different type of reaction would be to demand more intensive and extensive control over the recipients if it comes to be argued that the inadequacies in development are to be attributed to the sins and deficiencies of the underdeveloped countries. The same result might follow from large-scale defaults when debt repayments fall due. Both responses are in fact quite possible. Countries not of any particular concern to major donors might be left by the wayside, whereas those in which the maintenance of influence is seen as important might be more closely controlled.

It is obvious that the advanced countries, or at least the major ones which in the past would have an uncontested claim to be great powers, have enough wealth, strength, and command of further scientific advancement to make the opportunities which they open to the United States and its communist rival or rivals of real importance. On the other side, one of the most recent commentators on the relations between the developed and the underdeveloped countries has protested that as a matter of *Realpolitik* "the fate of the underdeveloped countries has only the remotest direct connection with the survival of the great powers . . . because there is almost nothing that those countries can do politically to harm or help the great powers." [23]

All of which may be true and which presumably finds a reflection in the growing disinclination to continue with expansive aid programs; and yet I take it to be, in fact, almost wholly divorced from an actual *Realpolitik*. The opportunities in the underdeveloped countries may be outweighed by the limitations, but these countries will be courted for humanitarian, political, economic, and a variety of other reasons. It may well be that the major reason, like that which spurs on the climbers of Mt. Everest, is that they are there and occupy a great share of the world's surface.

NOTES

[1] I am grateful to Miss Joan Nelson both for valuable advice in connection with this article and for letting me see the manuscript of her *Aid, Influence, and Foreign Policy* (New York, 1968), from which I have drawn much useful material.

[2] See, for example, Robert L. Heilbroner, "Counterrevolutionary America," *Commentary* (April 1967).

[3] Jacob J. Kaplan has cogently contended that the resentment derives less from the particular strings than from antagonism to American views and behavior in the more traditional spheres of foreign policy, "an antagonism that has been the traditional fate of world powers, whether or not they were conducting foreign aid programs. Rather, the programs should be regarded in large measure as a technique for mitigating this normal resistance to predominance and leadership." *The Challenge of Foreign Aid* (New York, 1967), 226.

[4] The House Committee on Government Operations complained that the U.S. Congress and taxpayer expected more cooperation than they were getting from the government of Vietnam, adding that with half a million men and billions of dollars of U.S. aid annually, "we should

at least be able to count on the wholehearted cooperation of Vietnamese officials in relatively minor economic matters." New York *Times*, Aug. 28, 1967.

[5] South Korea is reported to be making effective economic headway, even though it continues to be afflicted by severe political divisions and shortcomings.

[6] Gayl Ness has pointed out in Chapter Two the value of the relationship of a subordinate state to a subordinate territory if far-reaching reforms are to be carried out by the former.

[7] "A Political Theory of Foreign Aid," *American Political Science Review*, LVI (June 1962), 301–309. Kaplan also explicitly accepts the proposition that aid should be used to supplement American diplomacy, interests, and ideals. "It is indefensible to deploy U.S. foreign aid resources as though they had no relation to the nation's international concerns." *The Challenge of Foreign Aid*, 249.

[8] *The New Statecraft: Foreign Aid in American Foreign Policy* (Chicago, 1960), 62.

[9] *Ibid.*, 97. See also John D. Montgomery, *Foreign Aid in International Politics* (Englewood Cliffs, N.J., 1967), 15ff. With reference to Spanish bases and other such concessions, he remarks, "The commonest forms of these international exchanges involve the use of a military base, air rights, and adherence to alliances, all of which have been 'purchased' with substantial economic or military assistance instead of cash payments," 16.

[10] *The Diplomacy of Economic Assistance* (Samuel S. Stratton Lecture, Middlebury College, Oct. 27, 1965, published at Middlebury, Vermont, 1966), 12. As examples of the dangers involved in tying political strings to aid, he cites the familiar cases of the overthrow of an Indonesian government and the rejection by Burma of further aid.

[11] Cited by E. S. Mason, *Foreign Aid and Foreign Policy* (New York, 1964), 49. Although AID held that such a community of free nations "offers the best prospect of security and peace for the United States," Mason expressed his skepticism that free nations would cooperate more with the United States than their view of their national interest would dictate.

[12] See my *Africa and United States Policy* (Englewood Cliffs, N.J., 1967), 44–45.

[13] See Richard Butwell, *Southeast Asia Today—and Tomorrow*, rev. ed. (New York, 1964), 108.

[14] *The Diplomacy of Economic Assistance*, 20–21. It is Professor Mason's belief that "political conditions attached to aid are unlikely to be effective except in that limited number of situations in which economic assistance is the junior partner in an extensive mutual security program designed to counter actual or impending aggression," 25.

[15] For one segment of this story, see Abraham F. Lowenthal, "Foreign Aid as a Political Instrument: A Case Study of the Dominican Republic 1961–63" in *Public Policy*, ed. John D. Montgomery and Arthur Smithies (Cambridge, Mass., 1965), Vol. 14.

[16] See Andrew F. Westwood, *Foreign Aid in a Foreign Policy Framework* (Washington, D.C., 1966), 85.

[17] Referring to Washington officials who allegedly linked delays in meeting a UAR request for wheat with American disapproval of Nasser's foreign policies, *The Egyptian Gazette* on March 19, 1967, rhetorically asked "who cannot fail to be amazed at the unashamed confirmation by Washington officials of the most cynical charges brought against its manipulation of food aid for the Third World as a lever to either destroy non-alignment, or, as in this case, to directly intervene in internal Arab affairs and shape the policies of an independent nation?"

[18] *The New Statecraft*, 45ff.

[19] Putting forward a proposition that may be seen as the reverse side of that advanced by Jacob J. Kaplan (see n. 3, above), Andrew F. Westwood has contended that the effectiveness of American aid in many situations, such as military assistance for Turkey, massive aid to the Diem government in early stages, and President Kennedy's endorsement of the Alliance for Progress, was due less to the specific aid provided than to the fact that it came with the backing of the United States, the greatest world power; *Foreign Aid in a Foreign Policy Framework*, 102.

[20] *The Politics of Foreign Aid* (New York, 1962), 252.

[21] According to Theodore Geiger, the Marshall Plan experience of Europe's ability to initiate and execute its own recovery programs led to unrealistic expectations for Asia, Africa, and Latin America. The reaction then went to the other extreme; the aid-givers, notably the United States and France, handled development programs largely through their own personnel at the expense of stimulating a sense of responsibility and self-confidence on the part of the countries concerned. "Lessons of the Marshall Plan," *Africa Report*, June 1967, p. 18.

[22] See Herbert Feldman, "Aid as Imperialism?" *International Affairs* (London), April 1967, p. 221.

[23] John Pincus, *Trade, Aid, and Development* (New York, 1967), 10. He also contended that, although aid is given primarily in order to secure influence over others, with the passage of time it has become increasingly clear that the elements of *Realpolitik* in the official rationale of aid are not valid. "The North has given aid to Indonesia, Cambodia, Ghana, Burma, and Iraq without winning their political allegiance or suffering markedly from their hostility. From the viewpoint of self-interest, it was largely money down the drain. Appeals to self-interest are therefore becoming increasingly implausible as a basis for aid," 14.

THE CONTRIBUTORS

Henry Bienen is in the Department of Politics at Princeton University.

Richard Butwell is the director of the Business Council for International Understanding Program in the School of International Service at the American
University.

Rupert Emerson is in the Department of Government at Harvard University.

Ivo K. Feierabend is in the Department of Political Science at San Diego State
College.

Rosalind L. Feierabend is in the Department of Psychology at San Diego State
College.

Benjamin Higgins is in the Department of Economics at the University of
Montreal.

Lloyd Jensen is in the Department of Political Science at the University of
Kentucky.

Wilson Carey McWilliams is in the Department of Political Science at Brooklyn
College of the City University of New York.

Gayl D. Ness is in the Department of Sociology at the University of Michigan.